Children

of the

Land

Children

of the

Land

MARCELO HERNANDEZ CASTILLO

HARPER

An Imprint of HarperCollins*Publishers*

HarperCollins books may be purchased for educational, business, or sales promotional use. For information, please email the Special Markets Department at SPsales@harpercollins.com.

FIRST EDITION

Designed by Leah Carlson-Stanisic

Library of Congress Cataloging-in-Publication Data has been applied for.

ISBN 978-0-06-282559-9

20 21 22 23 24   LSC   10 9 8 7 6 5 4 3 2 1

For my son Julian, listo mijo

Contents

[MOVEMENT AS A TRIX CEREAL COMMERCIAL] I

FIRST MOVEMENT: *DACA* 9

SECOND MOVEMENT: *Interview on Allegiance* 75

THIRD MOVEMENT: *Sentence Served* 115

FOURTH MOVEMENT: *Glass* 205

FIFTH MOVEMENT: *Asylum* 301

FURTHER NOTES AND OBSERVATIONS 355

ACKNOWLEDGMENTS 359

NOTES 361

Children

of the

Land

[Movement as a Trix Cereal Commercial]

==

There were moments when I didn't need to tell my body how to move, moments completely new to me and yet something inside me knew exactly what to do when they came, as if I had been practicing for the Olympics. Some deep-seated knowledge rose from the very core of me. But it wasn't instinct. It was memory. I was tapping into an inheritance that up until that moment I didn't know I had. In this way life appeared monotonous, nothing was a surprise, but my body never really stopped shaking, a small breakwater holding back the tidal wave of the past. The first time I saw a gun it was the gun that did all the talking and part of me didn't know who to listen to, or if I was listening at all or running.

*

It was a Sunday afternoon when I heard a knock on the door. The TV was on and the low sun had that familiar warmth particular to Sundays, blinding half of the screen through a crack in the curtains. My little brothers and I looked so still in our reflections. No one was really watching. Amá was in her room resting her feet, preparing to tire them again the next day.

And again, the knock, louder.

I opened the door and a man held it open, the words ICE stitched onto his vest in bright gold letters.

"We're looking for Marcelo Hernandez," he said, and before I could say anything he walked in past me, followed by three others.

It happened so fast that I doubted it was actually happening. They all had their hands on their guns at the ready because *you never know, right?* The gun looked larger than I imagined one would look in my head. It was 2006, in the same Northern California home my family had rented for eight years and would go on to rent for another decade. I was only a senior in high school; maybe it was high time I should have seen a gun by then; I was overdue.

*

I knew ICE was all around us and that a raid was just on the horizon. But I couldn't tell anyone what I was always watching for, what I was always anticipating.

I could hear Amá's words rattle in my head. "Never tell anyone." She didn't need to remind me. I knew.

I saw them everywhere. I saw agents in trees, I saw their heads popping out of the ground like tulips, I felt their hands touching every coin in my pocket. But my mistake was that I always saw them outside—never did I think I would one day find them inside my house. For some reason I thought our house existed beyond the limits of the border, as if it was a sovereign country of its own. It was the only place I didn't have to scrutinize myself, the only place the shaking stopped a little.

Green was still my favorite color. Their green fatigues had the afterthought of something living—green in spring, the green leaves of frangipani, iris, lily-of-the-valley overshadowed by so much color. I judged the ability of my body by its speed and weight. I judged how long it would take me to reach the back door and who would do the talking. They had the house surrounded.

*

"Is Marcelo Hernandez home?" he barked again.

"I'm Marcelo Hernandez," I said. He looked at the paper in his hands as if it was the first time he was seeing it, as if he needed to go outside and check the address to make sure they had the right place. That happened sometimes; they would get the wrong address but would pick up whoever was at the house they happened to storm anyways. It was better than coming back to the office empty-handed. It was a numbers thing.

"I'm looking for your father," he said, scanning the room. "Who else is home?"

My little brothers sat on the couch, staring at the swirls on the carpet. They were getting their first lesson in speaking only when spoken to, in answering only what was necessary. I did all the talking. In my head, I wondered if in ten or twenty years that would be *my* face printed on the warrant in their hands, if I was capable of taking more than just my father's name and blood.

It had been about three years since Apá was deported in 2003. There was already nothing left of him in the house except for some old tools in the garage and the dip on his side of the bed, the outline of his absence weathered beneath the weight of his stillness over the years. Beyond that, all that remained was the likeness of my gestures to his, the way I carried my body, the way my mother said I chewed my food. Even his spare toothbrush had been thrown away long ago. It wasn't on purpose; there wasn't any thought to it. One day it was there and another it wasn't. We didn't bother trying to go through the stages of loss. We were young but could already turn off the parts of ourselves that hurt like a light switch. In ten years, I would hardly remember any of it.

The tulips sprouted. All of the leaves fell from the trees.

*

Surely Amá heard the noises from her room, but I knew she was still there, I knew she would never leave.

"My mother is in her room but she has a heart condition and I'm afraid you might scare her. Can I please go back and tell her you are here and bring her out?"

"Okay," said the agent, and nodded to the others.

I went into the dark back room, waded through the thick smell of analgesic cream Amá rubbed on her joints at night. Amá asked who was in the living room. I told her not to worry. I said everything would be okay. I said it like that, *okay*, and grabbed her by the arm.

"Someone wants to talk with you. It will be okay. *Okay*. They're looking for Apá. Everything will be okay."

I never said the word ICE, but she knew what I was talking about. I walked her out of the room and didn't let go of her arm as we entered the living room. I knew we both had that deep knowledge of flight inside of us although neither of us had ever spoken of it to each other. This wasn't the fight-or-flight instinct we all have, it was particular to immigrants because although everything inside us told us to run, we didn't. I knew her muscles were tensing just like mine even if she wasn't able to run in her older age like I was. And yet, holding her, I wasn't sure if I was keeping her from falling, or keeping her from running away. I could feel her body digging up memories of past raids. What if my body ran away involuntarily? What if it left Amá behind out of instinct or some generational memory? I wasn't sure what I was or wasn't capable of doing.

*

The paper in their hands had Apá's picture on it. It was a recent picture. I wondered where they got it. It looked like the one they took when they deported him. One of the agents went into the rooms, looking in all the closets, and beneath the beds, ransacking the drawers. They shuffled through Amá's things and checked the bathroom to see how many toothbrushes there were. They wanted to find traces of him, and perhaps, if they were lucky, even the warmth of the bed where he slept next to Amá, not just the crevice.

But they only found the life we had to make up without him, nothing more.

According to their records he had never left, or perhaps they thought he had returned. At first I thought it was a clerical mistake. Someone, somewhere in a small office lined with plants, may have hit a wrong button, and because of that, ten or so ICE agents surrounded our house and three held their guns pointed to the ground in front of us. I was certain they knew everything about me, my crushes, my fears, my deep longing to wander. I was sure they had been watching me for a very long time.

*

"How long has he been gone?" the agent asked my mother, and I answered because he asked in English, which she did not know. I did this often to avoid the brief and awkward silence that followed when such questions were thrown at her. I had always been a good translator; all of our doctor visits translating for my mother had trained me for this. I took out my phone and showed him my contacts and pointed to the bright little screen. It said Apá with a number from Mexico. I didn't have a calling card to dial out of the country and knew it would be expensive to call him without one but called anyways. I called as my only proof that he was indeed in Mexico and not with us, but he didn't answer. I thought back to the times I wished he didn't answer only to hear the familiar click of his phone coming on. I called again, hoping this time Apá would answer to tell them how far away he was, to describe everything around him as if he were on vacation, talking to his friends back home about how pretty it was. Again, no answer. How else could I tell them that there was nothing here for them; not me, not my brothers, not my mother, and certainly not my father? Sometimes I stuttered when talking to adults, but in such situations I was calm as if the panicked part of me *had* run.

The other agents came back after looking for evidence of him and finding none. Our house looked like he had never been there. The agent took my phone and wrote down the number I called. "We'll be in touch," he said, turned around, and left as quickly as he came. They all shuffled out the door. It was quiet again, but our ears were ringing.

Such a small mistake, such a small event. Maybe they took pity on us. Maybe we weren't worth their time. If so, I had never been more grateful to be that worthless. Maybe one of them had big plans for the evening and didn't want to bother with the paperwork, it was Sunday after all, there was a football game that mattered more than us. On paper, we were dangerous. On paper we were all of the things that people said about us on the news. But in our dim home, peacefully resting on a Sunday afternoon, we weren't even worth the ten-cent zip ties hanging from their belts.

*

We stood there, frozen, unsure of what to do. The inner urge to flee was replaced with paralyzed submission—we were cemented in place. In that moment, if anyone wished to do so, they could have walked through our door, commanded us to cut ourselves open, and we would have probably listened. Through the window, I saw many armed agents get into three vans and drive away. The vans were un-marked; the only sign of who was inside was the tires, riding low from all the agents packed inside.

When the last van drove away, we clicked back into movement as if someone had hit the pause button until then. They could have taken us all if they wanted to. Perhaps the fact that they left us *was* their punishment—*We'll be in touch*—a message that there was no-where we could hide, that they were always watching. They let us go only to let us know they could always just as easily pick us up again. We would never again close our eyes, we would never again release the tension in our bodies. Never again would Sunday afternoons be quiet. The voice in our heads that told us someone was watching would from that point on never stop, even if we tried to bang it out with a hammer. I would have paid anyone anything to make it stop. But I would never again be able to unwind at home, to take my shoes off and completely let my body go. Home was suddenly something to add to the list of dangers. I had nowhere else to go.

Outside, things continued as they were. The TV was still running. The sun was still making everything move slower beneath its Sunday gold. As if we ever doubted their perpetual presence looming above us, they came when we least would have expected it. They wanted to disrupt any semblance of normalcy that we might have attained after having lived in the United States for decades. But in order for a disruption to occur, they first had to recognize that we lived a normal life, they had to accept that we, too, were like everyone else, falling into the habits and routines of peaceful American life. Once they accepted our commonality, they used it against us. They stormed.

*

Nothing was safe. We sat in our living room and held each other as we sobbed quietly. For a moment immediately after their departure even holding each other felt like pinpricks. Amá had lost us once before to the immigration system, and she held us tight because she thought she was going to lose us again. We were separated as children, and even though I was much younger that first time, even though I was beyond despair, I feared deportation more than I feared ending my life. If I failed or succeeded, the rest of the family would be investigated and split either way. I had long ago embraced futility before I knew there was even a word for it.

Even though we weren't taken on that quiet Sunday afternoon, we knew we easily could have been, and that possibility corroded us from the inside. I forgot what my mother looked like before the perpetual panic draped itself over her face. I couldn't imagine her any more beautiful. But since it was only my first and my mother's fourth (?), fifth (?), eighth (?) raid, perhaps she always looked the same, and it was just my vision that had gotten clearer.

From that moment forward, I never stood still, my nervousness spiked unimaginably high. We never opened our door or windows again. What was once sweet now had the bitter aftertaste of uncured olives.

*

It didn't matter how good I was at hiding, I knew they would always find me if they wanted. It was useless to blend in, to not bring attention to myself—*speak neither too loud nor too soft*. It didn't matter if I perfected my English—*speak like a person who is wandering but not lost*. It was useless to try to negotiate two worlds at once when only one of them was visible while the other one threatened to collapse. And yet I tried, but it came at a price. So much of my energy was spent trying to avoid getting caught. I wonder how much more I could have done with my life if I'd been spared the energy it took to survive.

The next day I went to school. Amá went to work. I ate quietly with my mouth shut in the cafeteria. I had to tell myself when to swallow. Things no longer happened by themselves, I had to tell my body how to do them. Even laughter required some kind of effort. I had to remind myself: this is funny, this is how you laugh—*laugh now, laugh hard, spit out your food*.

FIRST MOVEMENT:

DACA

1.

I am trying to dissect the moment of my erasure.
—WENDY XU, "NOTES FOR AN OPENING"

I never knew where my grandfather Jesús was buried, only that he's been lying somewhere in the desert of Sonora for the last sixty years. Our family thought he was buried somewhere in a town called Empalme. We were almost sure he got a proper Catholic burial, but there was nothing proper about it.

Six miles above the earth, on a flight returning to the country of my birth with my wife, Rubi, after a twenty-year absence, I looked out the window at the desert below to see what my grandfather couldn't see six decades before—how, despite its seeming endlessness, the landscape did have limits, it did have an end. From the sky, anything seemed possible. We were in the space between two countries, along that indiscriminate line where perhaps even time was irrelevant. In the sky, I could stand still, something I couldn't normally do back home, something no one in my family was ever able to do. We were traveling from the Midwest to see my father for the first time in ten years since he was deported to Mexico. It was 2013, and I thought I was still young enough to want to start things over between us.

Flying thousands of feet above the border, I felt fluid. I positioned myself against powers larger than me.

Apá could not, and did not, return to the U.S. after his 2003 deportation. My mother had warned him not to test his luck by continuing to go back and forth under precarious conditions, but he wouldn't listen, and he ended up paying the price for it. I had just received DACA and applied for an "advanced parole" permit, which allowed recipients a special pass to leave the country and be allowed to legally return only under "extraordinary" circumstances in the face of an emergency. Apá recently had prostate surgery, and I didn't know if this would be my only window of opportunity to see him. Simply not seeing a father for a decade would qualify as an emergency in any situation.

As it turned out, due to this visit and my legal reentry into the U.S. with the advanced parole permit, I would be allowed to one day apply for a green card through marriage without ever having to leave the country. Without it, I stood a chance of facing the same ten-year exile from the country that he was facing. DACA, and advanced parole, was my only hope of avoiding a life that looked anything like my father's: moving back and forth between countries until being forced to stay in one. And yet I still had a reason all to myself for returning, a reason that had nothing to do with immigration, or my father. I wanted to go see a mountain.

[First Movement Before Me Against the Wall]

====

My mother was the youngest child of seven, and her only memory of her father Jesús is when she was four, in 1958, and hearing him whistle as he approached their ranch on the mountain, La Loma, after being gone for months, working in the U.S. under the bracero program. He was a kind man, tall and slender. She could never remember the song, but she could always still hear the tune in her head many years later. Her father dropped his small bag near an avocado tree, and she ran up to hug him around his waist. He asked her to wash his red bandana, so she brought a bucket, filled it with water from the trough, and rubbed it between her hands. He wrapped it around his neck to cool himself down, and they finished the song together.

*

In her memory, his face is blurry, but the red bandana and the tune are as clear today as they were in 1958. It was the color, it was the sound. They say she looks like him; they say if he would have lived longer, she would have grown to be his favorite; maybe she already was. Because she was the youngest, she was spared from having to work in the fields. She spent her days stealing eggs from the henhouse and trading them at the store for candies and a box of cigarettes to give to her older brother. She would also place batteries on top of a hot rock in the sun to give them a little more juice. When that stopped working, she rolled them carefully over a fire, hoping there was even a minute more left in them for the radio. At night, Amá would climb up to the roof of her house, click the batteries in, and carefully tune to stations as far away as Laredo. They sold a cow to buy that radio. She liked boleros, rumbas, and danzón. She listened closely through the static at the soft voices of romantic cosmopolitan trios. She didn't know how far Laredo was, but she knew it was in the direction of where her father came from, where he would leave again and would not return.

Her father would be dead the next year in Sonora, on his way to the U.S. The gangrene began in his foot and slowly crept up his body like endless tendrils of a seed. They told him not to go, but he would not listen. For generations, one thing was clear; the men in my family seemed experts at ignoring the warnings of the women.

*

Amá's earliest memory of her mother, whom we called Amá Julia, is of them sitting beneath the same tree outside the courtyard walls of that same ranch, La Loma. Her mother wrapped her in a shawl and they sat huddled together on a rock, listening to the birds roosting for the evening in the trees. It was the evening chorus that makes birds feel as if they are as large as their songs carried over the valley, announcing themselves, saying "I'm still here," as if there were any doubt about it. The stars were innumerable and soon the night would fall with its absolute darkness, because no one had electricity up on the mountain. It was so dark that everything seemed to be on fire when even the slightest light from the sun emerged in the morning, as if by noon it would all be burned to the ground. Amá said that never again were there as many stars in her life.

When the news came that her husband Jesús died, Amá Julia and her seven children all wore black dresses for six months as a rite of mourning. Julia, the new widow, turned every single picture of Jesús hanging on the walls around so that his face looked away— his head pushed against the cool adobe clay. The frames stayed that way until her own death many years later. My mother's entire time in that house was spent looking at the backs of frames. Neither she nor any of her sisters were ever allowed to turn them over to see what their father looked like. They were obedient; these were traditions of the past, not to be trifled with.

*

In his final years, Jesús drank himself into debt. When he ran out of money, he used the land he inherited as collateral. It was said that he would give an entire plot of land in exchange for a bottle of tequila. All he had left to trade was the ranch of La Loma, but he died before he could sell it. Amá Julia worked the rest of her life sewing dresses, selling her cattle's offspring, and growing corn to pay off his debt. She never remarried. She said she didn't want another man living in her house because she had too many beautiful daughters.

Years after Amá Julia's death, when they were certain her spirit would forgive them, the family finally decided to turn the pictures on the wall over. They mailed the pictures to the U.S., and for the first time since she was four, Amá saw her father's face. All those years she had dreamed of him and what he might look like. All those years that his face was just a smudge in her memory left her feeling guilty, guilty that she remembered a useless piece of cloth and a meaningless whistle instead of her father's face. And all those years he was right there, pushed against the wall, looking away.

Although she doesn't drink, Amá admits that she likes the smell of tequila. Like their father too, her sisters like to smoke now and then as they sit around a table playing cards, taking small sips of mezcal, raising a cup to their father, who now looks straight at them, hanging from the wall above their heads.

2.

On the plane, I wondered if there was an exact point when we were no longer in one country and inside another, or if there was ever a moment when I occupied no country. If ever that was possible, it was possible up in the air. There was no clear correlation between what was happening down below and up above. I had heard that at the official port of entry there were turnstiles, just like the subway, ushering the travelers forward. If such turnstiles existed, you could map the precise moment when half of your body was *here* and the other half was *there*. I could measure; all I wanted was that little gold stamp that said I clicked past onto the other side, I entered, I returned, I was measured, counted for, recorded.

Would a sudden coldness come over us when our bodies moved over the actual line of the border? Wasn't that how loneliness began, with the coldness of our bodies?

[First Movement Before Me as Salt]

Amá Julia poured salt into the shapes of crosses at the edges of her fields to save the crops and protect them from evil—whispering a soft prayer beneath her breath.

I imagine her in a long wool rebozo during the rainy season, walking out across a damp meadow in the morning, with a small bag of salt in one hand and a rosary in the other. One part of her religion was as ancient as olives or bells, not written in any biblical text. It was meant to save her seven children from hunger.

Amá, too young to work, walked through the damp field with no shoes, the soft dirt parting beneath her soles. The only sounds came from a distant wind, the earth muffling her steps as she counted seeds in her hand. It's not possible to imagine any other sound in that moment. The sisters could go days without talking up on that mountain, without hearing anything louder than a bird's call. And sometimes, Amá said, the air was so thick and heavy that it smothered even the bird's songs, so much so that you felt like you were walking underwater—your clothes and your shoes weighed you down to the earth by the stillness. She said you could feel the penetrating silence on your clothes, as if it was something you could wash away, or something you could carry with you far away into another country. And my mother did carry it around like a glove that had no pair because her silence always felt like it was missing something. How I wished I could go even one day without uttering a single sound.

Perhaps the only sound was that of Amá Julia, shaking salt at the edge of the field, salt falling over her like snow, glittering in the air. So much salt that the crops no longer grew in the fallow corner. So much salt that they didn't even resemble crosses anymore, just small white mounds broken only by her dark wool dress dragging behind her in the morning breeze—her thin lips mumbling a soft prayer through her teeth. Eventually her children would go north and leave her. They would be back with their own stories and their own children, with their own silences, some of whom she would never meet in this life.

3.

When I developed black-and-white photos in my high school art class, I erased all the grayness from their resolution because I believed you didn't need gradients to understand an image. I believed in black and white and nothing else. I won an award because even though I deformed the images beyond recognition, people could still see through them and understand them. I wanted someone to look at them and know what they were looking at despite everything I had done. Everything was either light or it was a tree.

You were either in one country or you were in another, there was no in between. Black and white. I had no patience for gray.

There was nothing I could do to stop the plane from charging forward. It felt like we were going too fast, I was afraid I would miss the moment we would officially cross over. The border existed both outside me as well as within. I smiled at the flight attendant, who smiled back, I ate my wife's Biscoff, and I pressed my face to the window.

[First Movement Before Me as Myth and Knife]

===

During a storm, my Amá Julia lifted her hands high and made the sign of the cross in the air with a knife. Before her time, her mother Josefina, whom they called Pepa, used to make the sign of the cross with a child and recite the Magnificat until the storm subsided. "My soul magnifies the Lord . . . Because he has regarded the lowliness of his handmaid . . ."

The child would die in the process of the prayer, but the crops would be saved. It was the price to be paid to save an entire family, or perhaps even all of the ranches on the mountain. It was the price paid to avoid hunger. Maybe that's just what they told themselves, that the child died from the curse, not wanting to say that it died because it went hungry.

4.

When I came undocumented to the U.S., I crossed into a threshold of invisibility. Every act of living became an act of trying to remain visible. I was negotiating a simultaneous absence and presence that was begun by the act of my displacement: *I am trying to dissect the moment of my erasure.* I tried to remain seen for those whom I desired to be seen by, and I wanted to be invisible to everyone else. Or maybe I was trying to control who remembered me and who forgot me. But I couldn't control what someone else saw in me, only persuade them that it was an illusion. There were things that I could not hide, things that would come out of me and expose me in my most vulnerable moments. It was my skin, my dark hair, my cheekbones, that I swore would give me away. I was afraid of the way I walked. It was easy to imagine being hit by a car, because even if they didn't see me, I would for once be able to feel my body as more than smoke.

[First Movement Before Me as the Blood Moon]

═══

Amá Julia believed that if a woman was expecting a child, she should not go outside during an eclipse and should stay away from the windows—lock herself up. She had to wear red underwear or at least something red on her and safety pins on her body.

When a child died, they never said it died, they said it was stolen. The ocean took her, the moon took her, or a witch who was jealous took her.

To prevent such thefts, the mothers wore red to fool the moon into believing they were dead or that they had miscarried. They stayed indoors and lay still to mimic their own death, since it was common for the newly dead to remain in the house longer than it is today. They needed at least nine days for the novenario.

*

Death was different then. It was something they allowed into their house. It was something they touched. The objects they placed on top of the soul-less bodies during the wake carried tremendous weight, almost as if to say "This will keep you down, this will keep you away."

The safety pins on the pregnant woman needed to be large, as if they were knives, the instruments of the mother's death. It was an act, it was theatrical, they needed to be seen. They put on a show for the spirits, for the moon, hoping to convince them that the child wasn't worth their time, that it was already stolen, that someone had beaten them to it, to move on to another—like the blood smeared over the door of the Israelites to protect their firstborn.

It was all for the sake of the visible, of things of this world, of things that with enough time could be holy to some. It was precisely the belief that ordinary things *could* be considered holy that bothered Amá. So she left the Catholic Church because her prayers could no longer be to a saint incarnate—to the statue of that saint, its physicality. The divine needed to be more than something standing before her, something she couldn't see, something she couldn't have the language for, something she couldn't even imagine or have a name for. Some people want physical proof of God; they want to see him just like they see their neighbor, in order to believe. But not my mother. She wanted a God who, like her, could hide in plain sight.

Maybe my mother didn't trust this world and the relics and saints of the world, however holy they may have appeared to be, to carry her message to God. But if it wasn't for things right in front of us, mediating our contact with God—the saints, the crosses, rosaries, and flowers—could our eyes stand such brightness? "I am that I am," God said to Moses when Moses asked how would the people believe him without proof, without something visible to show? My mother wanted Yahweh, the only substitute we have as the name too sacred to be spoken for, denoted by the empty space between the cherubs atop the ark of the covenant.

But if it wasn't for the blood, how would we know we were hurt? How would we know we were dying?

5.

I started to become undone, like a loosely coiled ball of yarn that was bound to come apart eventually. I felt like neither the U.S. nor Mexico wanted me and that I was between two opposing magnets and one was pushing harder than the other—my chest heavy beneath their weight. The U.S. was winning. How appropriate it would have been to die six miles in the sky with Rubi next to me—no footings on earth, a citizen of no country. How happy that would have made me.

I didn't want to find a home. What I wanted was an origin, which was different than *home*, to look and see if that origin had a shape, or if I could give it one. If I was not welcome in the country of my birth, I would be okay. I was used to that feeling. What I could not withstand was never finding that from which everything of *me* came from. Up until that point, I had only heard stories, legends, and myths of my family's past and what life was like on that mountain. I wanted something else that felt more real because I didn't trust my imagination enough to fill in the gaps.

If only I could have jumped in the air inside the plane until not even my body was touching the plane and hold still there for hours. I wanted nothing to touch me—to know what it felt like to be untethered.

*

I knew that I was supposed to be grateful to be able to go back because only two other siblings had been able to see him, each a few times in the course of ten years. I knew that there were countless others who would kill for even just a day to be able to come back to see their father. It was a story I knew too well: *Be grateful*. Rubi held my hand and leaned her head on my shoulder. She had never been to Zacatecas, and even though I was born there, it would be as if we were both seeing everything for the first time. We didn't talk much for the duration of the flight, we just stared out the window, looking at the landscape below. Being in the air, seemingly motionless, made me believe that I would actually attain it, that I would actually feel the moment we stepped over.

I needed to go to the place of my mother's birth, the house where she was brought into this world, the ranch of La Loma on that mountain where she played her radio late at night on the roof. Yes, it was selfish to only want to return for my own needs, but I wasn't done with the past. I could already feel the threads starting to unravel. What would be left of me when they all disappeared?

It was there, in La Loma, that I thought I could feel safe enough to uncoil what I had spent years wrapping tight around me. I had hid so much of myself through behaviors foreign to me, that I started to think those facades were in fact [me]. My whole life was an act, and it started to feel like a joke. I was a walking one-act play. I was tired because I had lost a sense of reality, a sense of who and what I was put on this earth to be. If in that moment at La Loma I became undone, I might be able to replace the center with something, to put something there and begin to wrap and coil myself together again. Maybe then I would be able to start a new life as myself all over again, the self that stayed behind when we migrated twenty years ago. I was returning to look for a five-year-old version of me, to tell him to stop, to hold him and tell him that things would be okay.

In a moment of great despair, I had tried to do this in California, but I soon found that the land, the country that is America, the foreignness of it, even if it was all I had ever known, would end me. Going to La Loma was the only way I could unravel and return to the world of the living. It happened when I was young, I wandered in the woods of the Sierra Nevada in the warmth of the summer, when the small mountain flowers and mule's ear sprouts were lush. I tried to open, I yelled and yelled and sang and chanted, but even the warm breeze felt like knives to an exposed nerve. And a few years later, I came close to that disentanglement again, but again there was nothing for me to hold on to, nothing of substance to replace the center, so I buckled up and tried to drive my car into the river. I didn't want to come back. And once this feeling of emptiness at my core started, it wouldn't go away. It was too late and it felt like I was becoming smaller day by day, unthreading, I could feel how much of myself I left behind everywhere I went. I was almost reveling in it because I felt it as a kind of ecstasy—parts of myself scattered over an entire landscape. A little of me here, a little of me there. My anxiety no longer mattered, my sadness, my invisibility, and my hopelessness felt foreign to me, which is to say, they were inconsequential. I withdrew and let the world move my body without me, I tumbled like dried grass. I didn't have anything like La Loma, with its thick walls built by my ancestors, to bring me back to reality. No semblance of permanence.

All I wanted was something to hold on to.

If I reached La Loma, I would replace the end of my thread at the center of me with a rock tucked close to my body, something heavy enough to keep me from moving—an anchor—one of those porous volcanic rocks that were found on my mother's mountain, and in my head I said it as if it actually belonged to her, "My mother's mountain . . . my mother's mountain."

We were always moving; I wanted to stay still for once.

*

I was going to take back what was stolen from me. My childhood was stolen, I had no memory of it whatsoever. It wasn't my choice to forget; there were things my mind decided were best I didn't remember. Maybe if I touched the places where I (and those who came before me in my family) were born, then something would come back to me. I couldn't remember being seven, or nine, or eleven. If I started the journey again, to go to Mexico only to migrate out of Mexico again, maybe it would be like living my life again moment by moment.

It needed to be a rock, it needed to come from the earth, because the idea of place had always evaded me. The places I inhabited were always tied to some kind of origin, but it was always an origin that I was never able to access. In the act of immigrating, I was always looking for what I had lost, perhaps forever. And so part of me, even a microscopic part, was always looking back.

Some part of me feared that I was going home to die. Where would I want to be buried? If I were laid to rest in Mexico, then so much of my family in the U.S. would never be able to visit my grave. Perhaps fate staved off my death in the U.S. in order to avoid betraying that little stone that was waiting for me to unravel on my mother's mountain.

Maybe it didn't matter where I would be laid to rest. Maybe it was just one long stretch of land where people seemed to lose their minds. This moving back and forth felt like an endless repetition. We had been doing it for a hundred years and still here we were again. Maybe we would be doing it for a hundred more.

*

I was also going to reverse my parent's journey; walking backward to what led them to cross in the first place. I was mapping. I was a cartographer. I would reach and keep reaching. It was an act of dissection, an opening up. *I am trying to dissect the moment of my erasure.* Something had been stolen from me.

Rubi held my hand on the armrest and nudged closer to me, trying to calm me down. What could I tell her? I looked down and noticed that the landscape had changed. We had been in the air for about two hours and were approaching what would be the border below. I felt myself getting smaller.

[First Movement Before Me: Amá and Apá]

═══

There was not much courtship between my parents before they married. It was more of a convenience and numbers thing—this ranch had X number of sons, and another ranch on the other side of the mountain had X number of daughters. It was math.

People were carrying a statue of the Immaculate Virgin Mary of Fatima to every ranch on the mountain. My parents met at the gathering and procession of a saint known for secrets.

When they married, Amá and Apá went to live on a part of the mountain called Mala Noche, which means "bad night." They had a small shack made out of adobe, which didn't have a roof, only a plastic tarp that didn't stop the rain from pouring onto the dirt floor. Amá said it was one of the saddest days of her life when she left her beloved home, where she didn't have to work, where she rested beneath the sun during the day and still listened to the radio at night, for Mala Noche.

Apá was gone mostly, so Amá was left to feed and care for her firstborn daughter alone, as well as maintain the ranch. She herded cattle down the mountain, gathered firewood, and walked three kilometers to fetch water. It was hard work that she wasn't used to, but she said those years at Mala Noche made her realize that she was on her own, even when Apá was home.

She would tie the baby to a tree with a rope so she could go work on the farm, and she left her faithful dog by the child to protect her from coyotes or snakes. On cold, wet nights, the dog would sit at the entrance to the shack and growl every now and then into the darkness. It was just her and her little girl, who at one point chewed on a straight razor she found on the floor because she was teething and her gums were itchy. Amá spent days cutting small pieces of onion for the child to bite on, hoping the onion would soothe and disinfect her tongue and gums that were tattered from the razor.

Amá doesn't remember what happened to that dog, her only companion, the only one who knew her sadness, the only one who didn't say to her "You've made your bed, now lie in it."

6.

From the air, the actual borderline looked like a long thread of hair—but nothing in the landscape around it held a particular shape for long. This is why I turned to nature for answers—because it reminded me of inconsistencies, breaks in a pattern we work so hard to preserve. Even the perfect little squares and circles of cropland were bunched together to make an amorphous shape out of many perfect ones. They all stopped at the foot of the mountains, where farmers could no longer exert control over the land.

I felt like I always had to redraw myself back into the landscape in one way or another—to my detriment, I was light-footed, I never left a trace of me behind. I usually used cash because it couldn't be traced and because there was no other option; for many years I didn't have a bank account. None of my family's cars were registered to our names, so it felt like we weren't even there. Every time I went hiking I felt the urgent need to turn over a stone and move it. It was always obvious to me that I didn't belong in the landscape of the West, the rolling foothills of Northern California leading up to the Sierra. Yes, I was aware I was entering a sacred space and I didn't want to disturb it, but I wanted to let someone know that I was there, that I meant no harm, that I too had been scarred.

From above, the border looked so obviously out of place, so obvious that it didn't belong, an encroachment to the snaking valleys, hills, and mountains. I heard that parts of the wall were made from old landing pads from the Vietnam War. Its point *was* to stand out, to be "other-than-the-landscape." Its geometrical consistency was jarring to the eye, violent in its precision, stretching for hundreds of miles without a single curve even when everything around it was curving. It announced its presence. And even in the past when there was no wall, there was still its vivid presence breaking two things apart.

I knew there were workers down there maintaining it, repairing broken sections, putting up more wire, clearing bushes for trucks to drive alongside it; they were marking the earth. Without those small interferences, it would be swallowed by the landscape. It would not last a single decade.

Given the nature of decay, perhaps that was not the same border we crossed decades before. How much of it had been replaced—as if it were a living thing that replaced its entire makeup of cells every few years? And yet it was still there, quite unchanged.

*

I ventured to believe that the function of the border wasn't only to keep people out, at least that was not its long-term function. Its other purpose was to be visible, to be seen, to be carried in the imaginations of migrants deep into the interior of the country, in the interior of their minds. It was a spectacle meant to be witnessed by the world, and all of its death and violence was and continues to be a form of social control, the way that kings of the past needed to behead only one petty thief in the public square to quell thousands more.[1] The biggest threat to immigrants who succeeded in crossing was the fear that the apparatus was always watching you. It was the idea that was most menacing, that infiltrated every sector of a person's life—total and complete surveillance. It was the unrelenting fear that was most abrasive on a person's soul. And on the Mexican side of the line, it stood as a symbol for those wanting to cross, announcing: "This could happen to you if you dare cross." We had all seen what happened to bodies in the desert; we knew the dangers of coyotes.

I always felt like it was on my back, looming just above me, the omnipresent nature of the beast. The border didn't just exist in the Southwest, but rather, everywhere. I had possessed its lesson; I knew that *place* wasn't somewhere I traveled to or lived in; the border had taught me that it had to be something else. I wanted to exist in a place that had no relationship to the border-at-large or to immigration or to my status or my family's. I just wanted a tree, a beach, a mountain, even a bird, not tinged the color of all of my fake documents. But where could I go that didn't involve a border in one way or another? Where on earth is a border irrelevant? How could I create a small landscape of memories divorced from that spectacle? Maybe this *place* could be independent acts of love that transcended the limitations of time and memory associated with borders, as in the phrase "I don't remember where we kissed, all I know is that we kissed." Place as memory. Place as disassociation . . . dissociation. There was no escape, so over the years I started drinking to create my own spectacle.

I knew that it was not simply birds, trees, and dirt down there. There were ghosts, very much as real as the trees around them. There was blood down there that didn't possess the magical ability to dry, to wither away into nothing, to be forgotten.

How easy it would have been to look down and see nothing but sand. How fortunate for those who couldn't or, better stated, refused, to see the bodies strung like sweaters on clotheslines beneath the water in the Río Bravo. I felt like I'd lost control of my body, like I was already dying six miles above the earth. There was death down there, and to some, it hardly made a shadow, it hardly made a sound; to others it was deafening, it started to sound like hammers.

[First Movement Before Me as Mist]

＝＝

Throughout the 1970s and '80s, when Apá left Amá to come work in the United States, he came to labor camps along California's Central Valley, mostly in Stockton and Modesto and sometimes as far north as Yakima, Washington. He slept in basements along with thirty or so other men without electricity or running water. A bucket in the corner was the latrine, and they rolled dice to see who would empty it next. Rent and food was deducted from their pay, as were their tools (marked up, of course), and the company usually and conveniently owned a small store to supply the men with any other provisions. Whatever was left in their pay they would send back home. There never was much left. Yes, he left Amá alone in Mala Noche, to fend for herself, to feed herself, and to care for their child by herself, but he was trying to get their small family ahead. It was the price to be paid for any kind of comfort.

*

Apá said that on some weekends, when they felt festive, they would invite girls from town to the camp, borrow a guitar, buy cheap tequila, and have a makeshift baile, or party. Since they were only ever able to bring a few girls at a time, the remaining men would dance with each other, holding themselves by the waist to a polka or ranchera, cheek to cheek, drunk, never to mention this to their wives back home until decades later.

The next day they would be back in the fields, picking one red and ripe strawberry at a time. Immigration raids were more common then. They were more public, it was part of the show. They also came in vans, but back then, they were marked in large green letters. They would come to a screeching halt and agents would surround a field like cowboys herding cattle. There was chaos and screeching, and flailing, and ducking, and "Stop, inmigración" in thick American accents that always sounded like they were part of a Hollywood western. There were heavy-metal-bumpered Bronco pickups with big tires that kicked up a dust storm when they came to a halt and also when they peeled out. Everyone knew the drill.

Sometimes if the bosses didn't want to pay their workers, they would call immigration themselves. During a raid, those who had papers never ran; they kept their heads down, continuing to pick their fruit as if nothing in particular was happening around them, as if they didn't see their friends jumping off their ladders, or jumping in a hole, hiding in a tree. One day a raid came and Apá just kept calmly picking his fruit, a bluff. It worked. The agents left without bothering to ask him anything. They came and went like ghosts. He laughed about it with his friends at lunch a few hours later when they returned from hiding, drenched in ditch water, or scraped up from hiding in the branches, laughing a little as to why they didn't think of it themselves, sighing because a bluff could only be done once.

*

Working in the fields was hard, but there was pride in it. The dirt felt good in your hands, and you were making your own living wage, much more than you would ever make back home growing corn, or anything else that came from the earth, even though it was the exact same earth you were cultivating up north as well. At the end of the day you could look back and see all the trees you stripped clean of their fruit. It was visible in the way other things were not. Sometimes there was no greater joy than sitting in the middle of a watermelon field, breaking open a melon and burying your face in the juicy red pulp. And on the hottest days, Apá said it almost felt nice when the crop dusters sprayed the neighboring field, how cool it felt when the pesticide mist poured over them with the slightest breeze.

7.

As we descended into Guadalajara, Jalisco, I began to worry about being able to return. My provisional document relegated my admittance back into the U.S. to the discretion of whichever individual border agent I happened to get at the checkpoint. If they were in a bad mood, they could deny me reentry and I would be stuck technically in Mexico but also in less of an actual "place" than I had ever been before. That feeling first came upon me when I boarded the plane back in Sacramento, when the stewardess announced that the doors would be shutting and wouldn't open again until our landing. But as we approached Guadalajara, it felt more pressing. As we got closer I could make out the houses, which looked like compounds with large walls gating them off from the outside world. I could see into people's courtyards, I could see the tiny dots of potted plants that I remembered having as a child in our courtyard. Even from that distance, I was starting to remember.

Ten years can do a lot to memory. I didn't know who my father was anymore or who he had become. I wanted to know if he had changed beyond just appearances. Had I?

*

I was fifteen when he left, and he was fifty-five. Upon my return, I was twenty-five and he was sixty-five. Our birthdays were one day apart. We were both Aquarius. He left me as a child and I was coming back to him as a man. I had a mustache and beard, my shoulders had squared, I was taller, maybe as tall as him, and I had a wife whom I'd met shortly after his departure and who fell in love with me over many nights talking on the phone about the man I was now returning to see.

I wondered what he would think of Rubi. I wanted to hold her the way he never held Amá and to show him the kind of respect a husband should have for his wife. I wanted to be heavy-handed about it with my body because I knew I couldn't talk to him directly. I always had to relay everything through symbols, images, and body language. We never spoke *to* each other, we spoke *about* each other. I wanted to prove to him that I made it just fine without him. And it was true. Had he been in my life at the critical times between fifteen and twenty-five, he would have probably told me not to go to college. I would find a way to tell him this. I would try to look him in the face and not say anything at all.

*

The day he left, he spent most of the morning packing old tools into the back of his 1970s Ford pickup, his favorite style of truck. He always drove stick shift and tried to teach me once, but I could hardly reach the pedals, and the gears were old and difficult to shift.

"Shift into third, shift into third," he screamed, which didn't help me shift into third any faster.

He went to Mexico often because he felt like he was rotting from the inside if he went too long without going back. With each trip, he packed his truck to the brim with farm equipment and old tools to sell or barter back home. Because I was small, he had me hunch inside the camper and arrange all the boxes that he handed me from the garage. This was always my job. I had to arrange them exactly right, otherwise they would not all fit.

"Not like that goddamnit!" he screamed when I put a box sideways when it should have gone longways. He grabbed the heavy boxes filled with screwdrivers and made the truck shake from side to side with his shuffling on the bed, trying to fit the box exactly where I was going to put it anyway if he had waited.

It never took long for my father to laugh off his rage and leave it in the past, while we were still left scrambling with remnants of his emotions from three or four episodes before.

That day, packing his truck for what I thought was just another of his trips to Mexico, I was almost happy that he was leaving. I felt that at last I would be relieved of the weight of his rage looming over my shoulders. Perhaps I wasn't sad because in my head I was certain that he would return.

Most of the money my dad made in the States would be sent back to Mexico to buy land, or a truck, or to pay off one of his many debts. My mother, on the other hand, worked for rent, gas, electricity, food, but my father worked for a separate reality that envisioned us all living again in Mexico. They never brought up the fact that the realities of their futures never crossed, it was just always in the air, most prevalent with a heavy sigh or a slammed door—never actually spoken.

When the truck was completely loaded, he went inside and took a shower. Apá made it a point to never look presentable. It's not that he didn't care about how he looked, because he did; he wanted to look ragged. He wanted other people to feel sorry for him. He wanted my uncles to think that my mother never cooked for him or cleaned for him, which in Mexican communities was the currency of worth for a married woman. He was controlling my mother's image to others more than she could herself. The reality was the opposite. My mother's constant struggle was for him to take a shower and to change clothes; she always begged for him to eat at home, not on the streets. He did it on purpose, perhaps to justify his leaving for six months at a time. If he could convince himself that in fact he had a terrible wife who did not care for him, then it wouldn't take much for him to enjoy his trip away from his family. Sometimes I thought he left only to be away from us; there was joy in his leaving, even though his joy looked nothing like any of ours. We each had our own definition of joy and kept its secret hidden as if in a secret box. No one would share their key; no one would allow anyone else to see inside their box.

Many times he would come home and scream at my mother that he hadn't eaten in two entire days, which was a lie. "The food is ready," my mother would respond, pointing to a pot on the stove filled with freshly boiled beans or squash. He would grumble something under his breath and walk away. He always wanted to make sure that he occupied the role of the victim. Nothing was ever his fault. And he fought hard to preserve and own that image of himself, even if he had to beat it into my mother to prove his victimhood, his woundedness.

*

When he got out of the shower, he put on some new boots I hadn't seen before. They were dark brown with intricate white designs and floral patterns. He wore polyester wranglers, a crisp button-up shirt, and a palm sombrero, and he had shaved his beard except for his mustache, which was long and pointy. He looked handsome. He looked like someone who was loved or at least in love—a dapper older gentleman with a family. He combed his hair to the side, like he always did. Even for his age, his thick, lush head of hair never had much gray. Balding isn't something passed down in my family. But I would have gladly preferred that rather than everything else I inherited: my anger and lack of patience. He's always had a large potbelly. He doesn't drink, so it's not from beer, but rather from all the food he eats on the street to avoid my mother's cooking, so he can complain about not eating a home-cooked meal. His belt is barely visible beneath his tucked-in shirt and belly spilling over.

Everyone says I look like him as a young man, and that soon I'll start looking more like him as an older man. I have a picture of him in his early twenties, and I do in fact bear a striking resemblance beyond even the obvious father/son connections—our cheeks, our eyes, our thin faces.

As he was getting his bag ready, a small tan leather duffel, my mother began crying. She always cried for the departed, perhaps because she had to do it so many times. Her eyes swelled up, but Apá never looked up to console her. He merely kept shuffling through his duffel bag to make sure he wasn't forgetting anything.

I was thinking about what I would be allowed to wear now that he was leaving. To anyone else who didn't know him, that would sound silly, but most of the fights between Amá and Apá were about how we dressed. My mother didn't really care how we dressed as long as we behaved and had good grades. My father, on the other hand, equated wearing baggy clothes with being morally bankrupt, with being looked down upon as a thief, as a gangster, as a useless miscreant, which stemmed from a long history of antiblackness and anti-indigenous xenophobia in ours and many Mexican families. He had a low regard for black culture because he equated it with so many negative stereotypes, and thus had a general mistrust of the black community in our low-income neighborhood. As a child and preteen, I didn't have the language to articulate his antiblackness, but I see it now. Perhaps, in an ironic turn, he saw blackness as quintessentially American at the same time that America distanced itself from black life and people while co-opting their culture.

I wanted to be like my friends whose parents didn't care if they wore baggy pants, or red shirts, or listened to rap and hip-hop. He saw it all as evil, a stain. I remember watching BET or VH1 or MTV when I got home from school and quickly changing the channel when I heard his truck pull up the driveway. Like many older Mexicans, he had conservative ideas of what was good and what was wrong in the world, and no one would change his mind.

I always had to wear fitted jeans, and I had to tuck in my shirt. It was a struggle to be allowed even to wear regular crew-neck T-shirts and not buttoned-up collared shirts all the time. Shorts, of any size or length, were strictly forbidden. I could not comb my hair slicked back, or too short; it had to be combed to the side. I was absolutely forbidden to shave my head. I always needed to wear a belt, my jeans (and only jeans) always needed to be snug, nothing baggy, and I always had to carry a wallet with at least one dollar in it. If it was up to him, we would also be wearing cowboy hats to school. The strangest thing to me was that he wouldn't let us wear tennis shoes until a certain age, and once he did, the only requirement he would not budge on was that he mandated that they could never be white, or majority white. I could never understand what white sneakers meant. I knew why he didn't want us in baggy clothes, but what did he have against white shoes? I came to the conclusion that to him, white shoes were for women. He didn't want his three boys dressing like women.

Maybe I snuck around him with baggy shirts because I wanted to get him mad, but more than that, it was because I didn't want to stick out. To wear boots and a sombrero was to imminently be called a naco, and if you were labeled a naco in my middle or high school, then you were also read as undocumented. He didn't care if people knew he didn't have papers because he never wanted to belong here, he never had the desire to fit in with six hundred other high schoolers. Why couldn't he see that I didn't want to bring attention to myself, that I wanted to hide? And wearing a cowboy hat, boots, and tight jeans to a high school mostly populated by kids of color was not the way to blend in.

The house where I grew up was in a neighborhood called Wilbur Block that was run by a relatively small gang of Norteños, but it was the largest concentration of Norteños in town. He knew this. He saw them hanging out in their yards, walking the streets, sitting at the park. They were all my friends. We grew up together, went to school together, and yet he wanted me nowhere near them.

Often I woke up unnecessarily early for school just so that I could comb my hair like my friends and leave before he got up. I laid my clothes out and sometimes packed a larger shirt in my backpack to change into once I got to school. I liked to spike my hair up or slick it back, which he hated. I chose my clothes the night before and carefully laid them out by my bed along with my shoes so that I didn't make any noise looking for them in the morning. I opened the bathroom door slowly because it creaked sometimes, and I turned on the faucet just enough for a small trickle to flow. The aerator on the tap made a loud hissing sound, which I wanted to avoid. It took a while for a small puddle of water to collect in my closed palm, which I rubbed together with gel and ran through my glossy hair. I tried to be as quick as I could.

Sometimes he would wake up quietly too and sneak up behind the bathroom door, which I had to leave cracked because closing it would have made too much noise. He would peek through the small opening of the bright bathroom, illuminating the hallway outside. His surveillance was obsessive. I never knew when he was watching me so I assumed he always was, and he would catch me and take the belt out. It was about control. The days that I didn't hear him sneaking up behind the door, he would catch me and slam the door open, startling me, and grab me by my hair with his fist.

"Hijo de tu pinche madre," "You son of a fucking bitch" was a favorite phrase of his.

Everything needed to be done his way, and his fights with Amá were somehow always our fault, the kids. According to him, if only we would dress respectably, like real men, like machos, then all of this could have been avoided. If only we wouldn't talk back to him, even when he was wrong, then there wouldn't be any problems. If only, if only, if only. Of course, there were always problems, but to him, none of them were of his making.

*

Clean-shaven, showered, and with fresh new clothes, he stepped out the door with his tan duffel bag in his hand. My mother followed behind, fiddling with something in her hands as if whatever she was holding would come to life and fly away. "Well, that's everything," he said to my mother and leaned over to me. I didn't know where my younger two brothers were. They should have been there, but they weren't. Perhaps my mother sent them away because she didn't want them to see their father leave yet again, which was silly because they knew he was leaving either way. My father shook my hand, gave me a light pat on the back, and said to take care of my mother and brothers. It was a firm handshake, the way he always taught me to shake. I would be his little hawk, his little accomplice. I would be the man of the house. Besides, I was named Marcelo too.

There was nothing special about that day, nothing momentous. We didn't know that his plan of being away for six months would turn into a deportation of ten years. It was a few days later that we got the call. He was charged with having violated the terms of his visa, which had been revoked. He entered Mexico no longer with the glee of visiting for as long as his money lasted him, but like a dog with his tail between his legs. His first plan was to buy a house in our hometown of Tepechitlán, Zacatecas; his second plan was to make us all come back with him, but that proved harder than he anticipated.

We didn't know then that we would have to stretch our memories to last us ten years. I would have paid more attention on that last day that he left. Maybe there would have been a party where our joy would slowly morph into a sadness that still didn't feel completely like sadness but had all of the consequences of sadness.

[First Movement Before Me as Good People]

It was easier to cross back and forth when Apá was young and still working the harvest seasons up and down the West Coast. He used to be more daring because the stakes were lower back in the 1980s. If they caught you, sometimes they just let you go and you would just turn around and try again the next day. Apá said he had friends who were sometimes caught three times in a single day. Still, one could never be too careful, so he crossed with larger groups because it was safer. In one of his trips north, he crossed with a group of about ten that included a pregnant woman who also had another small girl walking beside her. They walked mostly by night. The child tired quickly and often. The woman tired often too, and said her feet were unbearably swollen. The group stopped for them because that's what anyone would do.

They stopped again and again, but they figured if they stopped anymore to rest for her, they would miss their rendezvous and would all be in danger of being stranded with no food or water. No one said the words, but everyone was thinking the same thing. They were all hoping that one person was brave enough to say it, to say, "We can't stop anymore" and keep walking, or simply not say anything at all and just keep walking. The rest would surely follow, absolved.

Apá always said time stood still out there, like it was broken and would never work again no matter how many watches you wore, which meant that one step was no different than another—they were going nowhere.

*

They were good people, honest-to-God people, hardworking people. They didn't mean to keep walking, but Apá said that no one outside that moment would understand. No one was meant to understand.

Maybe they had to pretend not to hear her anymore. In their heads, it wasn't as bad if they simply didn't turn around to see her—action disguised as inaction. They must have told elaborate stories to convince themselves that it was all a dream, that they were making it all up. There were ten of them, never twelve.

And so they moved on, empty, vacuous, everything ahead of them monochrome, buzzing in a low electric drizzle.

*

Apá stayed behind. It wasn't that he was more courageous than them, not abandoning the woman; maybe it had nothing to do with choices. It was their fate to keep walking, and it was Apá's fate to stay behind. I want to believe that morality had nothing to do with it. No one questioned the higher powers that descend to the lowly depths of people in the desert. They do as they do and, in the moment, do not ask why.

Night fell, and they huddled together. Apá opened his large coat and nestled the woman on one side and her daughter on the other. When morning came, they set out again. A day passed before they found a road. There was no sight of the group, most likely picked up the night before just as was planned. *There were nine, not twelve.*

Apá waited by the side of the road for a long time until he saw headlights in the distance. He flagged down the car and asked the driver to take them to Los Angeles, which the driver kindly did, seeing the precarious situation they were in. They didn't care if it would have been immigration that they flagged. By that point, "immigration" was only an eleven-letter word and nothing else, except a chance to drink some water.

The woman's family, nervous that she didn't arrive with the rest of the group, buried their heads into my father's shoulder when they arrived in Long Beach, trying to stuff dollars in his pockets, which he didn't refuse. He said he liked the attention and told the story over and over about how he draped his jacket over them to keep them warm at night. They killed a pig in honor of Apá and threw a party with music and drinks and carnitas from said pig. They paid for his trip farther north, to the sister towns of Linda and Olivehurst, where we would eventually end up again a decade later.

If only the group had waited. Years later, I doubt they ever think of that woman and her child. But every now and then, I'm sure it returns to them, the memory, and there is nowhere they can hide. They didn't mean to. They are still good people. They will create elaborate stories to rid themselves of doubt, but nothing will work. Maybe they will even bump into her without ever knowing.

In one impossible scenario in their heads, to appease their regret, she is still somewhere out there, holding her *two* children, now adults, by the hand.

8.

The plane finally landed, and I felt the weight of my country above and around me. It happened, I could feel it in my bones, I had arrived. When the door opened, a wave of petroleum fumes wafted in, mixed with the smell of burnt rubber and a slight hint of soft, damp earth. It looked like it had just rained, but I didn't see a cloud in the sky. We took stairs off the plane and walked onto the tarmac to the terminal. Of all places, we agreed to meet at a Burger King inside the airport. Rubi and I walked closely together, lugging our suitcases behind us. I didn't want to look like a tourist, so I pretended to act bored, like I had done this a hundred times, but Rubi could tell it was an act. I looked at her nervously. She didn't care what people thought about her, and I envied her for that—I always had. She wore a large sun hat and a long dress. From afar, or up close, it was obvious we weren't from Mexico, at least not recently. I didn't have a question for her, but I hoped she had an answer.

It was so strange to hear everyone speaking Spanish. The attendants, the soldiers in the airport with their long assault rifles hanging across their chests, and the announcements over the intercom—all of it, Spanish. That was the first thing that disoriented me. I had never functioned in a space like that. I couldn't remember carrying my body in Spanish, completely in Spanish. Back home, even in private moments the atmosphere was still English: the TV was English, the cardboard cereal box labels were all in English, as were the unopened letters and bills on the table, and everything in the fridge.

It was hearing Spanish through the vehicle of authority that shocked me most. I realized how little is made up of words and how much of it is something more ethereal. The energy was different. I changed my dollar bills for pesos, and the man behind four inches of bulletproof glass in the exchange cubicle waved me aside for the next person in line with an uninterested glaze across his face. Even the flicking of his wrist felt like it was in Spanish, quicker to the point, frustrated.

I approached Mexican customs and immigration thinking I had something to worry about, thinking I had to prepare myself for the worst, as I always had. But then a sudden relief came over me, as had never happened before. I was a citizen of the earth on which I was walking; I pertained to the same body that could be elected president. There was a small moment of pride that died as soon as the officer said, "Are you Marcelo Hernandez?" The police were the police were the police, no matter.

[First Movement Before Me as Animal]

——

The first time my mother came with my father to the United States, she left the kids back in La Loma in the care of her mother, my Amá Julia. They promised they would only be gone a few months and would be back as soon as they made enough money. When they crossed into the U.S., they wandered the desert alone for miles without food or water. They were still young; maybe they still loved each other, or would soon start to. Every direction seemed like it was north, as if it was always noon in their heads. They moved because regardless which direction they faced, they trusted what was ahead more than what was behind them.

*

After a day of walking, a pack of wild dogs appeared to Amá and Apá out of nowhere. At first they thought it was a hallucination, the first signs that their minds were going. Both parties stopped to observe each other. The animals were real. The humans were real. After miles of indiscriminate turns around arroyos and brush too thick to enter, almost a statistical improbability, they happened to find each other at the precise moment that fate ordained. In a way, every decision they had ever made, even in childhood, led my parents to those dogs. Every song my mother played on her radio as a child led her to those dogs, every bird my father shot led him to those dogs, every heartbreak, every dress she sewed, every cup of warm coffee in the morning.

Two of the dogs left, uninterested surely, but one stayed behind. It approached them with its head down as if to say "I will not hurt you," and rubbed its head against Apá's leg. It walked right past them and continued ahead, slowing its pace and looking back to make sure its new friends were following. And indeed they followed.

They followed the dog because they thought it must have known the way to something—anything. The dog moved through trails hidden to Amá and Apá. Trails that only dogs are keen to. It turned with precision, and intent, as if it knew its decisions were the difference between life and death.

The dog led them to a ranch where men were working. They told the men their situation and asked if the dog was theirs, but they said it wasn't.

They're still not sure if the dog was real or not, but they remember it so well—its jaw slightly open, its head hanging low like a wilted flower. Maybe there wasn't a dog, and when those ranchers stumbled across my parents, rambling about a dog that no one else could see, dehydrated and wild-eyed, they simply shook their heads and said "Yes, yes, here, drink." My mother has never wanted to own a dog since.

*

The men gave them chicken soup and plenty of water, but not too much at once, because they heard it was bad. They tried to eat slowly, they tried to eat quietly. Even half dead, they still remembered that they were guests in a stranger's house, they still remembered it was bad for the body to drink so fast when it was thirsty.

Amá cooked a few days for them until the boss arrived with his provisions: food, water, and beer. They would have gladly stayed but the boss said he couldn't take them because they had children waiting for them back home. He was nice enough, though, to give them a ride to Los Angeles.

Years later, while driving my mother to the doctor, the radio will come on and a special episode on the border will say that a body only lasts a few days in the desert before it completely disappears—

no trace of it ever existing, ravaged by scavengers. Sometimes the bodies slowly make their way up a mountain, pulled up little by little by those scavengers moving their hunger in the same direction. And I will quickly turn it off, reluctant to admit a hint of gratitude that she doesn't know enough English to understand. They said that out there dogs return to their owners with a hand in their mouth and drop it at their owner's feet. Perhaps the hand just lies there on the ground, waiting for the authorities, because it is a hand, because that is what hands do, pointing in one direction or another.

They said sometimes dogs will last days out there, like the dog that saved my parents, and come back with nothing in their mouths, wagging their tails with joy at the sight of their owners, licking and licking their salty faces, tugging at their jeans to play. No one asks how it is they survive so long out there.[2]

9.

What had ten years of solitude done to his body? I didn't really know about his personal life. I guess I never bothered to ask, or better yet, I didn't want to know. Had he been alone that entire time? Had he taken a new girlfriend that we didn't know about? I knew general things from other people: he had a dog, he drove a truck, he liked to spend time up in the mountains. I had probably only spoken with him a handful of times in the ten years he was gone. And even then, it was only because my mother pushed the phone into my ear to use up the last few minutes of a calling card. Was his voice still the same?

He always avoided taking pictures, the only times I saw him was when someone came back from a trip to Mexico with pictures to share. He was there, caught off guard, in the background of someone else's picture—always in slight profile or walking away, never staring directly at the camera. That was something people did often. They would return and distribute any pictures where a family member of ours happened to pop up, almost like a footnote to their vacation, or perhaps as an excuse to tell us all about their vacation. It was bittersweet. The pictures were always so full of joy. We wondered how we could inject ourselves into that joy.

"Look, there's your dad," an aunt would say, pointing at a picture with my father lurking in the background and her daughters' enormous heads squished together in the foreground eating a ripe mango sprinkled with flakes of pepper. "Thanks, Tía," was all I could say.

I almost preferred to keep our interactions that way, filtered through someone else's emotions—it was easier to borrow them and give them back. His solitude, and ours, masked by someone else's joy. He was always caught in the middle of doing something—moving a bucket, crouching down to sit. It was in those rare moments that we got to see how he lived. I could tell a few things about my father's life simply from the way he leaned back in his chair, the angle of his head, the placement of his arms.

I liked that he wasn't taking the picture for me, it felt like I was watching him one frame at a time. In a way, it was like catching him in a moment of unfiltered sincerity, a moment that couldn't actually exist given his stoic nature, one isolated by circumstance and time. Had I been there during the moment the photograph was taken, I doubt he would be acting the same.

Sometimes it felt voyeuristic, like I shouldn't be looking at him without his permission. He didn't know that weeks later I would be sitting alone on my bed sifting through pictures where he was a small blurry dot behind my cousins smiling on horses. But that moment was ours, it was ours to keep and ours alone. I knew he would never give me anything like it if I asked.

If he was laughing, it wasn't for the camera, it wasn't for us, only for him, only for the moment. But I wasn't ready to confront him, so I was grateful for that removal of self, mostly because he wasn't aware that those pictures were coming back to us. He wasn't posing for the camera like my cousins in the frame.

[First Movement Before Me as a Tuft of Clover]

In one of those early trips of the mid-1980s, before I was born, Amá and Apá decided to make their life a little more stable and stay in the States for a while. They brought their two eldest children with them back from Amá Julia and began the slow work of settling down in Northern California. Yes, children are mobile and don't necessarily tie you to one place, but for Amá and Apá, who didn't have papers, to have a child born in America meant something different. Amá became pregnant in the States, and she had a home birth inside the doctor's house, which had thick ivy winding over the windows.

The child died only a few hours after birth, and they snapped a picture of Amá holding him in her arms, inconsolable.

The day he was to be buried, they couldn't afford a gravestone, so Amá spent the entire afternoon memorizing the exact placement of the trees and the bushes in the cemetery, counting how many steps from the path to where her child was lowered into the ground so she wouldn't forget. She was mapping a gravestone in her head to make up for what others could not see just beneath the surface.

"There's a tuft of clover nearby, he's three steps after the olive tree."

*

He was named Manuel for the four hours he was alive. They would have given him a name even if he had lived for two, or even if he died in her womb; he would always be Manuel. But no one would ever call him that. He would hardly ever be mentioned.

She wanted to mark it somehow, so that no one would step there, but anything short of a stone would be thrown away. She promised she would mark his grave one day. Soon after, they decided to return to Mexico, leaving the child behind. Besides, it was his land, he was born there. They gave up any hope of settling down, and after that, we never really stopped moving. It was too much to live near the clover, and it was too much to leave as well. Each paycheck she received, she handed over to Apá. There was never any chance for her to set aside a little for a stone. I always wondered, walking through a cemetery, avoiding the marked graves, how many times I was stepping on the unmarked graves of the poor. She didn't go back to say goodbye to the child; she knew he would be there when she returned.

*

Out of everyone in the family, it was Manuel who remained in place. And over the years, they kept coming back to that town where he is buried like distant moons orbiting a planet. It's where we eventually settled again somewhat, where the children had children. Something magnetic pulled us closer and closer to him.

Every time someone asks how long we have been here in this town of Marysville, California, they follow it with "why." "We don't know," we tell them. Thirty-six years after he was buried, Amá still lives within five miles of his grave. She has never forgotten how to find him.

There's a tuft of clover nearby, he's three steps after the olive tree.

We don't know if the olive tree is still there; surely the clover is gone. And still, no one has gotten a stone for him; afraid that in looking again, we wouldn't know where to find him, or that another marker would be there instead, placed by another family due to a small clerical error, always small clerical errors. We prefer to leave things the way they were, exactly as they were. We couldn't do anything then, so we won't do anything now.

10.

The Guadalajara airport seemed urban and rustic at the same time because it was the only choice for people from the city as well as people from the surrounding rural villages. I began looking at the faces of every older man I saw. I didn't know how long it would take me to recognize my father. Maybe it would be instantaneous, or I would look at him and keep looking in disbelief as if I was looking at myself for the first time through a dirty mirror. Streams of travelers spilled through two large double doors into the lobby where family members lined a pathway behind a metal barricade. It looked like a parade of weary travelers walking down the aisle with families cheering on either side, as if we had just finished a marathon. There were smiling faces, and people hugging, and tears. Was it always like that? How many other people on my flight were coming home for the first time too, how many were seeing some relatives for the first time in years? The mood in the air was one of joy. The workers, who had to witness this parade every half hour, seemed jaded, unfazed. Reunions only meant more trash for them to pick up. The salespeople standing beside their kiosks of lotions and perfumes straightened up for the newest arrivals.

That is the nature of airports. It is in airports where two countries actually meet. It is in the embrace between two people, wherever they might have been, that countries collide.

*

Rubi had seen Apá in pictures but wasn't really sure what to look for. I knew what to look for. In the distance I saw a white palm sombrero and a man beneath its shadow, waving at us. I immediately recognized Apá. I didn't know if I should hug him or punch him in the face, but my body took over, walked up, and embraced him.

Up close, I could see the changes in his face. He was much smaller than I remembered. His eyes were a little sunken, but his large pot-belly still hung over his belt. He was clean-shaven except for his large mustache, which curved at the tips. It was the longest I had stared at my father directly. I had always been afraid to look at him in the face. I used that moment as an excuse to do so, to examine every wrinkle, every scar. I knew I would never again be able to look at him straight in the eyes for that long. It wasn't like us.

It would either take another ten years of separation or death to be able to concentrate my vision on him completely, to take him in and hold him there. I was looking to see what ten years of solitude had done to him. I was looking for regret in his face—in his eyes—but I wasn't sure what regret looked like, only that Apá smelled like dried sweat and blackberries.

*

"Apá, this is my wife, Rubi," I said to him, and pointed to Rubi, who had been standing to the side. She shook his hand and gave him a hug. "It's wonderful to finally meet you," she said, and wiped her eyes. On our wedding day, just two years prior, Rubi asked to speak with Apá. I never knew what she said to him, and never wanted to ask. She sat by herself in her long white wedding gown in a far corner of the room and cried on the phone before hanging up and had to touch herself up for our wedding pictures.

I thought we would be leaving immediately after finding each other, but to my dismay, the "friend" my father paid to drive him three hours from Zacatecas to the Guadalajara airport decided to get more bang for his buck and include another pickup, so we had to stay and wait for those people to land. A bus would have been easier and cheaper but Apá insisted that a personal car was better for reasons unknown to me. I was very hungry, but I didn't want to eat in the airport. I wanted to save my appetite for some good home-cooked meals. I wanted my first bite to utterly destroy me. I had more confidence in food to welcome me home than in my father, so I had saved my appetite. I hadn't eaten all day. We decided to wait for the other passengers at the Burger King. Rubi got some fries, and I tried my hardest to resist them but I couldn't, I was too hungry. I carefully ate one and then another, hoping that would stave off my hunger until we got home—or my father's home, I still wasn't sure what to call it.

I didn't know what to say to my father. Could I show him love and anger at the same time without one erasing the other? I couldn't look at him for long anymore. That moment came and went. Now I could only examine him in short spurts and had to quickly look away. How quick, the moment his face opened for me before it disappeared beneath the shadow of his large hat again.

Five long hours passed before the other passengers arrived—a man with his son, who was a little younger than me. All six of us, along with our luggage, finally left the airport and headed toward the car. As I was walking, I heard someone behind me grab my bag and shake my hand. He asked where our car was so he could help us with our luggage. Apá quickly grabbed the bags out of his hands and waved him away. "Trucha, mijo," he said and took my suitcase himself. I felt bad for the man. I wanted to give him something, but my father refused. He knew this country more than I did. We crammed into the car as best as we could. I was irritated that we had to wait so long for the other passengers and even more so when I found out I had to sit on Rubi's lap the entire way, hunched down. The other father's son took the front seat so we squeezed into the single back seat and headed off. It was almost midnight. By the time we reached Tepechitlán, it would be close to two in the morning.

*

It took us about forty-five minutes to drive through the industrial city. There was a serene quiet to the gated yards full of commercial trailers illuminated beneath the orange lights of the city. It looked like everyone immediately dropped what they were doing as soon as night fell, and the hum of enterprise would pick up again in the morning.

I was already tired of hunching over, so I adjusted my body one way and another but couldn't find a good position. Apá and I were elbow to elbow, but I didn't know if it was okay to touch him. It was nice to be that silent, and to be that close to Apá, though I dared not lean my head on his shoulder to sleep. We left the city behind us and began the ascent over the mountain pass. The driver rolled down his windows and they got stuck. The night air was cold against my face as we drove through the winding road. I wanted to see the world outside, but it was too dark and the wind blowing in my face made my eyes water and my vision blurry.

By the first hour, the wind was unbearable. The driver said he could sometimes get the windows to work if he turned off the car, but then he ran the risk of the whole car not turning back on. The last thing I wanted was to be stuck in the middle of the Sierra at night. I wanted to be home already, but fate seemed intent against it. I changed positions with Rubi so that she was sitting on top of me, but I still felt a growing claustrophobia. I felt weak because I hadn't eaten or slept in almost twenty-four hours. The road was narrow and wound around sharp turns as we edged closer to my town. My father whispered to me that the driver had had a few drinks on the way. I wrapped my thin jacket around my head, mostly because I was cold, but also because I wanted to scream.

*

With each mile, I felt like I was going into myself, toward a point of singularity. I was afraid of both scenarios: that all of my questions would be answered and none. I asked my father the names of all of the towns we passed along the way: Santa María, García de la Cadena,

La Ceja, El Teúl. I'd heard those names before, and though I couldn't see them from the road, I imagined their town squares, and their churches all the same. I imagined the prayers of their mothers for all of the children stuck in El Norte and I realized that *we* were who people referred to when they said Norteños, we were the same shape of a mother's prayer in one of those small towns, except it wasn't really us whose return she was praying for.

My world was getting smaller. What I dreamed about was right in front of me, out there, hidden beneath the blanket of night.

The car began to slow down at the edge of a town that looked defeated in the orange haze of streetlamps. All around us were half-finished homes and empty lots. "We're here," said my father, probably just as relieved to be home as I was. I would have to wait until morning to see the rest of the town, hoping it was better than what I was able to see nearby. I was too tired to eat or take a shower. My father's German shepherd greeted us from the rooftop. At last I had arrived.

We made our bed in the spare room, and I told Rubi to shake the sheets to check for scorpions and look underneath the bed for snakes. It was a habit I didn't know I had. It came back to me unannounced but just as strong as if I had been doing it all my life, as if I had never even left.

[First Movement Before Me as Niños de la Tierra]

═══

They used to say that there were children living beneath the rocks on the west side of mountains. If you looked at their faces you would go blind, so you had to look up at the sky to avoid their stare.

This was a myth brought back to Mexico from the U.S. by braceros like my grandfather Jesús. I liked to think of these myths crossing the border as well, returning to their origin from thousands of miles away.

I remember climbing a hill the adults told me not to go near because Los Niños de la Tierra lived there. I looked up to the sky as I walked, careful not to look down at their faces, afraid of going blind.

Maybe those children belonged to someone, trapped in the north like everyone else, unable to return to the land of their birth. Or maybe that *was* the land of their birth, and they looked up because that's where all the mothers and fathers were.

11.

I woke up confused and groggy, with mosquito bites down my legs. It took me a moment to remember where I was and why I was there. The air felt damp and cold, as if I had slept beneath the stars and was glazed with a film of morning dew. Rubi, lying next to me, stirred but did not wake as I stepped off the bed onto the cold cement with my bare feet. Unlike me, mosquitoes never really bothered with her. In Spanish, there's a phrase for those who get bitten a lot: they call them sangrón, which means "bloody" (thus their attraction to mosquitoes), but it also means someone who is generally unpleasant.

I didn't want Apá to think that I was delicate; I thought I could pick up where we left off the day he left ten years ago, when I was his "little hawk." Mostly, I didn't want him to think that I was too good for unfinished cement floors, mud walls, and old creaky mattresses. I pretended I wasn't terrified of going through my luggage, which I accidentally left open on the floor, or the blankets in the corner of the room, piled three feet high, which I was certain were covered in scorpions. I recognized those blankets as the same ones we had sent to him over the years. We mostly sent him jeans, wool socks, and blankets because we thought there was no better gift than to keep our old man clothed and warm. Seeing the blankets tossed in the corner of the dirt floor for what seemed like years, with the most recent ones on top, made me think of everything I could have bought instead with the little extra I had.

I shook my pants in the air, peeked into my shoes, and walked outside, where it was brisk. There were dozens of large potted plants throughout the courtyard patio. Some were in large drying-machine barrels and others in plastic buckets. He had geraniums, and ferns, and bright morning glory growing everywhere. In the middle was a small garden bed lined with bricks where a few stalks of corn jutted out in random places. There was a stone washbasin in one corner of the courtyard, with clean socks hanging off the ends, and saddles were hanging off the brick walls. The air felt cold, but the sun was delicious. Even a single hour of that light would have been more than enough for any plant, more than enough even for me.

Because all of the rooms surrounded the courtyard and faced inward, I could see Apá darting through the kitchen, shuffling through some things. I didn't know what to say to him. Who would be the first to talk? Over the years, the few conversations we had on the phone had mostly been him screaming, asking me why my mother didn't want to return to join him in Mexico. Amá said she had never felt stronger in her life than when she told him she wouldn't go.

He appeared from the kitchen out into the bright mess of flowers and smiled. I could never answer him over the phone as to why Amá would not return, just as I couldn't answer him there, standing a few feet in front of me, when he asked me what was the first thing I wanted to do for the day.

I looked around—everything was his, only he had touched it. Here, in this courtyard, was the sum of his deportation ten years before, and his decision not to return every year thereafter.

My permit only allowed me to stay for a single week, so I had to make the best out of it.

"I want to go see my tías," I said.

"We can do that," he said.

*

It fascinated me that my father could keep a garden. That he could care for a plant, water it, prune its dead leaves, and turn the pot like a dial for the best light. I could see that he took care to put the ferns in the shade so the harsh sunlight wouldn't burn them. I could see how he wrapped the geraniums around the brick columns to keep them from breaking under the weight of their own blossoms. He didn't need to say much for me to see how lonely he must have been. I wonder if that was what solitude had done to him—if those petals were the soft edges of him I was forbidden to touch as a child.

I had heard talk of this garden from relatives who visited him in the past, but I never believed it. The courtyard wall keeping the outside world away seemed so large and absolute. Almost as if it was his intent to punctuate that solitude, and he pushed it as far as his property would go. He had a large bathtub in the middle of the courtyard and said he liked to take long baths in the sun, completely naked, because no one could see in. It all made me believe that perhaps he was happy, or at least that he could hide his loneliness better than others.

Since he'd always depended on Amá for domestic chores, he had never taught himself to cook, or clean, or wash, but in those ten years he had to learn it all. He had a clothesline with all of his jeans drying in the morning sun. He had a days-old pot of cold beans on the stove. The more I thought about it, the more I was certain that the large wall was there so he could make sure no one saw him washing his own clothes, doing what he said a woman should have been doing for him all along.

*

I never understood why he wanted to build such a big house. The living room and kitchen alone measured sixty by thirty feet, and the ceilings were about fifteen feet high. The house had four other rooms, one with a full bathroom. It was meant for a large family.

He built the house as soon as he arrived. He built it with the intention of using it as a way to convince my mother to leave the States and take us with her to join him after his deportation, but my mother would have none of it. She was firm in her decision to stay.

My mother could hide behind his deportation as an excuse to escape him. There was nothing he could actually do over the phone other than scream and plead. There came a time when my mother stopped answering his calls, not because she was too busy working, which she was, but because she was no longer afraid. She answered when she felt like it and hung up as soon as she thought his tone was starting to get too aggressive. "Bad connection, sorry," she would say, indifferently, the next time they spoke.

Apá still believed she was the same person he left crying on the driveway; he refused to believe that she would not listen to him and return to Mexico. But solitude did something different to her than it did to him. She was emboldened to finally speak up and say no. He, on the other hand, built an entire house around his denial, which stroked his delusion of power. Late into his exile, he bought a large dining room table that had enough room for eight people. It took up most of the space in the kitchen. It looked Gothic with its intricate designs carved onto the arm rests. He had it made by hand at the local carpenter's shop and even held the carpenter at gunpoint when it wasn't done on time. When we sat down to drink coffee that morning, he said it was the first time the table seemed somewhat full.

The large house must have sharpened his solitude, and made it more unbearable. I could see him walking those corridors late at night, perhaps whistling a song as he headed for the bathroom outside in the courtyard. I wanted to feel sorry for him, but hearing my echoes throughout the house made me clench my jaw and drink my coffee fast, burning my tongue.

*

He had always been one to overdo things, as I was always prone to overcompensate. Even the kitchen countertop had fourteen steel beams inside the six-inch-thick cement. Who would ever need a countertop made of six inches of reinforced cement? He said you could actually drive a truck over it and nothing would happen.

"Ten hurricanes could hit this house and nothing," he said.

"Apá, we're in the desert, there are no hurricanes here" I said. "No earthquakes, no tsunamis, we're even too high for a flash flood."

He had built footings into the earth for the kitchen countertop alone. The footings for the house were as tall as I was beneath the ground.

He probably spent a third more unnecessarily reinforcing his house. So much that I began to wonder if it edged on paranoia—his insistence on never again moving, his solution to all of the damage that his constant flux had caused. It wasn't extravagant, it was just thick and simple, like most of the other homes in the town—a few square parcels with a roof. He proudly pointed at the perimeter wall, which was made out of huge limestone blocks two feet wide by two feet tall by ten inches thick. He said it took four men to lift a single slab and drop it in place. He had to drive out of state to get the limestone from a special quarry, and proudly displayed a large scar running the entire length of his arm.

"Look, I cut myself open on the very first slab," he said.

I remembered that wound on his arm; at least, I remember hearing about it on the phone and imagining it in my head. The scar from the concrete saw now looked different than what I had imagined; it zigzagged through his arm like lightning.

The garage was even larger, easily twenty feet high, with an industrial curtain door so that it could fit large cattle trucks with tall railings to transport cows.

"Apá, we don't have cows," I wanted to say to him, but I kept my mouth shut and simply kept gawking and marveling to satisfy him. He spent the whole morning going through every detail of construction, from the placement of the outlets to the lights and the sewage system. He kept repeating that it wasn't a bad job for someone who only went to second grade. And indeed it wasn't. I was genuinely impressed. His greatest accomplishment, according to him, was the fact that the entire house was flat—there were no bumps or steps of any kind. He said he was thinking about the future, when he would need a walker or a wheelchair in his old age. He wanted to make sure he would be able to get around his own house with ease. He didn't want to depend on others. Even the shower had no partition; there was just a walk-in space slightly sloping into the drain. It was painful to hear him talk about the future because I knew it didn't include me or anyone else in the family. I nodded along, walking with my coffee in hand, wondering if he knew he'd built a house he would most likely die alone in.

I knew he had always been selfish. This was nothing new. But seeing his house gave me something to hold on to, something tangible to measure his narcissism against. He could have used that money on so much more. I could see what was worth more than me, my brothers, and my mother, and it was all around me, the totality of his possessions. Deportation was conveniently final to him, just as it was for my mother. He could exclaim as much desire to return to the U.S. as he wanted without having to actually do it. And Amá could go on saying that the phone line kept cutting off and apologizing. In the end, it seemed like deep down they both wanted the same thing. It's a wonder I ever thought he would return at all.

So many times I had asked why he never came back, or even attempted to come back, why he had never hired a coyote, and the answers were finally in front of me—in the red and white geraniums, in his large tub beneath the sun, in each steel beam running throughout the house, and even in the blood he lost cutting the stone. This was all enough for my father, enough for him to stay.

Rubi had woken up by then and was marveling at the garden, too. I looked at her from across the courtyard and wondered if by chance we could ever have a life in Mexico—if this life could ever be for us. No more hiding, no more fear of being deported, no more waiting and waiting for the laws to change. Could we see our children here? I tried to imagine her standing in that same spot but with no urgency to leave, just standing, and six or seven months pregnant, on the phone with her mother back in the States.

We hopped in Apá's old Jeep Cherokee and headed into town to buy some groceries because his fridge was completely empty except for some orange juice in a cracked glass jug. No one knew that I had returned because I'd kept it secret. Mexico had changed a lot over the years, and it was best to keep a low profile. The town and the entire state belonged to the Cártel del Golfo, but things turned violent when Los Zetas contested for the same territory. Apá said things were okay, that the worst was in 2008, and that you just had to be careful about what you said and did in public because you never knew who could be watching.

I went house to house, visiting aunts and uncles I only knew by name, and all of them held me for a long time in their arms, in utter disbelief. My tías looked me in the eyes as if they had a story to tell me but they didn't have time, or simply couldn't.

"You were *this* little when you left," my tía Beatrice said to me, pointing to the ground, still shaking her head.

Standing in front of my father as he presented me to family I never knew, I had to learn how to be a son all over again. Despite my misgivings, something deep inside me still wanted to impress him, still wanted to please him, though it would never be enough. I was his son, grown, with a beard and a wife. He paraded me through town like a trophy horse, like a gamecock with fighting knives dragging on my feet.

[First Movement Before Me as Peligrosa]

Amá used to say that a pregnant woman should never plant anything in the soil because she would turn the soil barren.

When Amá was pregnant with me, she lived on the ranch of La Loma. She said she would deliberately go into the cornfield and sow a small seed in the earth. Apá, as usual, was gone often in those days, and as usual, she took up the heavy tasks he was supposed to do—fetching firewood, herding the cows down the mountain. She talked to her animals a lot. She said she worried often that I would die as her last child, Manuel, had died. But that baby was three thousand miles away, in the ground, separated by a border. Perhaps the distance alone would make for a different outcome. Shortly before my birth, her mother, my Amá Julia, died of cancer in the stomach, suddenly and without much notice. Amá was lying in bed with her to keep her warm the night she died. Amá said her mother stretched her thin legs outward toward the end of the bed and let out a small breath before she stiffened.

A year after that, Amá was pregnant with me.

If, when she was pregnant with me, she buried the seed and the field became fallow, then maybe that would be an indication that the child in her womb wouldn't die like the last one. It would mean there was actually something there inside her, and not just a stone, that it would live longer than the last one. She didn't want to begin to grow attached until she was sure. It was my gravity—me at the center; she, orbiting around me like a moon. Or she at an even deeper center, and me in her womb, orbiting around her, pulled by the first green sprout in an otherwise dying field of corn.

I imagine her digging in the dirt, glancing around, making sure no one was looking, and dropping a small bean into a hole. Men might spend months toiling over something that would never grow while she held me inside her, growing, completely her own, something divorced from the world, if even only for nine months. She knew what she was capable of. And I grew and grew.

*

Perhaps it wasn't only seeds she planted but objects—a small doll, hoping for another daughter, the wingless bodies of bees she found in the courtyard, all of her children's baby teeth she kept in a small cloth, hoping for—I don't know what.

During each of the six times she was pregnant, Apá never laid a hand on her.

Amá, tú eres bella y peligrosa.

12.

As we drove up to my mother's ranch of La Loma, I realized how little I actually knew about the land and its specific characteristics. In his white Jeep, Rubi, Apá, and I ascended from the valley below. Apá drove slowly, pointing at small ridges along the road that told him exactly where it had rained and how much. He was precise, he was raised to learn the patterns of rain, how it left its subtle footprint even in the way the leaves hung off the trees. Apá took his time on the bumpy road, and even stopped completely, pointing to lines I could not see in the landscape that marked property boundaries of those old infamous families, five or six generations removed, whose heirs would come to kill each other over that land. He knew the names of the shrubs, and the trees, and birds. He could tell from a distance who had sewn their crop too early, who had done so too late, and who was wise enough to time it just right. His knowledge of the landscape seemed vast and effortless, and I was shocked that it had always been there just beneath the surface, ready to be called on at any minute.

From afar, Apá pointed to a compound on top of a hill. "That's it," he said.

Water was hard to come by in those areas, but La Loma was prized in its heyday because it had not only one but two streams which were now dry. The smaller stream, el arroyo chico, crossed right through the middle of the property, and the bigger creek was about one hundred meters down below. The truck stopped, and we were all silent for a moment. I asked both Rubi and Apá if I could go inside alone.

*

The thick adobe walls, which had withstood at least two centuries of rain, were evidence that my ancestors had no intention of leaving.

They built the house once and never had to build it again because they built it out of the materials that were already there around them. Maybe that was why Apá built his house the way he did. Unlike us, he was thinking three, four, or five generations ahead. He wanted something to last as long as the pyramids of Egypt, of Teotihuacan, of Chichén Itzá. It was an internal clock that looked far into the past and as much into the future. I didn't possess that clock inside me yet.

I opened the thick wooden door to the courtyard and took in a grim scene. The roof had collapsed years before, and shrubs taller than me grew in each room, making it difficult to walk through. I could tell that there was life there once, that people were happy. I could also tell that grief abounded, not because of its state of decay, but because there was no one left who would take over its care. Later, I would show the video footage to my mother, and she would stare at the screen for a long time before telling me to turn it off.

I walked into the room where my great-grandfather León, Amá Julia's father, worked as a weaver. He made wool blankets using a small wooden loom and sold them down in the market in town. He was limited to the color of the year's offspring. He sheared the wool from his herd and spun it into yarn. Sometimes he would get almost a golden hue in the yarn, or a crimson brown. But mostly it was a dirty white, black, and light brown. Nonetheless he designed birds, and deer, and different shapes of his own making.

*

As I walked through the rooms, parting the tall brush ahead with my hands, the house felt like a puzzle that had finally revealed itself after years when I was given nothing but fragments. I only remembered small details of the house from stories my family would tell, and now I was able to fill in the rest. I walked through each room, touching the walls with my hands.

Who would have thought that almost no one would be left on the entire mountain? So many homes built to last, only to be abandoned. There were holes in the ground throughout the house. Over the years people had broken in and dug, looking for some lost fortune, believing my great-grandfather buried some gold, but they always came up empty-handed, as far as we know.

Everything seemed familiar because I had imagined it endless times growing up. During Christmas, during a birthday party, or even just on a Sunday afternoon, anytime the adults would gather, the only topic of conversation was always Mexico and the ranch. I found the pig corral where my mother fell in as a child and was nearly eaten by a sow exactly where I had envisioned it. The three large avocado trees that my mother dreamed about looked nearly petrified, and probably didn't bear fruit anymore, but nonetheless they were there, just as I imagined.

It was quiet; not even the insects announced themselves. I walked to the back of the house, which was surrounded by a stone wall. I picked up rock after rock and put it back down. I turned rocks around to see what was underneath them. My blood was in that earth; it was in those trees, and even in the walls themselves.

I wanted to change something about the scene, even if it was only moving a single rock around. I wanted it to be different because of my arrival, different at my departure. I wanted my ancestors to see that someone was still there, tending to their eternal home. I made a little clearing. Removed all the rocks I could pick up and placed them on top of the wall. I wanted them to know that a part of them, which was inside a part of me, was still breaking a sweat in the crisp morning air on that mountain.

*

I talked to them. I didn't know all of their names, but I didn't need to. They knew all about me. I knew they could hear me and knew why I had come, more so than I did. I said I was sorry. I said I would make things better. I knew a lot of things weren't my fault, in fact most weren't: why the ranch was abandoned, why my father drove us into debt, why he was deported, why the family couldn't just stay a little longer in the U.S. after baby Manuel's death to get their green card under Reagan's famous amnesty order. How different our lives would have been if only they had waited. But although none of this was my fault, I wanted to take the blame, to let it all fall on me. If all it took to reverse any of this was for me to be punished, I would have gladly taken the beating.

I closed my eyes and saw the ranch in its glory days. I could see my mother as a child running through those meadows, laughing and swimming in the arroyo. I held my mother's small hand as she guided me through the house. We played games, we made clay pots at the river bed and pretended to drink tea. She knew who I was, she knew what the future held for her.

There was a sapote tree with its large fruit hanging from its branches that looked new, as though it came only after everyone left, as if it was waiting for everyone to leave.

I wept quietly at the center of my blood.

My mother's small hands led me to the courtyard, and there she was with all of her sisters, none of whom had been married yet. I could see them all sitting in the sun, sewing together, making dresses to wear into town, laughing at riddles they would tell each other to pass the time.

There was the room in which my great-great-grandmother Josefina died. She died on a cot near a wall. As she was dying, it was said that she kept digging her nails into a small crevice in the adobe wall. They said she was hiding jewelry in that hole, or that she was signaling to those standing around her that something was there. She died with her hand in that hole.

When I entered that room, I looked for the small crevice, and sure enough found it, right where my mother said it would be. It was just large enough for my palm. Nothing was inside. I took out a pen from my pocket and buried it in the wall.

*

I sat in a clearing in the courtyard. At my feet and around me were stalks of corn that sprouted haphazardly here and there. Gone from my vision was Amá and my tías in their youth, sitting in a circle, replaced by tall stalks of corn that came from those loose kernels dropped on the floor. For two hundred years my family had sat in that very courtyard repeating the same steps of desgranando mazorca to make nixtamal for tortillas.

I felt a sense of largeness come over me. I wanted to take my clothes off and touch every single adobe brick with every part of my body. I wanted to dance in the middle of the clearing and let all of the snakes hiding in the weeds come join me. I felt a sharp pain, like a wire wrapped around my throat and getting tighter, like something sectioning me in pieces. If the moon came out I would bow in reverence, I would unravel before it and speak softly into the dirt.

I envied the rhizomes sprawling beneath the earth, their secret language. I, too, wanted to touch that many things at once, to stretch for miles, connected by a single fungus, and to pulse through the roots of countless trees.

*

If I could, I would have left a part of my body behind. I rubbed my skin with a rock until it turned red. I knew the landscape would outlast me, that the border would still be up long after I died, that the trees would continue to be just that—nothing but trees. Apá's house would still be there, as would the walls of La Loma. I wanted so much more, but I still felt that I was missing something. I still felt like I was opening a small box with another box inside it, and it would go on forever. Maybe the point was the box, not what was inside it; the point was those walls that no amount of rain or hail could crumble. The point was that they came from the earth and were in no hurry to return. It's common to carry a small piece of dirt from your homeland when you leave. Knowing they will never return, some people eat it. I wouldn't know where to begin collecting dirt.

We left the ranch and began our descent into town. Apá seemed annoyed that I had taken so long. Perhaps he was upset that I didn't want him with me, that I wanted that moment to myself. In my hand I held a small rock I was hoping I could sneak past customs. They don't allow dirt of any kind to be brought into the States. I put it in my pocket and rubbed it gently with my fingers.

The next day was Christmas Eve. We sat in the patio of Apá's house with a large fire in an oil barrel between us. We were quiet, listening to the frogs and crickets in the darkness. At exactly midnight, and unannounced, Apá opened the main door to the courtyard, walked out to the street, and fired six rounds from his .357 Magnum revolver, which I had no idea was tucked beneath his jacket and which he had been carrying all day. I jumped at the sound of the shots. He came back in, locked the door, and sat down without a word, a slight smile across his face. It was his way of celebrating Christmas. No presents, just six hollow-point rounds into the air. In the distance I could hear others doing the same. He laughed a little and tucked the gun into his jacket. He said every man should know how to hold and fire a gun and that he would teach me in the morning.

Interview on Allegiance

1.

Rubi immigrated to the United States with her family only a year
before I did, in 1992. Although she came from the coastal state of
Guerrero, after living in Washington State and San Jose, in 1993 she
and her family settled in Yuba City, California, the same town where
I had just settled in from Mexico. We lived in the same government
migrant labor camp for many years and must have, at one point or
other, crossed paths as children.

All of the kids in the migrant camp knew each other, but it wasn't
until high school that Rubi and I became better acquainted. We
were both in a cultural dance club at school, and eventually started
dating in 2005. I wrote my very first poems to her and would slip
them into her locker, and she would show them to her Spanish
class, who would then try to interpret them, even though they were
in English. I wanted to write poetry because I believed any practice
in the English language would distance myself from my identity
as an immigrant and I thought (naively, ashamedly so) that the
farthest association from an immigrant was a poet. How foolish I
was. Little did I know the lineage of immigrant poets I came from
and would follow. But more than that, I wanted to write and speak
English better than any white person, any citizen, because in the
unthinkable case of ever getting caught by immigration, I thought

I could impress them enough with my mastery of English to let me go. What a stupid idea.

It took me months before I was ever able to muster enough courage to confess to Rubi that I didn't have papers, after which she admitted that she had only gotten hers a few months before. She was the first person I trusted enough to confide in about my documentation status, but it wasn't easy. We kissed before I told her I didn't have papers; I told her I loved her, and she said it back, before I ever mentioned I didn't have papers; we made love, we fought, we met each other's parents, before I told her I didn't have papers—I didn't want her to leave me before telling her I didn't have papers, if it ever came to that.

We married six years later on September 10, 2011. We chose the date specifically because it was 9–10–11, and thought the sequence of numbers was a once-in-a-lifetime chance. I liked things that felt rare and intentional. It was difficult to convince myself that people weren't saying behind our backs that I only married Rubi for her papers, so I decided to wait a while before filing an immigration application. It was a way of saying, "I'm in no hurry, I'm with her because I love her."

*

She finally submitted a petition for me to get a green card. It wasn't a single process, and could sometimes take up to sixteen years, depending what route people take. Because I was able to leave the country and reenter legally with my DACA permit, I didn't have to leave the U.S. for my immigration interview. When we submitted the form, again I said to Rubi, "You know I love you despite any of this," to which she laughed and said, "I know."

2.

The order to appear for my interview came in 2014, in a letter printed on special thick paper. Getting the notice to appear meant that I had met all of the requirements needed to receive a green card if all went well at my immigration interview. The interview was set for July 28, 2014. I was twenty-six, twenty-one years after I first arrived.

*

An immigration interview follows the same rhetorical form as any other interview. The rules you're expected to follow are the same. It's a structure so common that I sometimes took its usefulness for granted. It happened every time I waited in line at the bank, at the store, or even when I made love.

"Do you love me?" I would say to Rubi in our first one-bedroom apartment with no AC.

"Yes," she would say.

"Isn't it love even if we don't change?"

"Amor, I don't understand the question." We were so young and so much in love that we thought love could be anything we wanted it to be.

I repeated those words over and over. Sometimes in my head to myself—"Is it love even if we don't change?" I wanted to approach questions as I would approach a large body of water, as things in which I could drown, knowing how easy it was to drown, knowing exactly the limits and dimensions of my body and what it would take to drown it.

*

If I ever stood in front of a crowd, I would like to interview them in secret to see what they thought of me, to see if I would allow them to love me. We would all be knee-deep in water.

I would want to know what their collective answer would be. I would hold my finger to my mouth and tell everyone to quiet. And they would. We would know things about each other at the end of it that we did not know at the beginning. We would all nod our heads but some for different reasons. There would be small cubes of cheese at the end and wine to wash them down.

*

The day of the interview, I took out my entire closet for the right thing to wear.

"What shirt says: I want to be an American?" I asked Rubi, holding up two blue collared shirts in each hand. One was slightly lighter, the blue of open ocean, and the other was of the deeper ocean, where bioluminescent creatures lurked.

Maybe if my cells tried just a little harder, they too could light up just like those creatures floating a mile beneath the surface. Why not? They carried inside their scales everything that was already inside me.

"I don't care which one you wear," Rubi said, "but hurry, because we have to go, it's getting late."

We got in the car and drove to the city. I chose the shirt that was the color of an expensive velvet dress I saw an older white woman wear to a symphony, the darker one. It was my first and only symphony I had ever attended, and I was wildly underdressed. Maybe I *would* light up, maybe I would drown inside my car from so many questions as we practiced what we would say.

3.

I used to daydream that I was somebody famous. That people wanted to interview me on TV and radio, and I practiced my coy giggle with embarrassment. In these interviews, I balanced a very fine line between being humble and cocky in a way that was endearing to the crowd. They hated and loved me at the same time. Someone would walk up and give me flowers and I would thank them profusely, then walk away and toss them, even if they were still looking. Everyone wanted to be me.

Interviews reminded me how much of my life was lived through questions—interrogations—how much of it was just someone waiting for me to tell them an answer—how good I got at avoiding giving one.

"Where were you born?"

"Where do you think?"

But when I had no other choice but to answer directly, I still found a way to curve the truth about me; I took everything that was inside and put it outside, like how we don't really know how some deep-water creatures really look because by the time they reach the surface, the change in pressure has deformed them. It was how an unknown became a known.

Things always moved in a single direction, from the interviewer to the interviewee. Even when the person being interrogated responded, it was in the direction of the interrogator's next question, always moving forward. The U.S. government was good at asking questions, and it got in a lot of trouble when people learned just how it got its answers—it was a simulated drowning, but a drowning nonetheless.

*

In late-night talk shows, I saw beautiful people sit sideways on a chair with their legs crossed, drinking from a mug with the show's name printed on the front—it always conveniently faced the front. I always wondered if it was actually coffee they were drinking that late at night. They leaned over a chair, crossed their other leg over, and smiled with a mouth full of large teeth, almost too many teeth, which were so white they seemed to glow in the dark. Sometimes they wore sunglasses even though the only visible lights were the ones from the televised backdrop of the cityscape at night. Los Angeles was so pretty from above.

They let you see into their lives, just enough to pique your interest, just enough to stay barely scandalous—careful not to seem sad or garner pity. No one likes a sad and washed-up star, but everyone loves a star that is on the verge of getting there, on the verge of breaking. Sadness itself is sometimes a good thing. Sadness is hot, sadness makes money, sadness has soft filters and ashtrays and turns a young Elizabeth Woolridge into Lana Del Rey cruising through Venice Beach on a Harley drinking PBR.

The hosts ask questions they know will not be answered, but that is not the point. The point is for the celebrities sitting in the hot seat to shy away from their questions ever so slightly. The point is for them to say "Stop, you know I can't talk about that in public," or "Well, you'll have to ask them, not me." And then they all laugh because they're supposed to laugh. And the audience laughs and coos, and the hosts drink from whatever is in their mugs and chuckle again and turn to the musical accompaniment for additional commentary, which is underscored by a snare drum and "we'll be back after this commercial break." I loved every minute of it. I loved the live band. I loved the witty banter, which seemed so effortless, how quick and smooth they were with their answers, how everyone seemed to be a few seconds ahead in the conversation than the audience—ahead of me.

Then there was the moment when things went wrong. When someone didn't follow the rules. People don't like surprises. For instance, after a barrage of attacks, Cher (rightly so) tells David Letterman that he is an asshole. Her sadness stops being pretty to him. Though later it will turn out to be staged, Joaquin Phoenix stares inwardly from the reflection of his glasses, oblivious to the audience, and the world witnesses either a piece of performance art or a man who has lost his faith in an industry. The host, David Letterman again, aptly ends the interview by saying, "Joaquin, I'm sorry you couldn't be here tonight." Joaquin doesn't lean over his seat; he doesn't whisper anything in anyone's ear. He isn't playing along like he is supposed to. You can see that he doesn't want to be there; he doesn't want to take part in the soliloquy. At least his portrayal indicates that. *I'm sorry, you couldn't be here tonight*, as if you can be anywhere else.

In a more haunting episode, Crispin Glover, who played the dad on the *Back to the Future* franchise as George McFly, reads newspaper clippings about himself at a nightclub and seems surprised that he is being filmed at all when the audience erupts into laughter over his antics. He stares out toward the audience and looks directly at the camera as if wanting to see who is really there on the other side of the lens, who is really watching. He continues to read what the tabloids have said about him. He insists on arm wrestling David Letterman, who eventually walks offstage, visibly upset. A door has been opened that cannot be closed. The forward motion has stopped. Some of them were asked back on the show, and some weren't. Some apologized, others tried to explain what it was they were doing in front of yet another camera, in front of another person asking them questions.

[Second Movement: Hometown Pageant Queens]

In 1991, two years before we left Mexico, my sister was voted pageant queen of our home town of Tepechitlán, Zacatecas. She was fifteen. Her dress was red, and velvet and long. Her king, another boy from school, was dressed in torn and dirty rags, "the ugly king," as tradition goes. He groveled at her theatrical contempt.

No one knew what opulence meant, so her court tried their best in their suits and gowns two sizes too big, making grand gestures with their hands. For a moment she said she felt famous, except there were no cameras.

She was paraded through town on the hood of a truck, waving to the crowds.

The band, walking ahead of the car, asked for her favorite song, but she didn't have one. She was touched by the Holy Spirit and wasn't allowed to listen to worldly music. She knew the subtle art of fainting on Sunday mornings at church when she went up for the altar call as the pastor rubbed olive oil on her forehead and pushed her stiff body back.

Although the oldest, she was still the only girl, and though Apá reluctantly allowed her to participate after days of pleading, he grew furious when he saw her atop the truck and pulled her down. He yanked her arm all the way home, with the long train of her dress dragging behind; the music from the band continued playing, the party went on without her, without its queen.

The next day her pastor pointed to her in front of the congregation and proclaimed that she was a sinner. She was banished from leading the choir and had to beg forgiveness from God and the church for parading herself on top of a truck, a very worldly offense. She raised her hands and fainted every Sunday and rose back up as if she were a bored Lazarus who was tired of resurrection.

Apá sat her at the kitchen table and read off Bible passages to her even though he hadn't gone to church in years. The town took the dress back and said they would use it again for next year's queen.

4.

I drove an hour into the city and asked Rubi to record a short video of me saying something—anything. I wanted to document my voice so that I could look back later to try to remember that moment.

"How do you feel?" asked Rubi, holding her phone up as we walked away from our car toward the federal building in downtown Sacramento.

"I'm fine," I said, wringing my fingers together. Whatever happened after my interview, I would look back to that video to search for any signs, to see if something was trying to tell me that things would be okay. Maybe I would see that something in the background was trying to warn me to turn around, even if it meant giving up the prospect of ever getting a green card. If the interview didn't go well, I knew I could be sent into removal proceedings.

We entered the large federal building with our lawyer. It seemed like no one was inside, as if we had just entered a building dedicated entirely to myself, to granite and paper. This was a place built for the questioning of people and their stacks and stacks of papers, a simulacra of human lives. I wondered who cleaned the building at night because I could almost see my reflection walking below on the granite floor.

The first floor was dedicated to ICE removal operations, and the second floor was Homeland Security business. Most people think they're the same thing, but they're not. People—for the most part—were removed from the country on the first floor, and others were considered for entrance on the second floor. We were going to the second floor. My father's paperwork, gathered over the years, was probably somewhere in a box on the first.

My lawyer looked preoccupied with something else, relaxed, even bored. It must have been so routine to him, like dropping off mail, or waiting at the drive-through for a burger. The wood paneling made the whole second floor seem more judicial than the first, like a court-room where we were either confessing or swearing allegiance already, even though there wasn't a country at the other end to receive me. If we succeeded, there was a paper, not a country; I still belonged to Mexico.

*

After quietly waiting in a lobby on hard wooden benches, instructed not to speak, our names were called and we were led into a comfort-able office that looked like a guidance counselor's office with a large framed poster of Barack Obama smiling down on us, with all of his hair still dark. The picture was certainly taken on the day of his swearing-in to office—before the drones, before the quarter million deported on his watch, when things still seemed possible. Everything still seemed possible then.

Small indoor plants lined the window, and soccer pictures of someone's kids adorned the walls. My lawyer edged closer to whisper in my ear, "We're lucky, we got the good one," and I wondered if he said that because of the soccer pictures and the ficus plants or if he actually knew the officer. And by "good," did he mean under-standing, compassionate, or jaded so as to not really care about the impacts of her decisions anymore? He knew more than me. He had surely been in that very office before. He sat back in his chair as if his job was done, as if we had passed the test already.

I wanted it to be like TV. I wanted there to be variations of a laugh track to the mundane answers of my uneventful life. I wanted my uneventful life to sound eventful, thought-provoking even—"You mix eggs with what!?" But the room was quiet. Unlike the interviews on TV, I didn't have a mug to drink from on the table. I didn't wear my sunglasses indoors, and there was no musical accompaniment to punctuate our comebacks.

In effect, what I was yet again doing was crossing the border, inside that small office, with Obama staring down at me.

I wore the bluer shirt because it reminded me of the water at Bridgeport, a swimming hole up in the Sierra Nevada in Northern California. It was the only place where I felt absolute stillness, where I could comfortably dive until my head felt like it was going to collapse from the pressure. I had been that deep before in the ocean, but only at Bridgeport did the pressure feel both safe and not. Unlike the ocean, where it seemed like you could go in any direction forever and the pressure would only mount, there at the river, it was shallow yet deep enough to provide the feeling of being pushed toward your center, so I was never afraid of descending, never afraid I would go too deep without being able to rise. I could see the finite dimensions of the river—I knew what was at the bottom, I knew what was at the top. I knew how long it would take to get there. I wore the darker shirt because I imagined that like those bioluminescent creatures, even I could be capable of light—the kind of light only visible from the bottom, looking up.

*

We knew how we were supposed to answer, and they knew how to expect us to answer. It was a show. There was nothing new about any of it. I asked Rubi the questions as we climbed into bed at night. I found them online one night and printed them out. On some nights, however, we didn't interrogate each other with our interview in mind.

"Do you love me?"

"Yes."

"No, I mean, do you actually love me?"

"Yes, I do, why do you have to keep asking?"

"What's my grandmother's name?"

"Which one, Sarah or Julia?"

My lawyer held a large legal folder against his chest that detailed everything about me, and yet nothing. It had dates, addresses, pictures, and names, but it didn't have the things I was afraid of, nor what I longed for. It recorded the past but not what it meant for the future. I was interested in what would change about me after that interview. I wanted to record every moment to see if there was something I missed there in that office too.

Suddenly a woman opened the door, sat down at the desk before us and began the interview.

5.

It's a call-and-response. One announced the space into being, and the other filled it. "What is your name?" said the first voice. "Marcelo," said the second.

"Why are you here?"

"Because we want to remain together."

"And who is she?"

"I've known her almost all my life, she is my wife, and I love her."

Between us was a synonym for a barrier through which only certain things could pass. My name could pass, Rubi's name, how we met, how long we had been married. All of this could pass—information, which was free to move like air or animals over the border. However, there were still things that could not—how much we wanted it to be over, all the bad things we had to do over the years to survive as immigrants, and what I really wanted to say to the woman and to every guard I smiled to on the way up to her office. I still had to be polite.

I was speaking beyond the officer and to the entire country itself. Between us, a desk, but it might as well have been a long stretch of road. Long for its distance, but also for how narrow. She gave me something, and I turned it around and gave it back to her. Our language moved back and forth. It was like dancing reluctantly to a song that I hated—to a song that reminded me of someone I would rather forget. We were throwing stones into a deep pond and trying to figure out how deep it was by its sound. I would say something and see the ripples of its reverberation in the air. I would see it sink deep inside my interviewer as she nodded and pondered each of my answers to her questions, trying to decide if they were real. I imagined the entire building was vibrating with the small ripples of those afterthoughts when it was too late to take anything back— "I shouldn't have said that, . . . I should have said this instead." There were countless small rooms just like the one I was in where people nodded their head and said yes, or no, and watched a government worker scribble something on their notepad.

"Do you understand that marrying someone under any fraudulent circumstances in order to be granted any kinds of immigration benefits is a federal crime?"

"Yes, we do."

*

Her tone was casual. It almost sounded like she wanted to be our friend, as if she was inviting us to her spin class at the gym. Perhaps we had stood in the same lines at the DMV, and taken our dogs to the same dog park, and waited in line at the same bank with the same blank face everyone has on when they wait at the bank. Yes, there was nothing different about her. She clocked in and out just like I did at work. She went home and probably had the same problems at home as I did—bills, and dog shit to clean, and more bills. But behind her easy demeanor was something my mother taught me to fear—the warmth and tenderness of someone who could hurt you. She didn't look like La Migra. She didn't talk how I imagined La Migra would talk. But did I ever imagine La Migra as having a body, as having a mouth? Did I ever think it could be reduced to one person sitting behind a desk in front of me?

"Where did you two meet? I'm asking her now, not you, sir."

"That's a tricky question," Rubi said. "There wasn't one particular place, we were always just there."

I wondered if the officer followed the lives of the people she denied, or if each meeting was just another day at the office. I couldn't imagine her keeping track of that many people, years after their encounter. But no doubt there were a few cases that remained in the back of her mind. People's faces she couldn't seem to forget, their stories that haunted her in the shower.

"Where do each of you work?"

"We're kind of in between jobs right now."

"I see." She said and scribbled something on her note pad.

*

When someone asked me what I did for a living, I never said I was a poet. Instead I would cut the conversation short and just say I was a teacher, and after a smile and nod, no one would usually ask any follow-up questions. I preferred the terseness of such interactions. It was a boring response—it was safe. There was no more room for the imagination in that response. I didn't want to tell people I was a poet because I didn't want to explain (mostly to white people) what led me to writing, which would be followed by something like "I bet it was a great outlet of expression for such a hard life you lived." I usually had to spend a considerable amount of time trying to convince them (and perhaps myself) that I, indeed, *was* a poet. If someone asked my immigration interviewer what she did for a living, I wondered if she said she worked as an immigration agent, deciding who stays and who goes from the country, separating families as par for the course, or if she simply said she works in government, or perhaps she kept it blander and simply said "the public sector," yes, "I work for the state."

"How long did you know each other before you started dating?" she asked

"I'm not sure," I said.

*

I looked over at Rubi and remembered everything we had been through, like the time she left me in the summer of 2007, which led me to get a large tattoo on my back. When I saw her for the first time in the months after our breakup, I didn't know what to say, and the first thing that came out of my mouth was that I got a tattoo, which wasn't true. She asked to see it, but I said no, because there was obviously nothing there. Hours later that same afternoon, I went to the first tattoo shop I could find, pointed at whichever artist didn't seem to be busy, as if I was getting a haircut, and sat for four painful hours over the course of two days as they needled the largest cliché I could point to in their portfolio of pictures of red chapped skin with fresh ink from the needle. I stood up and held a mirror against another mirror to see, still a little bloody, and headed straight to Rubi with large wings on my back.

With each new question our interviewer was getting to know us better—testing the waters. Her job was one predicated on doubt. It was her job not to believe us. It was her job to unravel the story of us until it was replaced with one absent of love—an absence she could prove on paper, distill to its basest form, and perhaps even measure. And wasn't that what I did in my poems? Distill love into something that could never come close to love?

"What are his parents like? And same to you, what are hers like? Where do they live, and do you see them often?"

She trafficked in the images of legitimacy, trained in spotting the subtleties of body language in order to detect a sham green card wedding and tell it from the real thing. *How close do they sit to each other? Do they smile, do they look at each other when they talk?* It was our job to show her what we had shown the world, and to do it without thinking about doing it.

"What year did each of you enter the U.S.?"

"It's funny, we arrived just about the same time—1992 and 1993."

"Can you tell me all of the schools the other has gone to?"

But what if love had nothing to do with either her decision to legitimize our marriage or our decision to continue as such? If not love, then what? On what basis could they recognize us as a complete unit? Commitment? Were they looking for some kind of promise between two people? "I promise to pay half of the bills with you, I promise to not use up all of the hot water in the shower, I promise that if we ever have children, I will work tireless hours to give them a better life." Or were the characteristics for validity more physical— did I have a tan line beneath my wedding ring, which indicated how often I wore it? Did I have calluses in my palm from wearing it?

Some people could spend their entire lives together without love. I went to a therapist once who told me that after a certain time, love had little to do with staying together, that we build our lives around comfort.

"Do you plan on having children?"

"Not at the moment, ma'am, we want to finish school first."

If I told her, "Yes, I am married to this woman, but I am not *in love* with her. I will commit my entire life to her, but not my heart," would she automatically deny my application?

If I said, "I've been married to this woman and am *barely* learning to love her, but I know I am possible of loving her more in the future," would that be cause enough for rejection? What if I did not love her at that moment, but I was willing to let myself try? Would they take a gamble on me? Some people fall in love, and then they fall more in love with time. I thought about Amá and Apá. Maybe for them, the possibility of learning to love each other was disrupted when they were separated by immigration. Rubi and I had started to become distant since moving to the Midwest for school, even though we had been through so much. Perhaps I occupied the first scenario: "I am possible of loving her more in the future."

"How did you propose, sir?"

"She actually was the one who proposed to me."

What if I told her I loved this woman in particular, but I also spent many nights dreaming of a man? A no-name man who didn't do much in my dreams except sit by himself at a diner, eating a big piece of American apple pie? What would she do with our desires? I imagine a line in her notebook, and a box, and a checkmark, and a long pause followed by some notes in the margins. And it was true,

Rubi and I had begun to distance ourselves from each other ever since I came to terms with my sexuality. I told her I was bi that same summer, and she didn't take it as well as I thought she would. I told her nothing would change between us because of this revelation, but perhaps that's what bothered her most, that nothing would change.

What if my answer was the opposite of growth? What if I said: "I love her to death now, but I know I will no longer love her in the years to come, not out of choice but out of gradual neglect," what would happen then? I couldn't possibly expect them to believe that love was a constant, that once you had it you had all of it forever, that it was like an object you could hold and call yours.

"Where did you go on your honeymoon?"

"We never went on one, we couldn't afford it."

They wanted definite answers to the indefinite, beyond simply *is your marriage real*. They wanted the specific outline of love. Undoubtedly, between ours and the thousands of other interviews, happening in rooms just like that one, across the country with countless other dark-haired Obamas soon to be peppered with worry and compromise looking down, they must have believed that their data pointed to a collective consensus. Love equals [*blank*].

*

Of course our marriage was real, but she wanted to know if I married Rubi for the right reasons. And did I? In that moment, it *was*, if ever so briefly, that woman's job to determine what love was and compare her definition to what she saw sitting before her.

Did I look like I was in love? Did I carry my body like that of someone who dreamed of another? Was there something in the way I said "yes," or "no," or even "please?" I could always tell when someone was in love; I could see it in their eyes.

She asked us questions about our bodies and things that came in contact with our bodies.

"Are there any distinctive moles or birthmarks on your wife?"

"What color is her toothbrush?"

"What side of the bed does she sleep on?"

"Is your husband left- or right-handed?"

She wanted to know if we had moved beyond being simply intimate and into the world of the mundane. Had we moved passed the moments of mere sexual excitement and into the more repetitive spaces of domestic life? But there was not enough time to explain the intimacy of silence, of our own secret language, so many years in the making. I doubted she would even understand.

I wasn't certain if I knew Rubi's body the way the law wanted me to. Had I ever spent my nights looking at the shapes of her birthmarks, wondering what they resembled? Was I supposed to look at her the way some people looked at the sky and made animals out of the clouds?

"Yes, she has a birthmark on her back that kind of looks like the state of Texas," I answered rather abruptly.

Texas?

I hardly even knew my own body. We held each other at night not to count or measure each other but because we knew that we didn't have to. We didn't have to guess the shapes of our irregularities—our inadequacies. The world outside our bed was one that asked us questions that demanded answers—answers that had definite beginnings and endings, definite shapes. Inside, we could ask and ask and never feel compelled to answer if we didn't want to. We could spend the entire day in bed, naked, asking each other questions that would only be answered by other questions.

Inside, it was a world of feeling our way through each other in the dark. How could I tell our interviewer what I felt and saw in the hazy darkness of our room? How could I tell her what Rubi said at two in the morning as we both climaxed inside each other? I couldn't remember which side of the bed Rubi slept on. We didn't really pick sides.

*

How much could we possibly know about another person? I was certain that the amount of ourselves that we allowed others to see was minuscule compared to what else was there. Sometimes our secrecy is unintentional. Even six years after being together, one day Rubi discovered that I had a crown in my left molar. Shocked, she grabbed my face with both palms close to hers, looked me straight in the eye, and said, "Has that always been there?"

"Yes," I said, looking at her, confused.

"You're lying!"

"No, I've had it since I was little."

Had I never opened my mouth that wide for her that it took nearly a decade to see inside completely? I used to enjoy asking Rubi, "How many times do you think we've kissed? A thousand, ten thousand, a million?" My mouth was always so close to hers, and still she had never seen my crown's glint in the sun, even when I yawned. I wondered how many parts of her body I had yet to know.

*

We were under oath. We had raised our right hand and sworn to tell the complete truth. There was so much more I wanted to tell the interviewer, as if I was confessing my sins to a priest. Maybe telling her that I was afraid of clowns would ease my fear. In a way, it felt good to have someone give me their complete attention; her entire body was focused on every word that formed on my lips. But I didn't say more than what was asked, and my answers were short. I pointed at pictures of ourselves that were laid out on her table and recounted the moments when we were happy over the years.

It was strange to think that somewhere in a federal warehouse were pictures of my mother, my brothers, my senior prom, field trips in high school, graduation day, my wedding day, and mine and Rubi's first apartment together, among so many others. There were even ones in which I was doing absolutely nothing. It was those in which I was most mundane, most myself. It gave me a small joy to think of my monotony as a subject of interest, archived inside a box with a Dewey number, never to be opened. It reassured me that perhaps something of mine would survive this world after all. I was hoping that between the pictures and the documents submitted, I wouldn't need to choose what parts of myself to tell. But as personal as that information was, it wasn't the full picture. The intimacy of sharing those pictures did not escape me. Would the agent remember them on her drive back home that day? Would they remind her of her own marriage, or her own children?

"What would you do if granted the green card?"

"Nothing different, ma'am."

"I see," she said, and jotted some more notes on her paper.

[Second Movement: Hometown Family Album]

═══

Nobody could remember where we got the cameras. Amá, wearing bright red lipstick with her bangs puffed high in that early '90s trend, stood next to Apá for the picture. His face was stern and stoic, with his shirt unbuttoned down to his large potbelly.

In the picture, Amá still looked slightly happy, even though moments before, Danny was crying and Apá was yelling at him to stop, which made him cry louder. The only way Amá had permission to make herself pretty in a picture was if Apá was in it. The other time was if she went to church. Amá became a very religious person.

We went to a church where the pastor told us our poverty was all part of God's plan. "Believe," he said every Sunday, "believe that God is great and will recompense you tenfold." My mother fainted in the presence of the Holy Spirit every Sunday, and then she got up as if nothing ever happened, as if from one moment to the next the Holy Spirit was no longer in her—moved on to the next believer. I fainted too sometimes, but she hit me on the head and said, "That's not funny."

I practiced fainting in the backyard so she wouldn't hit me at church anymore, so I could be more convincing, and people would believe I too was capable of being emptied by the very hand of God.

6.

In preparation for the interview, I had to purge all of my social media accounts. I attempted to erase any trace of myself from the Internet so as to not let anything I had said be found. I was worried they would see something about me they wouldn't like. Would this country want another poet? I regretted having published so young on the Internet. I hoped they wouldn't conduct a background check, looking for some reason to deny me. There was nothing there *to* find, I had never committed a crime, but I was worried something would magically come up out of thin air. English was the language of misinterpretation.

Midway through the interview, the woman said, "I'll be right back," and returned after a tense ten minutes with my personal folder beneath her arm. I was sure they were looking for something.

"We just had some things to clarify and sort out with my boss. It says here you left the country and returned with advanced parole through DACA recently. How was your trip?" she said as she folded her arms and placed them on her desk.

"It was fine. I needed to go see my dad."

"How long had it been since you'd seen your dad?"

"About ten years."

"And why was he there so long?"

"Because he was deported."

"Oh."

She said the last "Oh," as if she was surprised that that was what happened when people got deported, that ten years actually meant ten years. It was one thing for her to see it on paper, and another to see it in person. I was that person, I was the product of one of those removal proceedings she might make again before her lunch without thinking twice.

It suddenly became clear that in all of the pictures we presented to validate our marriage case, still laid out on her table, my father was missing. Maybe I'd said too much.

"Well, Mr. Hernandez, I think that's it. I'm usually not supposed to say this to people, but I think you passed. It won't be final until you receive an official letter in the mail, but I'm confident you'll get that shortly. In the meantime, I suggest you take your wife on that honeymoon you owe her." She smiled as she said this, and I tried not to make my affectation too obvious.

She shook our hands with a firm grasp, smiled, and kept nodding her head. That was it. There was no applause, no musical accompaniment, and none of us would go home to watch reruns of ourselves late at night. We followed the rules, we passed the questions back and forth between each other. We got up to leave, but before we did, she said, "Welcome to America," as if I hadn't already been here for twenty-two years. I feared she could take back her decision at any moment so I kindly smiled, said thank you, and quickly walked away.

7.

Sometimes, when I had no business being nervous, even when everything in my life was calm and going well, I would still get this feeling of being sunken into the earth. Of walking through a deep sludge of mud. Thick mud. Dark mud. The kind of mud that exists where there is no water but no one questions where it comes from. I wanted the deepest roots of me uplifted. But there was another side to this feeling—it was sometimes good to know that I was at least holding on to something. That at least it was difficult for me to fall, even if I was going nowhere. That it was hard for me to burn.

After the interview, I wanted to go home and make love to Rubi and apologize for nothing in particular, just say "I'm sorry" over and over again and kiss her on her forehead and trace all of her birthmarks with my finger.

8.

Do other people who also undergo this interview think of this country as belonging to them? In effect, all the green card meant was "You can stay," not "It is yours to keep." I still saw it as temporary, something that could be taken away for even minor violations of the law. Besides, before even considering accepting the U.S. as *my* country, I had debts to settle with myself, the landscape, and its people. There would always be parts of me that would want nothing to do with this country and what it has done to many of its people.

For a moment, I understood my father a little better and his desire to distance himself from anything "American." More so than me, he came of age in the U.S. as a young farm worker actually hearing people say with disgust to him, "You cannot stay," "This is not yours to keep," instead of it being implied. So instead of being rejected, he rejected America first. Perhaps we had become too American for him. Maybe it wasn't us he didn't approve of, but what the U.S. had done to us. I could hardly keep up a conversation with him anymore. I felt his anger well up inside me, and I knew it was his anger and not mine because it came from an older part of me, a deeper part of my gut that had been hurt far longer than I had been alive.

Getting the green card and all of the benefits that came with it seemed like such a simple thing to ask for such a large price. All I was asking for was peace of mind, for protection, for basic human rights. And in return, for the duration of the interview at least, I was supposed to speak and look patriotic. I was supposed to show or prove an attempt at assimilation; that I aligned myself with undeniable American values—"values" that ensured the continuation of a system historically aligned against me. I had to align myself with a history of denial toward the violence committed on entire generations of people.

Perhaps to some, this was hardly a price at all. From their perspective, it was the other way around, how little I needed to give and how much was given in return. All I had to do was show a little love for a country that had given me so much, and in return I would be granted entrance into the greatest country on earth. *Be grateful.* Maybe it was my father's voice in my head, which sounded more and more like my voice, telling me about everything that this country had done to us that made the price of the green card heavy. I already had to erase much of myself, trying to survive; how much more was needed?

*

I should have been happy. Didn't I have something to be grateful for? Wasn't that so generous of them? The interviewer's final words rang inside me like the low baritone of a large bell, *Welcome to America.* Her message reminded me that there were people who actually believed I was not really here. That I was a ghost wandering through the corners of their eyes, easily dismissed as nothing more than fog.

She announced that I was finally here, in the flesh, whole, as if somehow before that moment there had been something essential missing in me, as if I was flawed before my interview and had been corrected by her generosity to grant me permanent residency status. *Welcome* [read]: you now have a name, [read]: come out now. *Be grateful.*

"How do you feel?" asked Rubi, holding her phone up to me to record as we exited the clean granite-and-limestone building.

"I don't feel any different. Actually I feel worse," I confessed.

This was supposed to be the end of a very long journey—a culmination of events all pointed at this moment. Our lawyer shook our hands and congratulated us. I could tell he was genuinely happy because his firm had been working with our family for decades. He had known me since I was little, when he was handling other family member's cases. His work would never end. Perhaps his generations after him would continue to become attorneys assisting my future generations in the same thing we were doing.

There were people entering the building as we left, all of them with a stack of papers in a folder beneath their arms, most likely going for their own interviews. They looked dressed for a special occasion, like a wedding or a christening. I wondered if they thought the same things I was thinking early that morning. "Which shirt says 'I want to be an American'?" There was hope in their eyes as well as fear.

No, there was nothing missing about them, there was nothing flawed. I could see them as well as I could see myself. There was nothing I had to be grateful about. What if I asked them questions? What if I asked if they were in love? "Who are you wearing? When did you know you were famous? Does your lover have a birthmark the shape of Texas?"

I entered that building the same way that I left it. I didn't want to make of this another border in my life. I was tired of dividing things in two. I wanted there to be a name for what I was doing that had nothing to do with papers, that had nothing to do with legality, that had nothing to do with anything larger than me. No, it had to be small, smaller than me, something I could carry. Maybe something that didn't even have a name, but just a sound. If I could call forth a sound that would embody what it was that I was doing, it would be low, an utterance not unlike the low moan an elephant makes that is carried just beneath the soil for miles. There should be a name for the time it took to exit that building; for the swiftness with which Rubi put down her phone and kissed me.

9.

We celebrated our new "entrance" into American life by going to a Mexican restaurant in midtown, which boasted a dazzling array of shiny hats hanging on the walls and murals of rural Mexican country life. We liked the irony. Chips and salsa were brought to us in a little plate shaped like a pig with its back hollowed out for the salsa. The fact that I was a permanent resident, the tall walls, the bright colors, and the cold AC blasting down on us gave me the sensation of falling.

"What's going through your head?" Rubi asked.

"I don't know, I'm just irritated."

I didn't know what to believe anymore. I still wanted to believe that the paperwork and the process were all artificial, that they were just numbers on a piece of paper made to make me believe that they mattered, made to make me desire them.

In the years before my interview, to pacify my anger, I tried to convince myself that having papers didn't matter because legal documentation was a social construct. And as a child, before I had that language, I said I was a perfect boy without them. By the time I was in college, I knew they were created by artificial laws founded on a history that was designed to beat us every time. I took what little comfort I could from telling myself that I wasn't going to give any more power to the systems that had gripped us by our throats for most of our lives.

At one point I felt the same way about the border, that it was just an artificial line drawn over a landscape that in turn was indifferent about its presence. That because we conceived it, that because it began as an idea, it was doomed to be returned by the landscape as nothing more than an idea if not for our constant upkeep—*Ashes to ashes* . . . The ecclesiastical meaninglessness of it all etc., etc., etc.

But the reality was that people lived there on the border. They made their lives and memories from such artifice, which meant it was hardly an artifice at all.

I could no longer pretend that they were just numbers scribbled down on a piece of paper. I always knew they weren't. They were as real as my hand, as real as my teeth; their consequences had a weight and shape to them. If I sharpened the edges of my green card when it came in the mail, I could cut myself open.

How little I deserved any of it, I thought, as I dipped a chip into the bright red salsa inside the little pig. The salsa looked too bright, a color not natural in peppers, as if they'd added food coloring. But surprisingly it tasted good. *Welcome to America. Be grateful.*

*

How many others deserved my green card more than me? I had waited so long for the day of my interview, but after it was over, I felt sick to my stomach. I didn't want to face my family with the news. Why couldn't I be happy for myself for once? What about me inherently negated joy at every point in my life? My joy was always elusive. It crumbled in my hands as soon as I held it. My problem was that I thought joy was something that was supposed to be given to me, or at least something that I was supposed to find, instead of making it myself.

That was my immigrant condition. I didn't know how to stand in one place without moving. I was suspect of any good that ever came my way and always turned it away. Nothing good ever happened for no reason.

"It isn't fair," I said to Rubi.

"What isn't fair?" she said as she looked up from her menu.

"How am I going to look at my mom?"

"What do you mean? She's going to be happy. You should call her."

I dipped another chip into the little pig. I didn't realize that I hadn't eaten all day, and before long, I finished all the chips and bright fluorescent salsa. What *would* I say to my mother? I was ashamed that I had been given something she had wanted for longer than I was alive. It felt like I had stolen it from her, it felt like I had stolen it from so many other people who deserved it more than me. If only it was like a seed and I could plant it and grow more. I would take my mother's picture, bury it, and out would sprout her own card. I would hand out the secret like religious pamphlets at street corners.

I left the table to call Amá.

Amá sounded eager to talk on the phone. What mother wouldn't want this for her son?

"Everything went well, Amá. They said I passed."

"Thank God, mijo. Thank God. What else did they say?"

"Nothing really, they just asked Rubi a lot of questions, but it went well."

Toward the end, her voice was cracking as if I had disturbed her prayer, as if she had never stopped praying, even though she must have known it was over by then, and was only waiting for my signal to cut her tie with God.

*

I had an international calling card in my wallet to call my dad back in Mexico because I knew he would want to know too. I always carried one just in case. Two dollars gave me fifteen minutes. I dialed the ten numbers on the card, then the ten numbers from the PIN that I scratched off like a lotto ticket, then the international code for Mexico (0–11–52), and finally the actual ten-digit number I needed to reach. It was a small miracle when the call finally went through, and even more of a miracle if the line didn't cut off while it rang, and more so if Apá actually answered.

"Hi Apá, I had my interview today, did you remember?"

"Yes, of course I remembered, how did it go?"

"Everything went well, I think."

"That's great, mijo. I'm happy for you."

We didn't talk for long. After a few awkward silences and asking how things were over there, and him asking how things were over here, and both of us saying the same thing to each other, I hung up. Leaving was always easy; hanging up took less than a second, and just like that, I was back in the restaurant, dipping more chips into the little pig, which they replaced with another one with green salsa.

Maybe if it took just as long to hang up, having to repeat the same process of dialing but in reverse, perhaps I would stay and talk for longer, maybe then I would be a different son.

"What did your dad say?" asked Rubi.

"Not much, just that he was happy."

I didn't want to sound excited over the phone because I didn't want to come across as if I was rubbing salt on an already infected wound. So instead I decided to keep it short and cold, which was not a difficult thing to do with my father, but it hurt to do so with Amá.

*

I wasn't sure if Amá and Apá would have passed if they took the same test. I didn't know if Amá ever really loved Apá, even in the beginning. Maybe they had a secret language of affection between the two of them that was hidden from everyone else. Perhaps leaving was his best way of caring for us and showing his love for us. I had never seen them be affectionate toward each other—never seen them kiss, no sly side-winks, no cute nicknames, nor had I even seen them hug each other for long. The closest I could remember seeing them was when they would get together for a picture, and even then Apá would always look mad, gripping Amá's shoulder tightly and letting go as soon as the picture was taken.

I, on the other hand, was always tragically, hopelessly in love with too many people growing up. I wasn't sure if I only liked girls, I didn't know what to call what I felt. I knew what love was, but I didn't know how to direct it. Maybe Amá and Apá didn't yet know they loved each other, even after so many years, just like I thought I knew what love was but didn't know how to love yet. When I was a child, when Apá was still present, I wanted some kind of confirmation that love was possible outside of the movies I watched and the Harlequin books I was too young to be reading. I watched Amá and Apá love each other in their mysterious ways, but I wanted to see proof of more. Maybe love had nothing to do with it.

*

After finishing our meal and all the salsa we could eat, we took the back roads home. Every few seconds, I looked down to check how fast I was going. It was a habit I picked up after years of driving without a license and which was heightened after the county jail, Yuba County, began cooperating with ICE by handing over inmates they suspected to be undocumented. A third of the inmate population in the county jail were ICE detainees awaiting trial. A simple traffic stop had suddenly turned into potential grounds for a deportation. The cautious habit never went away.

Sometimes I would spend more time obsessing over how fast I was going than paying attention to the road ahead. On a few occasions I almost crashed while going exactly somewhere between sixty-five and sixty-nine miles per hour on the freeway. That was a good range. I liked that range because it didn't look suspicious. That range told a story: it sent the message that I wasn't going anywhere in a hurry but that I had nothing to hide. It didn't draw any suspicion toward me. Anything less would have been too slow and made it seem like I especially didn't want to be pulled over. Going exactly sixty-five was too obvious, it was obsessive. Anything above seventy was too fast and started to get dangerous. Any cop on a bad day could technically call that speeding.

So I drove home trying to go in that sweet range. It made it difficult to concentrate on anything else, especially to follow conversations. Rubi scolded me for not paying attention to her, but I screamed and pointed at the speedometer and exclaimed that I was trying to concentrate. I apologized, and we stayed mostly quiet all the way home.

*

How many of these antics would soon loosen their grip on me as I became more comfortable, as I gradually eased into my position as a person with papers? A ticket could now be just a ticket, I didn't have to think of it as a deportation, but somehow it wasn't as easy as that. I knew the voice would still be in my head, telling me ICE could return for me at any minute, and the cameras would always be on, giving me the feeling that I was always being watched. The feeling of surveillance, I feared, would never go away.

What behaviors would be lost, and which ones would I keep? Would the fear nestled in every joint of my body finally be massaged away, so I could let go of the tension that I had been holding for so many years?

I had modified my behavior for so much of my life that I knew I would have to work hard to undo some of those habits, like staring down at how fast I was going, like staying quiet even when I should be screaming. Some of those behaviors could take years to undo, and others might have been irreversible. Being undocumented said nothing about me or my identity, but it did inform a lot of my behavior. There were things about me that became automatic, that over the years I came to do without thinking. I would have to pull myself back and adjust. I had to recalibrate—to enter the world as someone who was there, someone who was present. I finally had the liberty to do things as minor as saying my name out loud, and still at times I kept silent.

Maybe I wasn't as present as I thought; maybe my interviewer was right when she said "Welcome to America."

Laugh now. Laugh hard. Spit out your food.

10.

For years, to rid myself of anxiety, I got into the habit of asking myself questions in the second person in my journal. And I always answered as if having an actual conversation with myself. It was good to articulate and vocalize what was bothering me because it would fester if it just spun in circles in my head. I had been doing this long before my immigration interview. It was also a way to trick myself into saying something I might otherwise have not.

"Marcelo, are you tired?"

"Yes."

"Why are you tired?"

"I don't know, I just am, okay."

"Okay. Is there something bothering you, Marcelo?"

"Kind of . . ."

"Can you tell me?"

"Yes."

"Okay, so, shoot."

"The other day, you were there, remember, I said something out loud in class that I regret saying."

I wrote to myself day after day. I interviewed myself as if I was someone famous.

"So, tell me, who are you excited about these days?"

"Oh, you know, the usual suspects."

"I don't!"

"Well . . ."

"You don't say!"

It was a form of confession, and although I am not a Catholic, I believed in confession, in repeating the same prayer to dislodge whatever it was that was trapped inside me. I never went to church, but I wanted to confess to my friends all of the terrible things I had done to see if anyone would still love me.

But I was a coward. Instead, I interviewed myself and made fake Twitter accounts to anonymously declare what I was too afraid to tell anyone. It was a form of talking to myself, like a confession box. No one was listening, but that wasn't the point. My Twitter handle got followed by bots and shirt companies. They didn't care what I did. They just wanted to sell me things made in countries I had never been to by people in sweatshops who looked like me. As much as I tried, I couldn't find anyone I could tell everything about me.

Once, I tweeted to my actual account "I'm a terrible person," but people thought it was a joke. They replied with emoji faces that kissed or winked. I deleted the tweet and posted the same thing to my fake accounts and got ads for coupons, which I ended up using.

I never told anyone about these conversations, but one day, when I was teaching undergrads, out of some wild obsession to confess in front of people, to prove some point I can no longer remember, I told my students about my self-interviews, and they didn't believe me until I took out my laptop, connected it to the projector, and showed them. "Oh," one of them said, and the rest stayed quiet for the remainder of the class. We never mentioned it again.

I was just tired of keeping things inside for so long that I wasn't sure if I could keep them in me any longer. But still, there was no one I could trust enough to give all of myself completely. There were still things I couldn't say even to Rubi. Would there ever be, in my lifetime, a point in which I could say absolutely everything about myself with complete abandon, without fear of judgment or repercussions? I was always afraid I would say too much, but part of me drank with other people because I knew that was the only way to say anything significant about me.

*

I kept asking myself more questions in my journals day after day as I waited for my green card to arrive in the mail. "You look nervous, why are you nervous"? I waited by the mailbox every day for weeks, just in case it might arrive early. I didn't have much time because summer would be over soon, and I would have to fly back to Michigan for the start of the semester. On the day it was scheduled to arrive, there was construction on the road near my mother's mailbox, so the mail carrier decided not to deliver mail that day. It was as simple as that—there were a few cones on a Friday from a utility truck, and the mail carrier decided not to bother with maneuvering around them. The card was sent back to a main office in Texas and destroyed. It was their policy; maybe they didn't want any good cards floating around out there and risk being forged. They would have to make a new one, and I would have to fill out more forms explaining why.

After screaming at a post office employee who quickly told me I had to leave, or they would call the police, I sat in my car for what seemed like hours. I would have never screamed at a federal employee before. That was something new. I started the engine and drove away, going faster and faster down the road. I didn't care about going sixty-seven. I wanted to run a red light, to blow a stop sign, to swerve through the lanes as if something was chasing me. Maybe something *was* chasing me, but I didn't care if it found me anymore. Maybe the card should have gone to someone else indeed. Someone with kids to feed, someone whose parents were dying back home, and with it they could finally go see them. *Her toothbrush is red, I love her now.*

I revved the engine faster.

Waiting for my second green card to arrive, I had more of an urge to expose all of my secrets even if no one was asking, even if no one was around to listen: "I still wet the bed occasionally when it is cold, I don't always brush my teeth, I am jealous of so many people who have their first book published before me." It was a long summer. It almost made sense to be that sad. If I were my father, I would have sold my sadness for two dollars. I thought about my new friends back in grad school and wanted to paint their portraits from my memory of the day I told them I was undocumented. I wished that I had been raised Catholic so that I at least could go to church and do the real thing; confession. What I wanted most was to tell somebody, anybody, anything.

I wrote more interviews in my journals and covered certain words up with Barbie stickers that I bought at a Dollar General. It occurred to me, sitting in my car in the parking lot of that same Dollar General, in search of cheap balloons for a party which I did not care about, that I was allowed to be sad, the bad kind of sad, not the hot kind, or the glamorous kind, but the kind that makes people want to call for help or turn away. I picked out the brightest balloons, paid, and mouthed the words "happy birthday to you" in a dark room lit by everyone's phone cameras.

I entered all of my emails from five years into a cloud engine and the most used word was "okay." I spent many nights obsessing over the placement of the furniture. If I could, I would have given away my boredom, I would have given away my obligations, my desires. I would have given away the night I danced, and danced, and danced at a child's birthday party, drunk and by myself, pretending I was happy.

*

My time in California was up. I had to return to the Midwest, back to school for the fall, and the card would take months to resend. Still, my mother waited by the mailbox just as I did, just as if the card was for her. Every day she shuffled hurriedly with her slippers scraping the cement to see what had come. When it finally came, she asked if she could open it. "Yes, Amá, of course," I said over the phone. They shipped it to me, and I tracked it carefully on my bright computer screen, anxiously waiting for the next update—L.A., Phoenix, St. Louis, Chicago, Detroit.

They wrapped it inside the pages of George Orwell's *1984*—it was one of the only books left in my room back home, the only one I didn't bother bringing with me to grad school. I held the package tightly beneath my arm as I walked down the street. No one knew why I was smiling, but they did what good strangers would do, they smiled back. Maybe there were no cameras. I wasted so much of my life for nothing.

Third Movement:
Sentence Served

Suppose a father dresses his two-year-old child in cowboy attire and places him on a black mare with the intention of taking a picture. The mother watches from the window because there is nothing she can say to stop him. Suppose the father takes a picture and the camera shutter scares the horse away with the child on top. The mother walks back to the house out of shock, she doesn't want to see what she thinks will inevitably happen—her boy coming apart in small pieces behind a horse that runs faster from the weight dangling behind her, a body that might eventually look like a snake at some point—no hands, no feet, just a skinny thing of red.

But the child doesn't fall, he holds on to the mane of that mare with his small fists like pom-poms bunched together in the coarse hair, which makes the horse run even faster. Suppose a man down the road manages to stop the horse and grabs the child, but only the father, running up, catching his breath, can pry his small fingers loose. The horse looks shaken, her large eyes nearly jumping out of their sockets as if to keep running on their own.

Perhaps that man who stopped the mare knew something my father didn't, knew how to calm her with a child dangling on her mane. The horse didn't stop for my father because she wasn't supposed to. I wonder what that man said to make her slow down. Maybe it wasn't "Stop." Maybe it was something more like "Please." I imagine my father leaning into the mare, saying "I'm sorry," distracting her while he gently pried my small hands open.

Suppose the mother does not leave the house that day, rubbing aloe vera on the blistered palms of her boy. "Why didn't you just let go?" she asks, but he doesn't respond because he doesn't talk yet and it will take him a while before he does. The father sits outside on a plastic chair, mending the horse's saddle. He rubs it down with oil until it's soft and shiny. He walks over to the horse tied to a tree, still a little shaken, and says, "I'm sorry" while he caresses her muzzle and brushes her sweaty and muscular back.

1.

It took leaving California for Michigan to realize that there was a greater kind of loneliness to fall into, that there were even more ways an immigrant could bury his past. I took for granted how much growing up in California quietly consoled me just by being in the presence of people like me. But in the frigid Michigan snow, in its humid summers, in small corn-fed towns that I'm sure meant well when their people asked me "So what are you?" I had to recalibrate who I was to those around me.

Rubi and I had only been in the Midwest for two years, and already we hungered to reclaim and resurface the identities of our culture that we'd hidden for so many years. We were suddenly loud when speaking Spanish in public, and slowly the letter *I* started making its way into my poems. I was finally able to find enough courage to say even a little about myself, where I had come from, and where I was at in life. It took distance from all that was familiar to me, to be placed in a completely new environment for the first time, to see with some objectivity some of the madness I put myself through, and which in turn I was subjected to.

Rubi dropped out of school in Sacramento when we made the move. We didn't know what we were getting ourselves into, because I was the first undocumented student in the program's history, and I wasn't exactly sure how things would play out with funding and graduation requirements, if I ever made it to graduation at all. But I was given the opportunity, and I took it. I was grateful. *Be grateful.* On our first day in Ann Arbor, we sat in a bus looking at the Gothic architecture of the university buildings and I said to Rubi, "This is it, all of our troubles are finally over." I was so naive. But in the two years after we moved, things got considerably better. I got DACA, which was what allowed me to go see Apá, and shortly after I got my green card, which meant I had an ID, which meant I could finally go to the bar with my cohorts after the workshop instead of asking Rubi to buy liquor for me and drinking alone at home. I liked going to different bars just to slowly pull out my newly minted ID from my wallet like the punch line of a joke. Eventually they stopped asking me after I showed my face enough and became a "regular," but I insisted on pulling it out and making them look at it each time, slapping it hard on the marble slab bar. Being away from our family and friends was hard on both of us, and we both turned inward, away from each other.

*

In the warmth of our small apartment near campus in December 2014, surrounded by partying undergrads, I began packing for a flight to Ciudad Juárez to see Apá. After he'd waited ten years in deportation, his own immigration interview at the U.S. Embassy had finally arrived. Now that I had a green card, it was agreed that it was my responsibility to handle "matters of the family." It felt good to be needed like that; it made it seem like I was putting my green card to good use, like I deserved it. It made me not feel as guilty as when I first received it.

I took everything out of my luggage and spread it on the floor, a travel habit I acquired to make sure I knew exactly every single item that went into my bags. This would be the first time I used my green card to leave the country, and I didn't want anything to go wrong. I could hear drunken frat brothers screaming outside. They were always so loud, always so angry. I held my green card in my hand and felt the raised lettering on its surface—16 FEB 1988 M. I looked heavy in the picture. I had gained a lot of weight since moving to the Midwest. My long mustache looked like my father's, as did my hair parted to the side. The crooked smile was mine alone. The grooves on my fingerprint on the bottom right side swirled clockwise.

*

The winter air was a cold that I still was not familiar with, one that I didn't think I would ever completely understand. Just before evening, when I didn't know if the sun was still there or not—so far behind the clouds that it was only the idea of a sun—it looked like everything was crouching down a little—the cars, the houses, the trash cans lined on the road. Just then, and only then, when everything felt closer to the earth, like it was being slowly pulled by a thin rope toward the warmth at the center, a blue descended on the backs of everything—a kind of blue I had never seen back in California, a cerulean blue that seemed older than the things it touched, as if it was not from here but had taken a long time to arrive. And when it did, it felt eternal, though it only lasted about an hour before the boredom of the dark took over again.

And when the blue was gone, I felt like I could breathe again, like I could go back outside into the night and walk upright again. When it left, it was as if someone had unplugged a TV hissing its white noise in the background of a sad party where everyone suddenly blinks and looks around, aware for the first time that they're even *at* a party. You never knew it was there until it wasn't. When it left, it almost felt like it would never come back—it was hard to believe that anything like that could be done twice. And yet it did, it came back every afternoon in winter, weighing things down, making it difficult to move.

I found it hard to speak when the sky looked like that. It took more effort to open the hinges of my jaw. I had felt that way in the hot California summers too, only different. There was no blue, but a particular brightness. At the hottest time of the day, the air would stop. It was difficult to speak, people crouched a little lower too, a little farther from the sun. The stray dogs outside would walk in maddening circles, their heavy tongues hanging to the side like broken arms. But in the northern Midwest, there were different reasons to wander back and forth like aimless dogs. None of which involved the sun.

*

I finished packing my bags and put my green card on the table. The dark outside didn't interest me as much as the blue, which had long since left, transformed into the very things it weighed down. The dark didn't come from anywhere else, it was always there, it was as much a part of this world as anything you could buy at Walmart. It was cheap, it fit neat and orderly in every corner of the street. When I saw my father the next day, I would tell him about the blue. I would ask him if he had ever seen anything like it. I would ask if he felt the same ropes that I did, tugging him toward the ground.

2.

I liked to take walks late at night to get out of my head. "I'm going for a walk," I said to Rubi, who was wrapped in a blanket on the small sofa we bought at the Salvation Army. We were never planning on living in the Midwest for long, so there was no point in buying anything new. It felt like nothing in the house belonged to me, like I was just borrowing it from someone whom I would never meet. It felt natural to me to move and not be tied to any of my furniture. Never in my life had I bought a brand-new couch, not necessarily because I couldn't afford it, because there were times when I could, but because I had the feeling that our residence was always temporary. I hated to admit that it was easier to throw away a couch and buy another used one at a thrift store than to try to ship or move it.

I put on my heavy jacket, my hat, gloves, and snow boots. I liked having to put all of it on. It made even going outside for a moment feel like an event, like something special I needed to prepare myself for. It took a long time to put everything on, to lace my boots all the way up, and I appreciated that I needed to slow down just to be able to stand outside. It was never like that back home. The outside felt like the inside, especially after the ICE raid; there was not much to keep the two apart. One just turned into the other. It didn't feel special to go outside; you changed nothing about you, so once you were there, you hardly noticed. I stood there at the door fully clothed but didn't leave. It felt hot underneath all the feather down and fleece. "Did you forget something?" Rubi asked. "No," I said quietly after a moment, and opened the door to step outside.

I never knew what snow sounded like before moving to the Midwest. I didn't know it even *had* a sound. With my earmuffs, my steps reverberated inside my head. I could feel each crunch like rubber that turned into gravel or sand, like a medical glove grinding between my teeth. I felt the vibrations running through my bones, and I liked it for the same reason I liked putting on all those layers of clothes. It reminded me of each step. I could feel my body moving from one leg to the other, my knees bending, my weight arrowing down to my heel and pushing the snow aside. Any other time I just felt numb and withdrawn—apathetic.

I was seeing a therapist who told me about concepts that I jotted down in a small notebook and promised myself to look up later but never did. I made so many promises to myself that I never kept. The days had been passing without me, they blurred into weeks and months. I was moving myself only out of habit, and the small joy of hearing the snow with each footstep made me jump inside a little, it made me look both ways before crossing the street.

*

I didn't have anywhere in particular to go but liked wandering through the town. Everyone on that side of town was a young undergrad at the college. They took up so much space walking down the street and didn't care who overheard them, as if they wanted everyone to know about their bright futures—their unpaid internships, because they could afford to not be paid for three months, their summers abroad. Rarely did I hear anyone speaking Spanish on the street, but when I did, I wanted to run up to them and ask what brought them to that small town, to say anything to them and just listen to our voices muffled by the snow. I wanted to ask them where they were from, if they prayed to the Virgen de Guadalupe, and where was a good place to get some decent food. I had never before lived in a town whose restaurants called a torta a "spicy chicken sandwich" as they brought it to your table.

Sometimes I would take a bus to the next town over just to walk through the aisles of the only Mexican grocery store in the area. I liked to peruse the imported household wares, natural sponges wrapped with coarse horsehair bristles, a bar of Zote soap, which I was told by people who remembered, smelled, just like all of Mexico wrapped together, and all of the colors of the candies that were spicy and sweet—things that I could find nowhere else. I liked the butchers best, with their white aprons stained pink with blood, and how every time I entered they always greeted me the same, "Qu'húbole primo." And I would reply back with something familiar in my mouth, "Qu'húbole pela'o." I wasn't their primo, their cousin, but it meant so much more to say it there, thousands of miles away from my family, in a town where football was religion, where I had to take two buses to hear someone call me primo.

It didn't feel forward to be that cordial with a stranger; we both silently agreed we needed that intimacy, being so far away from whatever it was we called home. Maybe, if either of us stayed long enough, the next generation would call that town home. Each time we spoke, we were also saying "We made it here, we have both left people behind, but we are *here*." We were announcing the history of our pain. We didn't need to say much in the way of introductions—we knew enough about ourselves that we could guess what life was like for the other in that small town. The only things I didn't know, and what I dared not ask, had to do with returning. So when are you going back, primo, I thought—is your family here, is your mother here, or over there, or has she already left us? Some of those questions not even brothers asked of each other. "When are you going back?"

I always left that store feeling like I had just eaten something warm and savory. It was the only place I could find calling cards to call my father, and it was wrapped with the smell of meat drying on hooks above the cute young butcher sharpening his knives, the blades scissoring through the air like a deck of cards. I would often come home with things I didn't need, just to have them around.

3.

I spoke with my mother at least twice a day. Sometimes it was just for a second between classes. I wanted to hear her voice. She always asked how I was doing, and I never liked to admit that I was tired, even though my bones ached, my headaches were intolerable, and I felt fatigued for seemingly no reason at all, just generally lethargic. It was difficult to tell her I was tired when all I had been doing was reading all day and working on a few lines of a poem: "Yes, we drowned, then changed our minds, / then drowned again, / because we could, / because no one would know the difference. / Let's continue this drowning to remember what we look like." That was my new job, to read and write, and I didn't think I deserved that kind of comfort.

I wrote those lines in my journal. I tried to hold the words of my poems inside me like the sounds of snow, but they were nothing like snow, they disappeared as soon as I wrote them. Snow at least stayed until March, maybe even April. It didn't feel like I was doing anything important, or of substance. According to my director, I should have been writing something that caused great pain or emotion, or came from great pain or emotion, and I was its only vessel—"If you don't write it, no one will," I kept hearing at program meetings and bars. I scoffed. I didn't believe it. Everyone seemed to know what they were doing, seemed to know more than me.

None of my own work seemed to matter much to me because all it was, was words. I didn't know if the poems would ever be a book, I didn't know why I was there exactly, when I could have been home, helping Amá with her bills, maybe working hard enough to let her stay home if she wanted—real things, tangible things. I could have been useful doing something else. "Yes, we drowned, then changed our minds . . . because we could . . . because no one would know the difference . . . Let's continue this drowning . . . to remember." I was a lot more forward about who I was than when I first arrived, but I still felt like I was withholding so much of myself from people. I still felt like a fraud, and my poems reflected that, "you called it cutting apart, I called it song."

I changed the words in my poems around; I said them softly, and I could see the shape they made in the small cloud of fog beneath my breath as I walked farther and farther from home. That was my work, that was my labor, what they were paying me to do. Somehow it felt like I was stealing. They didn't take up much space, they hardly even existed at all. "Yes, we changed our minds to remember. Yes, we remembered, yes, we drowned, and changed our minds." I was losing my memory and I didn't know why, but Rubi was helping me restore it. "You called it cutting apart, I called it song." People kept opening and closing their mouths in front of me, and some days I was too depressed to nod along. My therapist said it would happen like this, but I didn't believe her. I wondered what kind of poems my mother would write if she was in my place, if someone would have given her the chance.

It didn't seem real to me whenever I spoke to Amá on the phone. It was as if I had been dropped into a different world. Unlike Apá, she was only a button away, her voice was clear, and yet she was geographically farther than Apá. There were things I could no longer explain, experiences she could only nod along to, though I knew I wasn't making sense. I didn't realize that because of my leaving, she too would be left out from a large part of who I would increasingly become. "That's great, mijo, that's great" is all she would say. I could feel our conversations steadily becoming more and more like Apá's—distant.

Nonetheless, we still shared the familiar set of words for being tired. I called her, stopped walking, talked for a minute, hung up, and continued walking. "It's a different kind of tired that you're feeling," she said, "but it's just as exhausting as anything else." I wanted to believe her, but I knew she said it to make me feel better, to make me forget about the longer hours she worked to make up for my absence back home. I nodded in agreement, even though she couldn't see me, and mumbled yes over the phone, because that was what any son would tell a mother who was tired.

*

I went on my walk so that I could tire myself enough to fall asleep, since I hadn't been sleeping well lately. I hated to admit that the only times I was physically tired anymore were when I went on such walks. I was used to feeling the aches of my body after clocking out from a long day's shift. I was used to lugging my body in heavy steel-toed boots caked with mud through the construction site. But here I ate soft cheeses at department parties where I laughed at terrible jokes I felt an obligation to laugh at. Eventually I came up with some terrible jokes of my own.

I taught poetry to dull-eyed business undergrads early in the morning who wrote about football, their fraternities and sororities, their family trips to Paris. I felt deflated when they demanded to know why, despite having *always* received A's in high school English classes, they weren't passing my class. No matter how long I stayed up, how many hours I spent crouched over my desk, it didn't feel like real work. No matter how much I wrote, it never felt like I got enough done, or anything done at all. The only way I've ever understood work was when my body was tired, when I ached, so I walked to make up for it.

When I was building houses back in California, I could see what we produced at the end of the day. There was no denying that I had gotten something done because the proof was right in front of me—a new wall, a new roof, a window. I could see my progress. But in that small college town, I felt like I was running out of time every day, and I would have nothing to show for it. I thought I would get left behind and couldn't allow myself even an hour of idleness. What was a poem compared to a house? I worked myself to death writing as many poems as I could to stave off the anxiety and guilt I felt for being comfortable while knowing that Amá and the rest of my family toiled just to make ends meet. What I wouldn't give to see my poems like I saw the houses I built—large things with many windows. But one thing was true: those poems were mine, and no one else's. Those houses never were.

Sometimes I wrote my name behind walls that would be covered up forever. Sometimes I wrote small phrases, "yes, we remembered, yes, we changed our minds," and carried these phrases with me to grad school, where they eventually made their way into poems. I fantasized someone remodeling the house years later, maybe a different owner, uncovering a board and coming across my small incoherent phrases. "Yes, we drowned."

*

I didn't only walk late in the evenings, I was always outside. I never felt comfortable being indoors or being in the same spot for too long. I called it my daily shuffle. I would start in one café on Main Street, and by noon, I was already sitting down in my third or fourth. It was very expensive buying a cup at each place in order to earn my right to sit down.

I especially couldn't be home in the midafternoon. The anxiety got worse around two p.m. The sun would hit my windows in just the right way to make everything feel dirty. Or maybe it was just the silence and unnerving calm of that hour of the day, as I sat alone with my thoughts, that made me leave. When I sat on my couch, a plume of dust particles swept up into the beams of light, and the dread would begin as soon as the dust settled back onto the couch. It was especially bad in winter, everything seemed dull and quiet, muffled by the snow, and perhaps even the clouds. Everything sounded like a variation on a bass note, a heavy thud. That silence reminded me that I was wasting time, that I hadn't gotten anything done and the day was almost over. My apartment might as well have been a hotel room, since I was only able to bear being there at night. I was the classic hardworking immigrant, but not by choice. I couldn't escape the traps I put out for myself.

I wanted to tell my mother I felt like I was dying, or that I actually wanted to die, to walk in front of a bus or out in the middle of a frozen lake with thin ice. I considered whether it was a mistake to come. I couldn't reconcile the two worlds that we were living in. When she asked if I was tired, I simply said, "No, Ma, I'm not tired, everything is fine, my head just hurts a little." She didn't know how much I was drinking, that I had gained a lot of weight from the Prozac, and that I came to graduate school only to lose my love for language. Back home, poems felt real, but after I'd been in the Midwest for two years, they felt like nothing more than bright store-bought balloons.

4.

It had been a year since I last saw my father. We still didn't know how to carry on our conversations over the phone, even though things should have been better since we reconnected after my DACA trip. Talking still felt like an obligation. Our conversations were dry and repetitive—"Hi Dad, how are things, are you cold, has anyone died, how's the dog, the young ones are fine, the older ones are fine, Mom is fine, I'm doing okay, I'm teaching now, I'm teaching poetry, no, poetry, po-e-try, it's cold here, no, I'm teaching poetry, Dad, I'll explain it later."

Every time I spoke with Apá, I had to repeat what it was that I did—"I'm a graduate student, Apá, but I also teach, it pays okay." He was obsessed with knowing how I made a living, and what I would do after I finished. He wanted specific details, a game plan. It was so different from how we had always made a living that I had to make up an ideal situation of my future to hide the uncertainty looming ahead.

Every time he asked, I would respond exactly the same way, and he would hum as if mulling it over, as if he was hearing it for the first time. The calls never lasted more than ten minutes. Most of the times we fit everything we needed to say to each other in less time. I asked him things I already knew the answers to but asked them anyway because it was part of the show. We didn't know what else to say. We checked each item off the list. We fulfilled our duties of father and son, and we both seemed content with it, even proud. I think he preferred it that way too. I wished we could have stayed silent on the phone the entire time, just to be in the company of each other. But our silent breath against itself would have been harder to pronounce than any apology.

*

Part of me believed that if we kept up the act, if we just repeated the motion out of obligation, we'd eventually find our conversations enjoyable, that practice would lead to sincerity, which would lead to something organic—that we would work our way up to affection.

*

There was a time when I believed in repetition, when I thought repetition meant things would be simple—predictable. Maybe then, when nothing changed, when all the variables were accounted for, I could move through the world in a way I had never moved through it before, how I imagined mostly everyone else made it through their day—intact, aware of what time, day, or month it was. If I drew the same circle a thousand times, I was certain I would see something different about the things around me.

Once, when my anxiety was so great that I thought my skin would actually peel off my body, I went out for a walk on a warm evening in California. I found myself in an empty parking lot beneath the largest moon I had ever seen. I sat down and stared until the moon started making faces at me, yes, actual faces. They would appear and disappear and move in circles. I sat there for what seemed like hours, not blinking once, and just letting my tears keep my eyes from closing. Joyfully weeping, I walked back to my mother's house and counted the steps it took to get there. I wanted to record exactly what I had done to repeat it for the next day. I wanted that feeling to last forever, and I was afraid that any small change would scare it away. I couldn't remember the last time I wasn't trembling with anxiety. Repetition as sustained attention made me pick up my body, walk home, and tell my mother I loved her in Spanish. It was so simple. I didn't even need a pen or paper to draw the moon, just trace it with my eyes.

*

I once read a book on Alberto Giacometti and his ritual of painting people's portraits. He would spend weeks painting over the same face; so much that the layers would start to clump. He would chisel away, polish, and start again. He said he felt like he was looking into a hole, something he could not see completely to the bottom. Was the hole in the face he was staring at, or in the canvas he was painting on? I wonder if he was looking for the right version of the same face, the one that few people knew existed. And in the end, you could tell there was something there behind the lines and scratches. You could tell that there was more than just a face, the emotion distilled behind the face; he always managed to find the right one. Somehow he captured the sadness of his lover, his friends or acquaintances. It could never have happened on the first try, it took him hundreds of attempts before he would be certain that he'd painted something worthwhile—all the while his models stood still, their hands folded on their laps, looking at his frustrated expressions. He wasn't interested in perfection, only in the process of getting there.

Did we, after nearly a century of my family's border crossings, come close to that repetition? Were we close to perfecting something that we knew we would never finish?

He said he would give up art forever if he could not find his way out of any particular painting. *Find his way out*, meaning he was lost. Maybe in the end, the final version was no different than the first—a complete circle—but the pain of repetition, of painting the same face over and over, made it something different in the end after all.

I wanted out, too. I walked to get lost, but I couldn't lie to myself that I didn't know the way back.

[Third Movement: Horses as Transitive Verbs]

———

I was supposed to die in 1990, dragged behind the horse in Mexico. My father was supposed to spend the rest of his life thinking about who I would have become, which is to say in regret. I was supposed to be only a story people would still be reluctant to tell even years later. I was supposed to be a story that led to a better story, a jumping point that led away from grief. Amá would be known as the woman who lost two children, the first to the U.S., the second to a mare. Apá would be known as the man who lost only one, because I doubt he would admit he had anything to do with the other.

I should have been a secret my family told new friends only when they were sure they would be friends forever.

I should have died again falling off my roof at the age of four, and then again a few months later when I walked into a corral where my father and other men were branding cattle and wrapped myself around the leg of the bull, which was already too tired and defeated from the burning iron to kick me.

I should have died when I swallowed a large plastic ball. My face turned purple and my feet dangled limp off the tailgate of a truck as they rushed me to the hospital. Before arriving, I looked at my mother's face covered in tears and said, "It's okay, Amá, it went down, you don't have to cry anymore." From then on my body was no longer soft.

I was never afraid of falling. I didn't think falling would hurt.

Because I did not die when I was supposed to, there were times I thought I wouldn't. I liked commotion, things that went fast. I liked the horses my father broke, even though they almost broke me. They would run around him in circles all day until they learned what it meant to go left, what it meant to go right, and eventually hung their heads low to the ground in defeat. They bucked and they kicked until they knew the common sign for stop, slow down, go fast. My father made a hole in the dirt from spinning on the same spot. He was like the shiny nail of a top, the horses lassoed to his waist, trying to run away from his hollering and his madness.

5.

We landed in El Paso and hopped in a taxi that would take us to Juárez. The borderlands were just as foreign to me as the Midwest, even though I'd measured so much of myself against that dividing line, living my life as a simulacrum of its possibilities and limitations. Just as from the air, from the ground too it seemed like the border retained an inherently elusive quality, unknowable, ever shifting. It existed for me as a myth, but in a time when myths were flesh and blood—a time when the gods would actually descend from the foggy mountain to keep an eye on things. It was both real and not real at the same time. Everything I dreamed about was there: the floodlights, the metal, the cement. It was the body of the name I had kept inside me for so long. It was exactly as I imagined it, exactly as it must have looked when I first came in 1993.

However, coming back this time to Mexico felt different than when I came with my DACA permit. I was now a legal permanent resident. If I wanted to, I could cross back and forth a hundred times in a single day. Entering Mexico with my green card, knowing I could leave whenever I wanted, heightened my pride and affection for the country of my birth. I felt like it was safe to love Mexico if I knew I could leave and return if I wanted, whereas before I was cautious of attaching myself too much to Mexico, since I didn't know if or when I would ever be able to return.

As we approached the checkpoint, I shuffled through my bag to get my passport ready. "There's no need for that, going into Mexico," the taxi driver said in a low tone, almost laughing when he said it. He was kind; he kept saying how long he'd lived there, as if time alone was proof that a city treated you well enough to stay.

We didn't stop. The car rolled right into Mexico. Perhaps because it was late and there wasn't much traffic. I was waiting for some kind of pause, something that would signal even the slightest change in velocity, that clicked us through. But the driver kept his pace and sped up as soon as we left the bright lights behind. It happened so fast I hardly noticed I was holding my breath.

*

The second we crossed, my phone changed service to a different communications company—either Telcel or Movistar. High above the wall, there was also a wall. It was invisible, it stretched up for miles in the air, it penetrated even the dust around my body. It said "From here forth, it will be different." And it was. I got a text that said "Welcome to Mexico." If my passport didn't say I entered, at least my cell phone did.

I could see the wall, I could see the guards and the floodlights through the car's mirror. It was something I could point to and say "That—*that*—was what hurt me." But when my phone switched, I realized just how hopeless and small I was. I thought there must have been a place where reprieve from the line existed. But I was wrong. There isn't a single square foot on earth that is not affected in one way or another by borders, even the oceans.

Perhaps it was different for people who lived on the border, who saw it as something routine, something so common that it felt like air. It was almost mundane, but behind that lay the very real threat. They lived each day balancing themselves on the sharp spine of a large beast. And wasn't that the most dangerous, when it felt like air, when people were so used to something that they forgot how easily they could fall off and break?

*

For so many years, I was resolved to think that I would never come back to the actual line and see the wall up close. It was a spectacle to behold, but just because it also served the purpose of optics as well as separation, that didn't mean the barbed wires weren't sharp, or that those weren't real bullets in the agents' guns. Its grandeur, its exorbitant budget, and its generally overbearing nature was typical of the U.S., just like the Empire State Building, the Hoover Dam, or Mount Rushmore.

When I asked other people what they would do if they were ever able to go back, their answers always had an air of youthfulness, as if by returning, they could start over again, perhaps differently the second time, and reverse their regrets and mistakes in life, as if their town had stayed unchanged—perfectly unwrapped—all those years they were away. Some said they would do nothing, "Just go to the post office and mail some letters, or go to the market and buy some milk." It was peace of mind they wanted, to not have to say anything particularly special in a letter—"How are you? The weather here is wonderful, soon it will begin to rain."

6.

The United States was never my father's country, so I couldn't really say that he was exiled. Neither he nor the U.S. would ever claim the other. He was already on the way out when he left; they just gave him the final nudge by revoking his visa at the gate and locking the door behind him. He spent a couple days in custody, and then they released him into Mexico. It wasn't his first time being deported, but he was certainly resolved to make it his last. He only now, after being away for over a decade, wanted to come back to the U.S. so that he could leave it on his own terms. Maybe he, too, could only learn to like it if he was allowed to leave whenever he wished.

And yet his departure so many years before still felt like an exile, not to him personally, but to us who were left behind. The rupture caused by his departure necessitated explanation—one I was reluctant to give whenever teachers, doctors, pastors, friends—anyone—asked his whereabouts. "He's fine, he's still over there . . . no, I don't know when he's coming back . . . it's just complicated." Most of the time I avoided talking about him altogether. It made people think he'd been gone much longer than he actually was. It made them stop asking questions. As the years dragged on, and each of his three youngest children grew, we increased our vocabulary of deflection.

I never liked saying the word "deported." It felt like a bad word—it was difficult to say in my mouth. It was especially difficult to say in Spanish because it carried an extra syllable—"de-por-ta-do."

Somehow even a single extra syllable made it infinitely heavier.

I would say everything that pointed to the word, but never it exactly—"he's over there . . . he can't come back . . . he's been there for five, eight, ten years . . ." and if I found enough approximations, enough euphemisms for he-is-never-coming-back-don't-you-get-it, people usually understood. I could use synonyms because they didn't carry the same kind of weight—"They sent him away, you know how it goes . . . dismissed, displaced, removed, transported," gone. The worst was when they asked about my mother: "So, are they still together?" People were so nosy. I was always ready with my response—"Yeah, they're together still, they still talk on the phone." "Together" meant different things at different times. There were months when I was sure they were finally through, but then Amá would break and send him a blanket, or some underwear, or socks. Or Apá would break and every once in a while send us a pair of boots or a cowboy belt, which we would toss into the closet and never wear—same as the blankets he tossed in the corner of the abandoned room and never used.

Who were the famous exiles? Seneca, Leon Trotsky, Marlene Dietrich, Pablo Neruda, Victor Hugo. What did they do during their time away? Their best work was completed in moments of exile—longing for home, trying to make sense of their distance, trying to build bridges any way they could. Hugo wrote *Les Misérables*, and Neruda wrote *Canto General*, both while in exile. How great was their longing to return? They stood at the edge of one land and looked back at another—perhaps standing outside their country, they could see what no one else could see from the inside. In Apá's case he first left Mexico, and from the outside, he saw the beauty and horror of Mexico—he longed for the beauty and looked past the horror. Then he was deported from the U.S., and from the outside, he saw the beauty and horror of the U.S.—he exclaimed at the horror and looked past the beauty that was hidden most of the time.

*

When my father was—*banished? sent away? excluded?*—he took part in this ancient tradition of exile, and what had he to show for his ten years away? Where was his *Canto General*, his *Les Misérables*? In those ten years away from us, he learned to build a house that wouldn't fall, that was warm in the winter and fresh in the summer, with a garden in the middle of a courtyard where geraniums tilted their small petals to the sun. It was enough. It took him ten years to learn to care for something like a pot of flowers for no particular reason; just for the sake of flowers. When I asked him why he had so many flowers, he didn't know how to answer me, as if he didn't understand the premise of the question. "Why wouldn't you have that many flowers?"

At least those years were not for nothing. Amá says that even though it was hard on us, I should be glad that he was gone when and as long as he was, because otherwise I would have never left the fields or peach orchards. His gift was precisely the absolute fact of his absence.

7.

I wonder why the government chose ten years specifically as enough time for a punishment before you can attempt to file for a return. That is, if you are allowed to return at all. Maybe in ten years, your fading memory began to soften the hard edges of your wounds, as if we were angry dogs put aside to cool down. *Think about what you've done.* It takes about ten years to master anything. What did they think we were supposed to master in that time away from each other? Our silence grew, and our estrangement grew. By the end, we were experts in nothing in particular, and Apá was just as sharp and hot as the day he decided he would learn to grow flowers.

Apá surpassed his ten years, in fact. He stayed for two more, just to be sure. Almost as if he were saying "I did what you told me and then some," as if he would be rewarded for his noble efforts. We were looking for a reward at the end of our sacrifice. We paid a price, and now we were getting ready to collect what we thought was ours. Apá would have the freedom to come and go as he pleased.

I guess we thought it would be automatic; that if he completed his punishment, that if he was a good boy and followed the rules, cooperated, then he would automatically be allowed to return—quid pro quo. But it didn't work like that. In reality, he was just waiting for his punishment to be declared. It would take them ten years to tell him he would never be able to return. And they needed to do so in person, on the spot, so that he could hear it with his own ears, instead of reading it in a letter that might ring empty in his head. They needed to deliver the most visceral kind of *no*, to get the point across that he was never to return.

To them, his punishment didn't mean anything; it was just a clock in a file somewhere with his name on it counting down. It was just a one and a zero, something you only read about in school. Ten years seemed like such an ancient number. It was a decade, which turned into a century, which turned into a millennium. Ten was everywhere I looked. The Ten Commandments God gave to Moses. Ten was the times the referee counted for the boxer, ten was in the verb phrase "to decimate," to reduce something by one one-tenth, which had something to do with the killing of one in ten soldiers as a punishment for mutiny.[1] Odysseus took ten years to journey home to Penelope, the Trojan War having already lasted ten, long enough for a corpse flower to bloom just twice, once every ten years, long enough that they could barely remember each other's faces.

*

I had an older friend who was deported and got the ten-year ban. Let's call her Esperanza. She thought the same thing as Apá: "I can do it. I'll follow the rules." Esperanza tried to make it work; she brought her children with her, those young enough to obey; the others stayed behind with her husband, and those who could cross tried to visit. But two years into her punishment, she realized that it was impossible to be separated from the rest of her family for that long. Even though she returned, things were never the same.

Upon being reunited for the first time in almost two decades, the first words an aunt of mine said to her son were, "Who are you?" to which the stranger replied, "I'm your son, Mom." They had always exchanged pictures over the years, and yet. My aunt looked down, slightly embarrassed or ashamed, and said, "Of course, of course."

Ten years was just enough time to learn how to live without someone and move on.

[Third Movement as Migration]

===

We had to leave Tepechitlán for many reasons. There were so many different ways to say we were tired, each a synonym for debt. There was a point when I knew the names of the birds in Tepechitlán and thought it was a good idea to eat the flowers in my mother's garden so that I could be a different color on the inside. I was too young to love, but I kept falling in love. I was convinced that, like me, the whole family couldn't sleep because they too couldn't remember the name of that bird with the yellow breast and black head.

Over dinner, Apá confessed that for the size of the town, there was a disproportionate number of suicides. He said it calmly, like he was talking to strangers about the weather, while he picked at his plate.

The events happened in order. First we lost our home, the home that Amá built with the little she was given after her mother's death. Then "It's a boy," the doctor said in late 1992 to Amá as he pointed to the blurry ultrasound. Another one, her last. She smiled and rubbed her stomach with her callused hands. We tried to pretend it was easy to feed a family of seven for as long as we could.

"Toña, you can barely feed the children you have, what were you thinking getting pregnant again?" my aunt Beatrice said to Amá when she told her the good news of the baby. Beatrice said it as if it was Amá's fault alone that she was pregnant, as if my father had nothing to do with it.

Amá had weathered a lot in her life, but hearing her sister say "You can barely feed the kids you have" was a breaking point. Amá gathered her kids and told Apá she was moving to the U.S., with or without him. She would prove to my aunt that her kids would never go hungry, by which she meant we would never return to Mexico.

My father, seeing her anger and conviction, agreed and sold his guns in order to afford the trip north. If we were to leave and cross to the other side, we would have to do it soon, before Amá's belly grew even larger.

We gave away our pathetic attempts at prayer, our small, irredeemable gods and their suffering. I imagined the afterlife as a kind of song played on repeat forever. We were selfish in our longing.

I, too, gave away what little I had to my cousins and friends, making them swear to take care of my things. I asked them not to break my toys because I would be back to reclaim them. How dumb of me?

It was like a Greek play in which everyone played the role of the chorus because we each thought we knew how it would end.

We made promises. We made promises.[2]

8.

Looking back into the distance from inside the taxi, I couldn't tell what was El Paso and what was Juárez because at night the lights all looked the same. Each patch of dark meant that no one dared, or could not, settle there.

But the buildings and their design differed on either side of the line. On the Mexican side, the homes, even the poor ones, had the flair of modern design—everything was a square on top of another square. Perhaps modernism was well suited to Mexico across class divides in a way that it wasn't in the United States, at least not in homes. The U.S. was still wedded, for the most part, to the Victorian, the cottage, the Tudor.

In Juárez, as in Guadalajara and, I imagined, most of Mexico, no one built with wood, which allowed for those small, intricate designs of ornamentation and peaked roofs. For builders, tradesmen, and journeymen working with steel and cement, the only way to go was modern—90 degrees by 90 degrees by 90 degrees. It made the most practical sense. One could say that modernism had caught up to the practicality of Mexico and most other non-Western countries.

The old colonial buildings like the church and the presidential palace in the oldest part of every Mexican city were the only buildings that really curved. They were adorned with the embellishments that harkened to the Baroque, neoclassical, and Rococo—all orbiting around the image of Christ at the center. Everything was gilded and emanated away from itself, as if it were meant to go on forever, as if their reign over the colonies would never end. Had it?

The opulence and sheer breathtaking scale of those older Mexican buildings sent a message to the (then) present but also to the future. The splendor of the vaulted ceilings announced itself as power, reminding every citizen and slave of its colonial presence—"We are always here, we will be here long after." Those buildings were meant to last.

Throughout Juárez, absent were the eaves drooping over the walls as they did back in the states, in the suburbs of anywhere USA. Absent were the pitched roofs that allowed for empty space that would, by design, go to waste and was only good for things like attics. Absent were the beveled cornices, the cantilevered fascia boards, bargeboards, soffits, and gables. When a house in Mexico caught fire, everything inside burned but not the house, made of stone, cement, and iron beams.

The U.S. was also enamored with the architecture associated with the centuries from which it was born and from which it gained its power. It held closely to the nostalgia of its eighteenth and nineteenth centuries, and never left. It romanticized the New England aesthetic—the house on the shore with a high-pitched roof and thin planks of spruce wrapping around—or the Craftsman bungalow. Although Mexico (in a strictly colonial sense) was a much older country, the vaulted arches still carried the same weight as they always had, still emanated the same message of colonial power.

*

Apá's house in Tepechitlán adopted the compartmentalized aesthetics of the early-twentieth-century avant-garde—out of functionality, not style. Rooms were separated by function in a much stricter sense, and nothing was connected. The kitchen was the kitchen and nothing else, the living room was the living room and nothing else; the bathroom, the bedroom, the store/feed room, the same. Newer American homes, on the other hand, always wanted everything open. They wanted to see everything happening in front of them, as if to say "Nothing is hidden in this house," one thing seamlessly leading into another and another—"We don't keep secrets." You could be dicing tomatoes in the kitchen while someone talked to you on a bar stool in the dining room as both of you watched football on the far TV in the living room. It was the American way of life, to be seen, splayed out; its entire aura said "Look at me, look at me, I'm happy."

Like so many other houses in Mexico, the compartments of each room in Apá's house in Tepechitlán affected how people inside interacted. The separation of rooms, all having a common courtyard, altered people's behavior. The act of having to leave, say, the kitchen, and go outside to the common courtyard in order to enter another room felt like a cleansing of the palate, an intermezzo, a small dash of sorbet to wash out the bitter taste left in the mouth after an argument at the dinner table. Leaving one physical space for another, you could start fresh, even better than before, forgiving those who had hurt you. It was the outside that did it, the fresh air, the act of situating your body beneath miles of open sky before coming back into a different room. That wasn't possible in most American tract homes, where all the tragedy happened under one roof and was never released.

In a way my father, just like, I figured, everyone else, was an extension of the spaces he inhabited. He functioned as they functioned; it was how he saw himself in relation to the world and the people around him. He could go from absolute joy to absolute rage in a matter of seconds. And he lapped circles around us between rage and joy while we tried to keep up. It was so easy for him to switch back and forth, as if he was walking from room to room in his head. Sometimes Amá would just shrug and continue with her business because she knew he would boil over and then simmer, almost embarrassed to admit that he had been stricken again. It was always so confusing to me, but as I got older, I soon began to do the same. I found my rage was quickly followed by laughter followed by rage. I had only lived in those compartmentalized houses for the first five years of my life before we migrated to the gabled and pitched homes of the U.S., but that was enough time to establish that pattern in my head, or I inherited it from him at birth. And in my head, I did feel like I *could* walk into a room that housed anger, turn around and leave, and then walk over to the room that housed love, sorrow, or shame, and stay there. *On/off, on/off.*

Growing up, I never knew how to approach my father because there was no sign of how he was feeling at any particular moment. There was no warning. He was never expressive to begin with, and the large palm sombrero he always wore obscured his features even further, casting a slight shadow beneath his eyes. If I laughed when it wasn't a time for laughter, I would certainly know it. If I was somber when I should have been happy, he would look at me and slap me on the back, shine a few crooked teeth at me and say, "Trucha, mijo." And I would let out a deep nervous breath.

That breath, a calibration. I was adjusting myself to his likeness, I was matching my rhythm with his so that there would be peace, so that we could just go one more day without screaming. That was my breath, led, as if by a leash, by the rhythm of his. It was a guessing game most of the time, and it took me many years to become a good guesser. Even then, I guessed wrong many times. I was always following behind him, going from room to room, whiplashed from the darkness of one room to the brightness outside, always looking beneath that large hat for any sign of what would follow.

9.

The taxi stopped in front of our hotel, next to the U.S. Embassy. I paid the driver and thanked him. He took our luggage out of the trunk and rolled it over to the entrance. I tried to help him with our bags, but he kept insisting that he should get them. I handed him a tip and thanked him. He was kind. "Thank you, sir, and good luck with everything," he said as he jumped back into his small Nissan, heading back to the airport. Although it was midnight, no doubt, he would repeat the same trip many times before the sun came up— from the El Paso airport to a hotel near the embassy and back.

The hotel was meant to accommodate people coming from the U.S., meant to make them feel at home, as if saying, "This isn't Mexico." It had stuccoed foam around its cornices, which made it look like a suburban tract home. Soft amber light tumbled out of the low windows of the first-floor rooms and lobby onto the narrow patches of bright grass that surrounded the building, and if you stood close enough, it almost made you forget you were in the desert. Water runoff from the sprinklers trickled down the sidewalk and pooled in the gutter for what seemed like hours. Such a waste.

We couldn't really afford that hotel, but we felt like we had no choice. We wanted all our collective energy focused solely on my father's interview so that he would have nothing else to think about other than what to say to the agent when the time came. We wanted to eliminate any unpredictable variables. It was next door to the embassy, it served breakfast, it had a copier and printer, and it was comfortable. We never thought, however, that it was the kind of place that Apá was not used to, that it was comfortable only for Rubi and me, that it was something foreign to him.

I saw my father waiting for us in the lobby, draped in that soft light, with his familiar palm straw hat, his tight denim jeans, his boots, his belly hanging over his belt, and his tucked-in plaid shirt. It was strange to see him in a distant city, far from where we'd last seen each other, back home in Tepechitlán. Unlike the last time, I was now arriving as a seasoned traveler with a green card, even though my only other experience was a single trip to Tepechitlán the year before. I didn't know where we'd left things between each other last, but as we approached, it felt less like a grand reunion and more like something I could see myself doing for a long time after—coming to see my father for short periods of time. It was a new way of being a son that I had never known before. Now I was the one coming and going, and he would be the one to stay behind, watching me leave. If things didn't work out, I thought, this would be how our lives would continue, him waiting for me to come back and going back to his life as normal after I left. I wasn't quite sure what to say, so we shook hands and came in closer for a hug.

*

He traveled an entire day and a half by bus to get there from the south, and we boarded a plane in Detroit and flew a few hours from the north. I fell asleep on Rubi's shoulder for most of the flight because I wasn't too worried. I was optimistic. He did his time, he was going to collect his reward.

We met in something of a middle. But in reality it wasn't the middle, at least not for him. The middle only existed for people like Rubi and, now, myself, who could go back and forth freely between the line. How much had changed in a year! Even though the U.S. was just a stone's throw away, we could have been thousands of miles farther south and it would still feel just as distant. Even if I took him to the actual wall on the Juárez side, and even if he touched it with his bare hands, scraping his nails along its rusted metal, the U.S. would still be impossibly distant, it would still be out of reach until he acquired his papers. There were only two conditions: either you were inside the U.S., or outside it. To be close or far away from it didn't matter, only whether you were in or out.

Yes, we knew our world by dichotomies, yes, it's how we made sense of things—we knew them by what they were not. There was always a price.

*

I held Apá longer than I should have, and he began to pat my back as if to say "That's enough, son, that's enough."

"How was the trip?" I asked him.

"It was fine, everything was fine. How's everyone back home? How's your mother?"

"They're fine, Dad. We'll talk to them in the morning. It's late now."

Even at the brink of his possible return to the U.S., I knew he was still asking, in one way or another, if my mother would ever return to Mexico with him, which either meant that he wasn't as optimistic about his interview as we were or confirmed my suspicion that even if he was approved, he would still live in Mexico. All of this commotion at the border, the paperwork, the tense nights before big mornings, it was old news for him. He had been in the same kind of situation on the same kind of night dozens of times before. He was used to those roads, those lights, and the darkness beyond them.

He didn't seem alert like we were, wiry with anticipation, our eyes tired and red. Our clothes looked outstretched from trying to sleep in them on the plane, the way they look when you've been wearing them too long. It didn't seem like there was anything different about Apá. He talked like he always talked, moved like I always remembered him moving.

He had been to Juárez many times, and it was in the Juárez/El Paso border station, that very same checkpoint we had just crossed, where they detained and deported him back in 2003. For him, it was just another city, just another attempt at crossing, something he had been doing for decades either by car, by foot, or by paper. Unlike me, he held no grudges against the border, or the city, or anything related to the situation of his deportation. He was able to forgive and forget, something I admired him for.

We checked in and headed upstairs. I wasn't sure whether to lead or to follow, unsure how to hold my body against the presence of his. I thought I would have learned all of that already since I last saw him, but I hadn't. I followed but told him the way.

We decided to get two rooms, one for Rubi and me and one for him. I didn't know if he wanted to stay with us and perhaps spend more time together, or not. My excuse was that Rubi wanted her privacy, but in reality, I didn't want to share a room with him. I didn't want to start sharing the formalities of daily living, only to be suddenly cut off. I didn't want to know what color his toothbrush was, if he wore undershirts to sleep, what side of the bed he slept on, if he preferred walking around with sandals or socks, or even how he organized his small bag, similar to the one he had when he left in 2003. His interview wasn't going to be like mine. They weren't going to ask him who he loved and if he loved them forever, they were going to ask him to say he was sorry.

There was the broader image of my father, which I knew well, and then there were the smaller subtleties that I had forgotten over the years, some of which I never knew. Even in the short moments we'd already had together, I could already observe he didn't like the cuffs of his shirt to touch his wrists, he kept a pen in his shirt pocket with a small memo pad filled with names. Between both the large details and the small, they composed the entirety of my father. I was content with having only part of him.

I didn't want to start something that we couldn't finish.

10.

It was like any other Denny's, with the low-hanging lightbulbs, the bright menus with enlarged pictures of sweaty meat, fries, and drinks. I thought it was appropriate to be eating at a Denny's, as if just by being in the restaurant, we were already in America. *Do you like burgers and fries, Dad? Do you like the unlimited coffee? The plates as large as your face? The ketchup and mustard and ranch dressing? Dad, does this suit you? The waiters with their name on their lapel, and the bright fuchsia-colored drinks dripping their excess on the menu? Is this all enough?*

You didn't need permission to enter the bright America that was Denny's, which was next door to the little America, the embassy, and everything was in stark relief against the big America just beyond. All you needed was money. It was easy to take part in the Denny's America, to sit down at a booth and listen to Britney sing "Hit me baby one more time," sometimes twice, to order an American beer with your very American burgers and fries from a nice waitstaff who wore their names on their lapels. It was easy because they didn't care when or where you made your money, only that you had it at the time of purchase. Money was your green card, they were selling their green card—"Verde que te quiero verde."[3]

I asked for water because I calculated in my head that the bill was already high, but the waiter brought me bottled water, which wasn't free. If I closed my eyes, I could still taste the iron and clay of the water from Apá's well tap, back in Tepechitlán. Unlike the cell phone waves, unlike the masses of people trying to cross, unlike even some of the wildlife scrambling through the desert floor at night, the water deep in the aquifers beneath us was one of the only things that moved freely back and forth. The large reservoirs that spanned both cities hundreds of feet belowground had nothing to do with us, with this system of walls, cameras, and paper. I knew that both cities were fighting for that water, and both were trying to claim ownership over it, as if it too could be divided. How flawed we were, and still are, to think that an underground lake could be cut in half like a piece of string.

The bottle sat there on the table, sweaty with condensation. Even in a place as dry as Juárez, there was moisture in the air. It made a ring around the napkin. I felt guilty drinking water, even just looking at it. I remembered Customs and Border Protection's policy of slashing bottles of water left behind intentionally by aid groups in the desert, in order to discourage more migrants from crossing, to deprive them even of a last shred of hope for survival. How many needed that bottle more than me? How many more were out there, beyond the city lights, in the dark areas that would soon be flooded with light in the morning, so much light that you wonder if one sun alone could be responsible? Out there were families who were just starting the journey we had been on for decades and were hoping to soon end. I twisted the cap and drank it all. It was so cold that it hurt going down, and it turned my stomach to look at the bottle standing on the table, so empty, as our food was set down.

*

Even though he wasn't paying, Apá spent the rest of the dinner complaining about the price of the food. It looked cold even as the steam was rising. It was Wednesday night, and his appointment wasn't until Monday, which meant that his complaints would last until Monday. The bill *was* too much for me to admit. I didn't want him to know I was counting every peso, careful not to spend too much, constantly looking at my bank account on my phone. I knew we couldn't afford to eat there every day, so I was relieved that he didn't like the food.

The check came, and it was almost six hundred pesos. It was Denny's America, which meant they charged like Big America, too.

Rubi took out her small purse that she'd had for years, which was starting to rip. She wrote down the expense on a small notepad and paid. I felt bad for her because all of my family's troubles were expenses that were paid directly out of her checks as well. It wasn't her father who was sitting across from us, and yet she treated him as such, perhaps better. She could talk to him in ways that I couldn't. She could calm him down and make him understand things in ways I struggled with myself. I never liked to look inside her purse because it always reminded me of how much she had deprived herself for me and my family, not because there was never any cash—neither of us ever carried cash anymore—but in the small items she carried. Recycled pens, a small coin purse, a plastic comb, a napkin, a small bottle of foundation, a Lotto scratcher. They were things that said, "I'm doing my best with what I have," things I found often while going through Amá's purse as a kid to see if she had an extra dollar anywhere.

Apá refused to let me tip, and called the waiters vultures, zopilotes. I felt bad for the young waiter who stared nervously as we argued. It wasn't Apá's money, but he still felt he had ownership over it. I saw a glimpse of the old dad, I saw it in his eyes. I knew he wanted to say something more, but he couldn't; I could tell that he was holding back because it wasn't his money. *We* paid the application fee for his interview years before, *we* got him there to the border, *we* booked the hotel, *we* paid for the food, *we* dished out all our savings to keep paying the lawyers, *we* paid for everything.

Time didn't stand still after he left. It moved and we moved too, we grew. But the more time I spent with him, the more I saw that it was he who stood still. Even all those years before he was deported, when he was going back and forth to Mexico, he was static, he saw the world the same, he dressed the same, talked, thought, and breathed the same. Nothing was different about him. Having to ask for our help, having us pay the tab, the hotel, the fees, was slowly eating away at him because he couldn't accept that we had grown up without him.

*

Back at the hotel, he went into his room and we went into ours; we locked our door tight, but he left his slightly cracked. He felt comfortable enough to leave it open. The city, and the country, was his home in a way that it wasn't ours.

"Go talk to him," Rubi said as she slipped into her pajamas.

"Fine," I said, reluctantly.

I knocked and pushed his door open. He whistled for me to come in, knowing it was me even before I spoke. I didn't go to apologize for talking back to him at dinner over the tip. I just wanted to set up the plans for the next day. He was lying on his bed with his shirt off in his underwear. *Noted.* He looked very comfortable.

"So, tomorrow we're going to do your biometrics," I said, trying not to look at him but instead looking at the TV, which he put on mute because he hated talking over it. "Yep, God willing," he said in a reverent tone. I couldn't remember the last time I had seen him without a shirt, let alone without pants. Even as a child, around the house, he was always fully dressed. He looked like a different person without clothes. I could see his bony shoulders (*noted*), his droopy chest with his large nipples (*noted*), and his thick legs (*noted*). In my head, he always had thick legs, unlike me. I didn't want to see how he looked when he was most at rest, when he didn't have to look a certain way for others. His whole body looked soft, in fact.

I remembered taking a shower with him as a child, and also seeing him in nothing but underwear. I was already taking showers by myself then, with the occasional bath. It was during the time when I was making that transition, when I started to become embarrassed of my naked body and would insist that my sister or mother no longer bathe me, or at least let me keep my underwear on if they did. Puberty was still years away, but I remember I didn't want to be seen because by then I had already gotten my first erection.

I got in the shower first and he followed, or he got in and I followed.

I wasn't as embarrassed with Apá as I was with my sister or Amá, but he told me to keep my underwear on, as did he, and I was old enough to know why but young enough to not think about it too much, and instead just have fun playing with the water. We let the warm water wash over us and we splashed each other with soap. It was a father being a father, making funny faces and spitting water at me with his cheeks blown out like a puffer fish, which made me laugh and almost slip. When we finished, I stepped out and took off my underwear to dry myself on the mat. It was okay because I was no longer in the shower. I put the towel around my small waist and left him in the shower. He had closed the curtain and was drying himself. It was a side of him that I had never seen even in my young life, and one that I would never see again. Something remotely tender. It was just that one time. Even a few more months would have made me too old for that. Perhaps he realized too late that he'd lost the chance for moments like those, and so was only allowed it once before I began to grow.

As he lay on his bed in the hotel room, I almost felt sorry for him. His eyes were starting to become milky with cataracts and other soft smoke-like tissue. His actual lens was turning opaque; it was doing it to itself as a way to protect the eye from the harsh light. He was making himself blind out of his own stubbornness; he refused to wear sunglasses in the intense sun of the High Sierra. He always said sunglasses were for women, and I thought of the saying "chíngate pues," which roughly translated to "Well, go fuck yourself then," which he did, which was why he could only see clearly out of one eye, chíngate pues. Seeing him watch the muted TV on impeccably white sheets, obviously ignoring me, it was almost difficult to imagine him as the same person I remembered as a kid, holding my hair tight in his fist above the bathroom sink, saying "Look at me, look at me, goddamnit."

After staring at the TV for a minute or two, I walked over and gave him a hug and said good night. Though his skin still looked tight around his shoulders and arms, it was loose when I touched it (*noted*). He was warm, and he patted me on the back as if, again to say, "Ok, son, that's enough, that's enough."

I went back to my room to take a shower because after traveling all day, I felt dirty. On the mat I slowly pulled my underwear down and took off my shirt. There was so much pressure from the shower head that I had to turn it down a little. I waited for the water to get warm, and eventually the mirrors began to fog over. I stepped in. One foot, then the next. I stayed there for a long time. I knew I shouldn't have kept the water running for so long. And yet I let the water pour over me. Gallons and gallons of water. I wasn't even scrubbing anymore, just standing there with the water on my face. It was such a waste, and rather than make me speed up, the guilt made me linger in shame. I wondered how many people I could have saved in the desert with all the water that was wasted in that shower. I felt like punishing myself. I turned up the heat until my skin could take it no more, until it was pink and tender, like the burger I left half eaten on the table.

[Third Movement as Migration, a Streetlamp, a Fruit Stand, and My Uncle's Mistress]

===

The butcher went to the other side. His son, the one with the amputated leg, also went to the other side. They settled in Georgia. The middle-school math teacher went to the other side—her cousin swore she could make forty dollars in a single day picking oranges if she was fast enough. No math required.

She wouldn't be fast enough.

The priest went to the other side, and left the believers to wander through the church, blessing everything they touched. The Virgen de Guadalupe and the Pale Christ abandoned the altar and went to serve food in a Denny's on the other side. They went by Chuy and Lupe, they took English classes at the library at night. The neighbors to our right went, but only half of the family; the other half sat anxiously every day, waiting for the mail to arrive. The mayor went to the other side to enroll his children in school.

*

Every Sunday the crowds that gathered at the plaza shrank by one or two. It was hardly even noticeable at first. The sheriff went to the other side and left his uniforms in the street to whoever would claim them. No one claimed them. The drunks who spent their mornings in the cantina went to the other side, as did their bartender, serving them drinks along the way, all lamenting the women who had left them. The young man who went to the national track-and-field championship tried to go to the other side but died in the crossing. His running was only good for circles.

The dogs went to the other side. The women waiting on the corner for their bus to the market went to the other side. The markets went to the other side.

The debts all went to the other side—the only things that death could not touch. All the paper in the town was taken to the other side, so people reverted to memorization. The stonemasons, their tools, the trees, the money, the nuns, have gone to the other side.

It seemed like there was hardly anything left except the mothers who sent their sons ahead of them.

Eventually, all that was left was a street post next to a fruit stand where Angelica, my uncle's mistress, sold mangoes to anyone passing by. No one passed by anymore, but she still waved the parched mangoes in the air, yelling, "Dos por diez pesos." She bit into a mango and spat the pulp on the road. There were still roads, yes, but no signs, so she might as well have been anywhere. She picked her teeth with her nail, trying to pry loose the small fibers lodged in her gums.

The streetlight turned on, and the mangoes got sweeter and sweeter in their box.

11.

I didn't sleep very well our first night in Juárez. I opened the curtains and flooded the room with morning light, making Rubi squint and turn over. Outside, Juárez was already bustling. I could see old buses stopping for students dressed in black oxfords and blazers. I could hear their groaning engines all the way from our room as they churned down the boulevard, transporting people to the factories called maquilas to make goods that would be used in other countries.

The air was fresh and slightly chilly as Rubi, Apá, and I walked out of the hotel after leaving three soggy paper plates with luke-warm eggs untouched at the breakfast bar. Even though it was still early, all of the sprinkler puddles had dried up by then. Apá looked different in the morning light, almost as if the light alone made him larger. But the difference was that he wasn't cowboyed up. He wore slacks and loafers, which I had never seen him wear. We walked conveniently across the street to the clinic for his doc-tor's appointment. The first step to getting his green card would start with a doctor looking inside him. The application required an archaic physical to screen for diseases, to determine if he was fit to enter the United States.

*

In the doctor's office, we sat quietly with our legs crossed. Everyone was either looking at the floor or trying to quiet their children. It was a new building, very modern. The metal benches were bright blue and looked even brighter against the chemical whiteness of the walls, which were still free from scratches and scuffs.

Maybe it wasn't a new building, but rather a building in which people did not touch anything. We were almost certain that the workers there were also employed across the street at the embassy. Or if not, we wondered how deep their channels of communication were. And so out of that wondering came stillness, followed by slow, calculated movement. We quickly took our seats and sat up straight, looking dead ahead as if our interview had already secretly started, as if there were spies reporting to the immigration agents across the street. If there was any conversation between the patients, it was simply a mumble, nothing beyond the occasional comment on the weather, or the waiting, always the waiting.

Each person was hypervigilant of the others and how much space they took up in the room, even if the room was empty, or especially if it was.

I looked for signs in the faces of the others waiting with us in the lobby, signs that could reassure us that our specific uncertainty and fear wasn't unique. Everyone in that room would be interviewed or was accompanying someone to be interviewed. Eventually others would come in to replace us as soon as we left, coming to a halt on the same blue benches, being careful not to peel any of the paint. I wanted to turn to my neighbor and beg him to tell me why he was silent, and perhaps he wanted to do the same. But we both just sat there, not touching anything.

Despite having arrived at the clinic from our own unique circumstances, places, and histories, whether we said it or not, at that moment, everyone in the waiting room was the same helpless person with the same helpless prayer. We had everything in common. We were all smelling the same sterile air coming in from the vents. We were all shuffling our feet and fidgeting with our hands—all leaning to one side and then another when we got tired. And that's all we did, waited. We were good at it.

I recognized one family who was staying at the same hotel as us. We looked at each other and nodded, as if trying to reassure each other that things would be okay. Despite our mutual uncertainty, and fear, it was a triumph to be in Juárez. For so many years, to sit at a table for an interview was not even an option. It was our version of the Emerald City. We had made it that far. But unlike Dorothy, we had been disillusioned long before we arrived.

12.

Shortly after entering World War I, the U.S. passed the Immigration Act of 1917, also known as the "Asiatic Barred Zone Act," which prevented immigrants from Asia and its adjacent countries from entering. The law also introduced a literacy test to screen and further exclude immigrants deemed "imbeciles, idiots, feeble-minded persons, persons of constitutional psychopathic inferiority (homosexuality), vagrants, [and those with] physical defectives."

It was around this time that Juárez implemented what the Germans would later call "the El Paso solution." Mexican migrants were subjected to screening practices at the border that were later believed to have partly influenced the Nazi gas chambers. They were forced to remove their clothes, wait in lines naked, and be bathed in a shower of different chemicals to kill the supposed lice, ticks, or typhus-spreading rat fleas they wrongfully believed the migrants were carrying. Although the war was over and the typhus scare ended, even though the outbreak never existed, the practice of "delousing" continued up until the 1950s.[4]

A living uncle of mine still remembers vividly the time he migrated in 1950 through Juárez and how they stuffed his clothes and shoes into large industrial dryers to "kill" any infestations. He remembers walking naked through the line to retrieve his clothes and the bad taste of whatever powder they poured over him. He said it tasted like grapefruit rinds, just like the bitter citrus of the fields on the other side, ready to be picked.

*

In 1919 my great-grandfather León Talamantes gave up the loom he used to make wool blankets to sell at the market in Tepechitlán and came to Juárez for the first time. He was twenty-one years old, newly married, and on his way to the U.S., where he would eventually find work with the Santa Fe Railway. I didn't know what it was he did for the railway company, whether he ever went as far as New York, or Chicago. I wondered if he saw those endless miles of stockyards that I read about in books like *The Jungle*.

León was a tall and slender man, born in 1894 in the same town as I was, Tepechitlán. It was rumored that León's father, my great-great-grandfather (whose name no one alive remembers), conceived him at the age of one hundred and died shortly after, leaving León as an only child to care for his mother. León became an orphan by the time he was ten in 1905 and worked as a servant for a wealthy older gentleman who never married. The great-great-grandfather whose name no one remembers was born in the late eighteenth century on the same mountain that houses La Loma. I found the church records of León's crossings online on an ancestry site. It was simple, all I had to do was type in my debit card and pay about thirty-eight dollars to see León's name on an official immigration bust card with his age, his height, his hair color, date(s) of crossing, and occupation—laborer.

León must have grown tired of life on the mountain. I wondered what he knew about the U.S. I wondered who was the first one to plant the idea in him that it was possible to go, that it was doable. He was the first to leave. Hundreds of years after the colonization of our town in the early 1500s, thousands of years after its settlement by its indigenous Huichol people, León left his beloved mountain for something else. I didn't know what "else" meant to him, but he went out there to look for it.

He too took off his clothes and waited to be deloused, to be cleaned of all "impurities." He crossed five times, but after the fifth, he never crossed again and instead went back to becoming a weaver in Tepechitlán. Five times he was sprayed with the latest chemical agent. I imagine his skinny frame standing naked before a white Texas Ranger looking him up and down, curling his lips, leaning his barrel chest forward to get a closer look at him, stamping his card before giving him the go-ahead to cross.

13.

Even after the practice of delousing stopped, the general policy behind the idea that immigrants were inherently diseased until proven innocent, and thus needed to be screened, continued until the present day. I too had to go through the process of seeing a doctor certified by immigration to check me for diseases—one of which was tuberculosis—and to make sure I was vaccinated before I got my green card, well before attending my immigration interview. Even after all those years of trying to get my papers, all that money spent on lawyers, all the endless paperwork, it never occurred to me that something that was once dormant inside my lungs could hold me back, could be reason enough for my denial.

We had only recently immigrated to the States when I was exposed to tuberculosis. Amá took me to a doctor who took a picture of my lungs, and I was told to keep my distance from other children for six months just in case. In case what? I thought.

The pills were large, and I could feel them edging down my throat, scratching parts of myself I didn't know were on the inside. They said it was in my lungs, but I couldn't feel anything. I had heard of tuberculosis before at school and church and thought I would start spitting out blood, but the blood never came. All I knew of TB was that famous people in history got it and it made me feel special. At church, I would hear the preacher talk about other ancient diseases like leprosy, and I would imagine myself among those banished, and being cured by the touch of Christ and allowed to return.

I liked the attention, even if it was only in my head; Amá told me never to tell anyone about the pills I was taking or why, just as she told me never to tell anyone I didn't have papers. She said people wouldn't understand. I barely understood myself. She took me again to the doctor, who told her I could stop taking the pills but that it would live inside me forever. I translated for her, and the word "forever" felt so much more permanent when I said it than when I simply heard the doctor say it—"Siempre." She nodded at the doctor as if I was not even there, as if she could understand him perfectly well, which was the sign of a good translator—to disappear in the maelstrom of conversation.

*

Just like my grandfather and great-grandfather before him, the U.S. also believed that I, along with every other immigrant, was diseased until proven innocent and had to undergo a physical, or "screening," before my immigration interview. I was more nervous about my immigration physical than I was about the interview because I was afraid they would find what was inside me. Lying in my interview was always an option, but I would never be able to hide what was inside my chest, inside my blood. I had gone so many years without thinking about the TB that I forgot it was there, silent, just beneath my breastbone. I wasn't contagious, I didn't actually have it, but it showed up in tests nonetheless.

They ran their tests and afterward handed me a sealed envelope with the doctor's name signed over the seal, covered in tape to ensure that it wouldn't be tampered with. The doctor was not allowed to tell me what was inside, especially if there was anything in there that would flag me.

She could have written anything about me in the envelope, and there was nothing I could do, I was merely the messenger, but also the subject. She could have said anything about me that would exclude me from becoming a legal permanent resident of the United States:

Have you EVER violated (or attempted or conspired to
    violate) any controlled substance law or regulation . . . ?

Have you EVER engaged in prostitution?

Do you intend to engage in illegal gambling?

Do you intend to engage in any activity whose purpose includes opposing, controlling, or overthrowing the U.S. government . . . ?

Have you EVER been a member of, or in any way affiliated with, the Communist Party . . . ?

Have you received public assistance in the United States from any source? . . . Are you likely to receive public assistance in the future in the United States from any source . . . ?[5]

Although none of those questions necessarily had to do with my body, I worried she could have said something that was easy to misinterpret, or even written her results illegibly and thus voided my admittance. Whatever was inside my chest was now on display inside that envelope which I could not open. I would have to wait until immigration received it to find out if I'd passed the test or not.

I mailed the envelope to my lawyer, who assured me that the process was just a formality, that unless I had an active case of tuberculosis, or syphilis, or leprosy, I didn't have anything to worry about. He also assured me that those were old rules that were put in place many years ago and were just never changed. It was strange to see that the U.S. still feared the spread of communism. The legacy of that law is what persisted. It assumed that the U.S. was clean, not to be soiled by the ilk of the world.

14

We had been doing this for a long time, moving back and forth. My family's roots felt like a sinewy thread that got thinner and thinner with each successive generation that stayed in the United States. I wondered what my children would think of Mexico. What it would mean to them, born in the U.S.? Would they feel that rope tugging at them like I did? Would they too spend their lives trying to help someone cross, still trying to get somewhere? I wondered when we'd ever get there.

I was always jealous of friends who were second- or third-generation immigrants because they could share their past with others. They all had vivid stories to tell about how their grandparents came and stayed to make a new life for themselves. And how their parents grew up speaking English and had American jobs like working at McDonald's, or a carwash. I had vivid stories, too, of León, and Amá Julia, and Jesús before he died in the desert, but I never spoke of them. I couldn't share my lineage with others; I felt like I always had to stop at 1993 because for many years, I couldn't talk about what happened before 1993—before our crossing. I couldn't give myself permission to have a past.

But I did have a past. We were still doing the same thing. I could track my family as far back as the 1700s, on the mountain where the house of La Loma was built. My past was one that moved back and forth.

And there we were, at the same border town where León was deloused. The same border town where Tío Miguel was deloused. The same border town where Apá was deported in 2003.

Apá would be opening his mouth for a physical, following the flashlight in the doctor's hand side to side, squeezing his large fist for a blood test, shaking his head to the list of diseases on a piece of paper. One hundred years after León's first crossings, we were still trying to cross, still moving in maddening helplessness, a revolving door without an exit.

When I thought of the past, I thought of one of my favorite lines of poetry, by Robert Hass—"All the new thinking is about loss / In this it resembles all the old thinking." I thought about what I had lost, what I continued to lose, and I realized it was the same thing we had been losing for centuries, the ability to say "enough."

15.

Rubi and I continued waiting in the blue chairs of the immigration clinic after Apá's name was called. After a surprisingly short amount of time, he reappeared with his sleeves rolled up and Band-Aids on his arms. They gave him vaccines which he already had but couldn't prove, they asked if he could raise his hands above his head, open his mouth, stick out his tongue, and touch his feet. They drew blood, and he was done. We waited for a few hours in another lobby for his results. Still, we touched only our own bodies and the handles of the doors we needed to open.

At last they called our name.

"Do you take a credit card?" I asked.

"Of course." The woman smiled.

"But it's a card from a U.S. bank, is that okay?" I asked again.

"Yes, that's fine," she said, and let out a quick laugh.

I gave her the card. It was $481, U.S. I put the receipt in my pocket, and she handed us a dark plastic envelope with my father's name on the front. "Don't even think of opening it, or else it's no good," she said through the small holes in the thick bulletproof glass, waving the next person to the window.

It was similar to the envelope I had received, and I wanted to look inside. I wanted to know what they could have possibly gathered in the short time that they saw him. We were simply messengers taking that package from one building to another, and we paid $481 to do so, to convince them that Apá wasn't contagious.

To say that the whole enterprise was a scam would trivialize it as petty theft. It was much more than that. It was an entire industry distilled in a few city blocks. There were hundreds, even thousands, of people moving between the embassy, the clinics, the hotels, and the mall across the street every day. They were all doing the same thing we were doing. They were paying into a system that was central to the engine of America—immigrants paying for immigration. In a way, I didn't see how this was different than paying a coyote to cross; both seemed just as corrupt. Besides, in the end both would cost just as much.

No—he wasn't sprayed with Zyklon-B. They didn't make him take off his clothes and stand in line. The guards didn't take pictures of the women standing naked with their hands over their bodies. The vaccines didn't make his mouth taste like the citrus trees of the Central Valley. But we walked away from the clinic feeling like something similar had been done to us; we felt dirtier than when we had entered. Our hands had a thin layer of grime, and I wanted to go back to the hotel to take a shower and wash away the shame.

16.

The first time I read Edward Said, I wanted to take a vase and break it into many pieces. The idea of the "other" was a Western invention. And so, in order to define itself, it needed to define what it was not. I was that idea of *not*.

When I showed up on paper, when I saw my real name finally authenticated by a government body, it was only by agreeing to their rules, by allowing myself to be screened for filth and disease. I should have ripped open that envelope and burned it—not that it would have helped, but it would have made me feel a little better.

[Third Movement as Migration and Imagination]

＝

We had to start again, from zero. All we could carry with us to the U.S. was a change of clothes. Amá wanted to bring her pictures too, but she couldn't. We let the dogs off their leash and let them run away; no one would take them anyways. They were already skinny and mean. They would do just fine by themselves.

We left the remainder of our things locked in a room because there still existed the slim possibility that we would return. It was easier for my father to leave if he knew he still had a bed stored away somewhere in Tepechitlán. Maybe that way it didn't really seem like forever.

In my backpack was a pair of jeans, a shirt, and an extra pair of clean underwear.

And so began our migration to the north.

It was Palm Sunday when we boarded our train in Guadalajara and passed through Nayarit, Sinaloa, then Sonora, before finally stopping in Tijuana—the beginning of Holy Week, the end of those forty days of fasting. We didn't give up anything for Lent. We didn't need to, since that was all we were doing. Soon we would be entering America, and there would be plenty more to give up there.

One by one we all got sick on the train. They say my grandfather Jesús went mad on the train. Something about the wind, something about the speed.

It was the end of Holy Week when we arrived at a relative's house in Tijuana. We ate at last. We drank coffee and talked around the dinner table. Amá didn't send me away to play with the other children like she always did. There was nothing she didn't want me to know. After many arguments and indecisions about how exactly to proceed, Apá banged his fist on the table, and Amá went to sleep in the other room. Nobody really slept.

I knew what we were doing. They didn't have to say that it was a game and I was supposed to run whenever they ran. They told me what we were doing, and I understood. I knew what they meant when they said "el otro lado," the other side. Maybe they *should* have hid it from me. Maybe they *should* have told me that it was a game we were playing, that none of it was real—the guns, the agents roving on foot with their large flashlights. We waited weeks for just the right time, but when would there ever be a good time for a family of seven to cross the border, and Amá waddling behind with her large belly?

Yes, they should have told me it was all make-believe.

17.

If all went well at Apá's interview, he would be able to cross almost immediately, but until then, for the next few days, all we could do was wait. We went to the mall across the street for breakfast at the food court, where they served better eggs, beans, and cheese with a decent salsa—the only food around that almost looked home-cooked. We spent the day walking around, window-shopping, trying on clothes we wouldn't buy. The merchandise was just as expensive as in the U.S.—all the same brands. There was a children's beauty salon. It was decorated in bright pink and purple. There were little girls sitting in high chairs wearing princess dresses and getting their very own mani-pedis. There was the Liverpool store, with guards at every corner. I saw well-to-do Mexicans looking at clothes, spraying on perfumes, and eating ice cream as they paraded down the aisles. They had everything they needed in Mexico; there was no need for them to go north.

Every day before Apá's interview was the same: wake up, cross the street to the mall for breakfast, walk through the stores for a few hours, and head back to the hotel before going back for dinner. We went to every restaurant in the food court.

We were tired of waiting. We couldn't bear the food at the food court anymore. We arrived on a Wednesday, and by Sunday, we decided to stay and eat at the continental breakfast bar in the hotel because at least fresh fruit and cereal felt different. We still stayed away from the eggs. We watched movie after movie in our rooms. Apá taught us how to play Conquian, an old card game that didn't use tens, nines, or eights. We didn't play for money, just for the satisfaction of beating each other. Rubi and I played by ourselves, or I played with Apá, or we all played together. It got old quick.

*

When we weren't watching movies that were dubbed into Spanish and always lagged behind the actor's mouth a little, we prepared for my father's interview. I sat across the bed from my dad and pretended to be the interviewer.

"—Good morning, Mr. Hernandez, how are you doing?"

"—When was the last time you were in the U.S.?"

"—What was the reason for your departure?"

"—Do you understand the gravity of your crime?"

"—How many years had you lived in the U.S.?"

"—Do you have a family, and where are they?"

"—Are any of them permanent residents or citizens?"

It went on like that for hours. We simply wanted to ensure he remembered exact dates and times of arrivals, departures, and residences, so that there wouldn't be any discrepancies in their records. All he needed to do was state the facts. We were afraid that any stumbling could be misinterpreted as a lie. I repeated his timeline to him over and over, as if he hadn't lived it himself, and asked him to say it back. I could tell that he was starting to get annoyed. I still wasn't sure if I would be able to enter with him or not. What could I add to his case?

In the background was a black-and-white movie from Mexico's golden age of cinema. My father loved those movies. They romanticized the ranchero, the vaquero, the hombre my father always thought himself to be. They provided all that was good in the world for him, as well as all that was bad. The women like María Felix and Dolores del Río always had long and gloomy faces; their sad eyes always looked slightly away as they sang atop a balcony dimly lit by the moon. The men like Jorge Negrete and Pedro Infante were well built, handsome, and they too could sing. They would break into song for any reason. Their songs were an extension of this general sadness. They too looked away from the camera. Tequila was always on the table.

I didn't like questioning Apá the way I had been questioned because I didn't want to assume that role, even if we were just pretending. I didn't want him to apologize; I wanted them to apologize for his solitude, for all of those years my mother was forced to work overtime and take up an extra job to raise us by herself. Why were we the ones who needed to apologize?

"I'm sorry, Apá," I wanted to say in the interviewer's voice. "For what?" he would say. "I don't know, maybe for this, for having to be here, for not being here sooner." I never said anything. I felt like everything was my fault, even things that happened before I was born. "I'm sorry, great-grandfather León, for what they did to you, I'm sorry, baby Manuel, that it took so long for them to believe you were dying."

A friend once told me that any time we apologized, we could instead turn it into gratitude. So that instead of saying "I'm sorry I am late," we could say "Thank you for your patience." In my head, the conversation continued like this:

"—I'm sorry you were deported, Apá."

(Thank you for letting your sons be raised by their mother.)

"—I'm sorry we never called you."

(Thank you for understanding that our Spanish was starting to fade and we didn't want to embarrass ourselves in front of you, or for you to think that the distance between us was more than just miles.)

"—I'm sorry we never came back to you, and that you were alone."

(Thank you for being proud that I went to college instead. Thank you for growing a beautiful garden.)

"—I'm sorry things never went as you planned."

(Thank you for letting us live in surprise.)

18.

On the evening before his interview, I thought it would be a good idea to have a Skype session with everyone back home. We had seen pictures; his face was nothing new. We had heard his voice over the phone throughout the years, so his voice was nothing new either. But we had never, in all those years we were separated, received them together. And we always thought it was enough of him to get by— voice but no image, image but no voice. We got pieces of him doled out to us, which, I suppose, made it easier to hang up, or to toss the pictures back in the drawer instead of hanging them on our wall.

*

I sat Apá next to the window near the light. Juárez was still buzzing outside. I placed my laptop in front of him and waited for the connection. The Internet at the hotel was slow so it took a while, and we sat there staring at the dark screen, our faces bright with the evening sun beginning to edge toward the horizon.

We were at the precipice of disaster. We felt it but we could not admit it, and it was strongest while waiting for the Internet connection, staring at ourselves in the dark computer screen. Somehow, we knew already the next day would not bring good news. The small buffering signal turned and turned until we heard a new voice in the room. It was a child's voice. Apá had never met his grandchildren before.

He sat there on the edge of the bed, an old man, the sun already gone. The lightbulbs with their soft glow made it look like a dream. A few words were exchanged. They didn't know how to talk to him either, I imagine they felt the same things I felt each time I opened my mouth to speak to him. "Ya, turn that thing off," Apá exclaimed, wiping his eyes. It caught me off guard, so I slammed the laptop shut without closing any windows, without saying goodbye to the small voices on the other end. And just like that, they were gone from the room.

The room was quiet except for Apá's heavy breathing. "I don't like that," he kept saying to himself, or to us, I wasn't quite sure. "I don't like that at all."

"I'm sorry, Apá," I said quietly. And in my head I turned it into gratitude: "Thank you for teaching me how to wait."

*

I wanted to ask him one more time if he knew his facts for the interview, but I decided not to push it any further. We had said enough, we had prepared enough—it was out of our hands, if it ever was in our hands to begin with. We had done everything in our power to better our chances. I had moved on to a new credit card to keep us going; we just needed another little push that required luck, not money.

I just wanted to be done with it, I wanted to leave that city already. I couldn't stomach going back to the food court and eating those same eggs, beans, and bland salsa. I just wanted to go home, as I knew my father wanted too. But I wondered if for him, home still meant Tepechitlán, or if now, after he'd seen the rest of the family in real time, if home meant California. Perhaps Apá's greatest gift, and what I inherited but had yet to fully understand, was that his conception of home was not singular but plural. It was malleable and could evolve, adapt to the situation. Maybe that's why he was so calm the entire weekend. He would make a home out of whatever outcome came from Juárez.

*

I went to my room and took another long shower. I thought about the times my brothers and I would shower together when we were little. We would play games about space and monsters until one of us inevitably left the shower crying because we wouldn't play fair.

I turned up the heat as much as my back could handle, feeling my hands over my tattoo. My nose ring was still new and tender and would bleed at times. Apá didn't ask me about either; he tried to avoid talking about them all together.

The piercing had gotten infected since I'd arrived in Juárez. The dry air made it break out with keloid bumps, and I kept picking at it, which made it worse. I dried myself and went to sleep next to Rubi; the other bed was still empty except for a pile of our clothes. I heard a small thumping from Apá's room next door. I tried to imagine what he was doing but I couldn't. The thumping continued for a few minutes until it stopped abruptly.

I heard a soft wail and I convinced myself that it was the TV playing a Mexican movie from the golden age, with those sad songs by men who looked slightly away as they sang.

19.

We packed our bags in the morning to check out of the hotel. I saw that Apá had packed his bags too. Everything he carried fit inside his small duffel bag, and he carried so little that I wondered if he even planned on crossing over. But whatever the outcome of his interview, we knew we wouldn't stay another day at that hotel. We kneeled in the middle of the room and called Amá. I put her on speaker, and she said a quiet prayer over us. Her voice was soothing and gave us a little hope. My father wasn't a religious man, but I heard him mouthing words of supplication, words of longing. I heard him repeat the words that my mother spoke, and it was like an echo. She would start and he would finish.

I held his hand, which I couldn't remember ever having done for a long time. His hands always felt larger than normal, cartoonish even. "Jesucristo—Jesucristo—Jesucristo." He squeezed my hand, and together in a circle on our knees (Apá, Rubi, and myself), we repeated my mother's words. It was a prayer not so much of sentences as it was of phrases—short and distinct from one another. The common language of the church. My mother finished speaking and I hung up, but the vibrations of her voice lingered in the air like the scent of a candle.

[Third Movement as Migration and a Flock of Birds]

═══

I don't know why I went temporarily blind in Tijuana while waiting to cross in 1993. It didn't happen all at once. It wasn't like someone suddenly turned off the lights. First it was the colors that started fading, then it was the shapes, and then shadows altogether. Or maybe not in that order. I could explain the colors leaving, I knew that the world sometimes did that—seemed grayer than usual. I thought it was clouds. I thought the gray came from the walls themselves, and the dried trees and the loose dirt. Maybe that's just what Tijuana looked like.

But it was shapes I could not explain. Their edges softening into the empty space around them until I couldn't tell where one thing started and another ended. I could see something was more of itself closer to the center, and less of itself farther out—a gradient. Maybe the soul wasn't just one thing but an assortment of many little things huddled together, like penguins keeping warm in a blizzard. Or like a flock of birds packed so tightly in a tree that you think they're all just leaves until a loud noise startles them, and they shudder the bare limbs loose.

The things in front of me slowly became less and less of themselves, but they stretched out nonetheless, beyond the edges of themselves, as if they no longer wanted to be whatever it was that they were put on this earth to be—as if they too wanted to get a little farther north.

Even the sky no longer felt distant but rather like it began right above my head. And didn't it?

When I tried to look at Amá and Apá, I saw an interchangeable thing. Part was more mother, the other part was more father, but was one thing nonetheless—malleable, connected.

The trees and the cars and the houses and the children felt like the same thing too. I could feel the dirt, I could feel the bricks along the wall and their grainy textures—how one square ended at the deep ridge of the grout. I could feel the grout, and I ran my finger along it until it scraped the tip. With time, maybe things would have separated again, maybe they would have gone back to themselves.

But initially, and because it happened so fast, it looked like someone went by and smudged the people's faces with paint thinner. I could hear Amá talking to me, but I could only see the darkness of her eyes contrasted with her light skin.

After colors, after the shapes, and after the shadows, all that was left was contrast—one thing held up against another. I could tell there was a chair not by what it looked like but by the things around it. By what it was not. It never went completely dark, just almost.

I cried and felt my way along the edges of the wall. There was no here or there, except the sounds of the cars outside and Amá and Apá fighting in another room about what to do with me.

"Mijo, can you see me?" I heard my mother say somewhere in front of me.

"What about now, can you see me now?"

Soon we would be crossing. Soon we would want no one else to see *us*—to go invisible too, to move through the mountains like a flock of birds shaken by a sudden clanging of a bell.

Wouldn't it be wonderful to slowly disappear? First our shapes, then the edges of ourselves, and finally our shadow, how we looked against the backdrop of the sky. How easy it would be to walk right past the guards so that Amá would not have to run with my baby brother knocking around inside her big belly. We could take our time, stand in the middle of the checkpoint and watch the faces of others as they nervously talked to the guards. We could look at the landscape instead of trying to run away from it, pick up a few rocks and toss them leisurely against the lights and laugh.

I could hear Apá grunt and complain that I was watching the TV too closely and that's why my eyes "hurt." He didn't say blind, he said that's why they "hurt."

"He'll be fine, just give him a few days," said Apá.

Was it something so ordinary, so common? *He'll be fine.* What was the point in worrying anyway? We had no money for a doctor, we hardly had enough money for food. All we could do was wait for my vision to return. And if it didn't, would they go on without me? Would they lead me by the hand and describe what was happening around me? "Here is a mountain. Here is a snake. Feel the coarse leather of this man's boot."

When it came back, it didn't return in the same order it vanished. Things were separate from themselves again—distinctly each their own. Amá was Amá, and Apá was Apá. The birds in the trees were again just birds.

I saw her face at last as she held me—rocking me to sleep. It wasn't smudged. I would need my rest. Her shirt was green. If we were in a meadow somewhere far away, it would still be the brightest thing in that field.

20.

We had finally arrived at Apá's immigration interview. Thousands of people clustered into numerous amorphous lines outside the embassy. We couldn't tell where the lines ended or why some people were in one line and not another. We figured they all must lead to the same place. "Remember what we talked about, Dad. You know your dates, you know your facts. Everything should be fine, just stick to your facts," I told him as we took our spot toward a bulk of people in the back before being sent to another line by a guard. I ran through every excuse in my head for them to allow me to enter with him—I'm his translator, I'm his son, he's elderly, he needs me.

Despite so many years of waiting for that moment, and having spent all of the previous week getting ready for this day, I still wasn't sure if we were ready. Anything was still possible. A future with my father was still possible, still imaginable. Or if denied, he would return to his town, his house, and his dog. He would not have to go through the trouble of making a new home for himself. A future identical to the present was possible.

After hours of waiting and moving from one line to another as we were instructed, a guard pointed and hurried us down.

"Whose case is being heard?" he said. I pointed to my father nervously.

"Only he can come in, no one else," he said in a loud voice. "You have to wait over there, outside."

"But I have to go with him, he's my dad, he needs me to translate." That's all I could think of, that he needed me as a translator. In the moment, I had forgotten everything I would have said and simply said that I was his translator.

"He won't need any translators in there—they all speak Spanish. And only the person whose case will be heard can go in."

Apá looked at me and reassured me that he would be okay. I gave him the thick portfolio of papers I was holding that he might need, his biometrics envelope, and hugged him. Rubi hugged him as well and held his hand for a moment. The guard grew inpatient and called again, in a louder voice. I should have been more persistent in demanding to enter with Apá, but I didn't know how. His words seemed so final, so absolute. I couldn't fathom any room for interpretation in what he said, or any alternative. It was my instinct to avoid conflict, obey, turn around, and walk away. They took him inside, and I watched the doors close behind him. He had done this many times before and was far more experienced in such matters than me, but I felt like *I* was now the parent looking after a child, watching him walk into his classroom on his first day of school, staying in place until the doors slammed shut.

I saw a crowd gathering to the side of the building. They too, whether out of instinct, defeat, or fear, dared not question the guards, and looked nervously at two doors where people were exiting the embassy. Every time the doors swung open, all eyes jumped to them, to see if it was their loved ones who were coming out. Rubi and I sat on the curb and waited, anxiously looking at the double doors from which Apá too would eventually emerge.

*

Every time we heard the doors open, I took a few steps forward through the crowd to see if it was Apá. I was absorbed by the faces of those who emerged. There were only two possible answers for every person who left that building, and their faces told the story. I could see in their eyes if they had been accepted or denied. Some showed it more than others.

A woman exited the doors and walked through the crowd, looking for her family, her eyes scanning the crowd as if we were at Disneyland and she had briefly lost her child. She had a manila envelope beneath her arm and was holding it firmly with her palm. Her lips were tight and her gaze was sharp, darting in every direction. I couldn't read her gestures, I couldn't tell if she had received good news or bad. I saw her face light up when she saw a man. Two girls joined them at their waist, and they quickly gathered themselves and walked away. The rest of the crowd watched them leave and went back to staring at the doors.

I was happy but also envious at the same time for anyone who walked out smiling, either because they were accepted or because they accepted their rejection with grace. We didn't even know Apá's decision yet, and I was already fearing the worst. In my head I thought of it as a give-and-take: one green card for someone else meant one less for us. There was some truth to that, there was a cap to certain kinds of visas, but I wasn't sure if it applied to us. I thought every person who walked out smiling was worsening Apá's chances inside. But maybe they just smiled for us and would cry as soon as they turned away.

Not many walked out smiling. In truth, the majority of those who walked out through the doors looked somber, some stricken with grief, a sadness about them that looked inconsolable. I could see tears running down their faces that they didn't bother to hide, looking at the crowds for their loved ones, their gaze locking on everyone as if saying, "Yours, too, are next." I didn't feel guilty about staring either. Everyone was staring. It was like the back door of a theater, and we, the fans, stood crowded outside, waiting for them, the stars, to exit. We, the paparazzi wanting a little taste of stardom.

I tried to figure out how long each of us in the crowd had been waiting and what it could mean, but there didn't seem to be any logic attached to the variety of wait times. Some came and went quicker; others had been there far longer than us. There was an unspoken bond between the ones who were waiting the longest, and we tried to cheer each other up with small talk, pretending it was normal, pretending we couldn't hear the growing anxiety in each other's voices as we spoke, or that we didn't see the others coming and going faster than us. My worry turned to panic when I couldn't recognize anyone who was there when we first arrived. What if something had gone wrong, and they detained him? We were already in Mexico, what were they going to do—deport him again?

Maybe if I was a citizen I would have exclaimed and said something. I felt like I was owed at least an explanation as to why it was taking so long. But having only a green card was precarious. I kept my mouth shut and waited.

*

The waiting became unbearable, and I was sure something had gone wrong. I started making plans in my head. People kept shuffling through the doors, but none of them were Apá. After what seemed like an eternity, I saw him emerge through the doors.

I tried to hurry up to him but was held back by a series of stanchions keeping the people in order and had to watch him agonizingly wind around them as he approached me, as if he was about to board a plane. I looked at his face. I was preparing myself for that moment. I almost didn't want to look at him because I still wanted to remain in the realm of possibility, of obscurity. Anything was still possible. But I could do nothing to change what it was my father already knew.

He had a slight smile on his face, and for a moment, as I held Rubi's hand tight, my heart leaped. But as he got closer, I saw that his eyes were red.

It was one of those rare moments when I allowed myself to look at him carefully again, to study his face. I stopped trying to look for something—change, regret, sadness, joy. All I saw was an old man who was tired of chasing a carrot dangling just out of reach.

*

"Apá, what did they say? What happened?" I asked him, as if it was mandatory to ask, even though I already surmised the answer.

"Let's just go back to the hotel," he said. We'd left our bags there with the concierge.

He didn't want to talk about it there, in front of the crowd. He was too proud to let his failure be seen in public. I knew they were all staring but didn't care. I suddenly understood the people who exited the doors before me. I went from being the voyeur to the observed without skipping a beat. I was now the spectacle, and I could feel everyone's gaze on us, trying to decipher our news—wondering if their fate would be like ours. How desperate they looked from that perspective; how thirsty for any kind of relief. Apá didn't stop to talk to me; he just kept walking in the direction of the hotel, not fast but not slow either, just steady.

We left the crowd behind to tend the limelight.

"What did they say, Apá?" I said, this time more demanding as I tried to catch up, now that he picked up his pace.

"It just didn't happen. Let's talk about it in the hotel."

I didn't have time to understand because he kept walking away. I didn't know what to say to him, or to Rubi, or to myself, so I just stayed quiet, and we walked in silence to the hotel.

There wasn't much I could say or do, there weren't many decisions for me to make. The decisions had already been made for us. The gears had been set in motion. It felt like we were at the beginning of a new era, as if from that day forward, our lives would be different. Anything that could have been would never be. Everything that was, would be forever.

21.

Apá said it was a young woman who had interviewed him.

"She was nice, and she was sincere. She spoke Spanish and was kind when she talked to me. She kept saying 'I'm so sorry, there's nothing else I can do, I'm so sorry, I wish I could help you.' And I think she was telling the truth," he said, looking away from me.

Perhaps the woman indeed was sorry. Perhaps she didn't really want to be there, having to deny people all day, changing the courses of entire families' lives with a swipe of a pen or a click of a button. Maybe she thought that the job would be different, that she was going to make the world better. Isn't that what we all think when we start a new job? Maybe she was just assigned to be at the border as part of her training to go elsewhere. "Just two years of this and I'll be in DC, doing other things," I could see her thinking. We were what she had to put up with to go on to better things, a story that led to a better story, a jumping point that led away from grief. *I'm sorry, I'm so so sorry.*

Couldn't she have helped?

Apá waited ten years (plus two) for them to simply remind him of his previous deportations, to point to them as additional reason for his rejection. Couldn't they have just told him that in 2003, and we could have moved on with our lives instead of living with a small iota of hope? If we had let go then, if we had moved on with our lives without Apá, what would have become of us?

For so long we lived with the hope that he was paying back his debt to society in return for forgiveness. We thought there was something at the end of this for us. If we had known that nothing could make his mistakes in the past go away, we would have told him to come back, we would have brought him however we could, however much it would have cost. Or we would have told him to never come back, and simply cut ties altogether. Either option was better than spending my entire adolescence and early adulthood in uncertainty about him.

*

How different, I thought, from mine and Rubi's interview. Rubi stayed close to me because she knew about Apá's short fuse, and though he had controlled himself the entire time we were in Juárez, we were both uncertain how he would react. She held my hand as we made our way to the hotel and waited in the lobby chairs for a cab. I knew it was a mistake to try to begin to know him too well, and I could tell that Rubi was backpedaling her mistake of trying to know him as well. Neither of us wanted to know what he carried in his bag, or how he shaved his beard at night, and the little that we did pick up, we were beginning to put back down.

"Rubi, Rubi . . . Rubi," I said as she stared at her phone.

"Yeah?"

"Let's make sure we have everything ready for the checkpoint, yeah?"

We were both polar opposites in moments of distress. My adrenaline kicked in, and I was always on top of things, making sure nothing went awry. And depending on the severity of the distress, it wouldn't be until weeks, months, or even years later that I would crash emotionally and reckon with the weight of that moment. Rubi, on the other hand, was the opposite. She retreated into herself at the moment of intensity and was strongest afterward. We complemented each other nicely. So while I was frantically looking for our passports, calling Apá's cab, making sure we still had pesos at hand to pay the cab, and figuring out logistics, Rubi had her earphones on and had checked out. I was okay with that because I knew I would need her in the future, when I would not be able to find any excuse to get out of bed, when I would need a half fifth of vodka just to make it through the day.

Our cab would take us across the border to the El Paso airport, and Apá's would take him to the bus terminal in Juárez. Our cab came first. I looked at Apá for any sign. What would come next? What was there left to do anyway? We put our luggage in the trunk, and I gave Apá a hug. I squeezed him tighter and tighter, as if I could squeeze him enough to fold him up and put him in my pocket.

"Okay, Apá, we have to go now," I said.

Rubi hugged him and held his hand again for a brief moment. She had her small purse wrapped around her shoulder, and it swung around as she turned to get into the cab. I gave Apá the rest of the cash I had, only keeping exactly enough for the cab ride. The small Nissan headed north toward home. We didn't need to say anything, I stretched out my hand, and he stretched out his to receive it. Giving him money would from then on be the best way we could talk to each other.

22.

The ride to the border checkpoint was quiet. The driver, too, must have known what had transpired, given where he picked us up from and where he was taking us to, and the silence between us. At the bare minimum, he knew we'd had to leave someone behind. He kept his eyes locked on the road.

Even though it was December, it still felt hot in the middle of the day, so I cracked open the window. Traffic was backed up for about half a mile at the checkpoint. We inched forward, unbearably slow. Either Juárez was tugging us back, not wanting us to leave, or El Paso was pushing against us, not wanting us to enter.

Walking down the lanes were street vendors with their merchandise hanging from hooks on large boards. Others carried large sticks with plastic balloon animals, cotton candy, popcorn, newspapers, and toys, so many toys. Their bright colors against the hazy sky made me want them as if I was ten years old again but knew better than to ask for a toy when there wasn't any money.

One of the vendors approached the window and asked if I wanted to buy a rosary.

"Here, el Cristito, so you can cross safely," the man said as he reached his hand through the cracked window. It was colorful and refracted the light inside the cab like a spiraling disco ball, tossing small triangles of God's supposed holiness onto the stained upholstery. I knew I could cross on my own, I knew I didn't need God anymore.

I entered Mexico much the same way as the light entered the rosary, and when we departed the corridors of its prisms, we did so no longer wholly intact either, a little broken.

*

I wanted something to remember the trip, to hold something that could stand for our time there, and burn it later, perhaps mail it to a friend and have them burn it and describe it burning to me over the phone. Unfortunately I didn't have any money, either pesos or dollars, since I gave it all to Apá.

"Rubi, do you have any cash left over?" I said.

"No, I don't. I gave it all to you," she said, still searching through her purse.

I handed the rosary back to the man, and the light scissoring through the cab faded away, leaving only the stains behind.

"Ándale, I'll give it to you cheap, here," he said as he pushed it back to me, insisting that I buy it.

"No, I'm sorry, I don't have anything left," I said, and took out my wallet to show that it was empty as I gently pushed it back into his palm.

"Ándale pues," he finally said, and took the rosary back, along with all its holiness. It would help us cross, he had said, but it was too late for that; we weren't the ones who needed help. If only we had met him hours before to wrap the rosary around Apá's neck, bursting open like sharp flowers.

*

The drivers in the other lanes looked bored. Some of them played their radios loud, and others looked as I imagine we looked— defeated. In the air, through the lanes, I heard the soft beat of a cumbia song. More vendors reached into the cab to hand me things I could not buy as they walked down the lanes. I wanted to get out of the cab and run, I wanted nothing to do with Juárez anymore. Not the vendors, not the embassy, not the miles and miles of open land, not the city with its incessant motion—none of it.

"You're going to have to get out and walk through the checkpoint on foot," the driver said. "I'll meet you on the other side."

"Why, is everything okay?"

"Yeah, everything is fine—it's just company policy that you have to cross over by yourself, and I'll meet you over there by the sidewalk." We grabbed our suitcases and walked.

The building was small, and there was hardly anyone inside. Ahead of us was a man in torn clothes with no shoes and disheveled hair. He chatted with the officers for a minute before handing them his card. They were friendly toward him, as if they saw him every day and knew him by name already. Their voices had an air of worry and care, and they kept nodding their heads at the tattered man as if saying "Take it easy, you're going to break your mother's heart." They gave him back his card and waved him on, a worried smile on their faces, as if he were a high school friend who had seen better days.

I held my passport and my mica, my green card, in my hand as we stepped forward. I could feel the ridges on the card, and I thumbed them gently. That's all that they needed to see—a piece of plastic with my name on it. I thought the card and the passport should at least weigh more, that they shouldn't be as light as they were. They were too important to be that light.

I handed my card to the officer, who was talking about a football game and looking over to the other officer; he hardly noticed that I was there. He only looked at me when he held the card up against my face to compare the two and waved me forward.

"I'm telling you, that catch would have won the game," he said, returning to where he'd left off in his conversation, looking over to his friend again, who in turn was looking at the scanning machine as my bags passed through the conveyor belt. We were an aside in a football commentary, a mere interruption.

"No, it wouldn't have, they would have needed a two-point conversion," said the other agent, avoiding me altogether.

They handed me back my card, and I walked through the metal detector as they continued their conversation. It couldn't have taken more than three minutes from the time I gave him my card to when I picked up my luggage on the other side of the machine. Rubi went even faster because she handed them her U.S. passport, and they were less cautious about citizens. Just like that, we were done. We did in three minutes what my father had waited ten years to do but couldn't.

*

El Paso looked different in the daytime. It looked like every other American city I had ever been to. It had seemed like a different city at night, when we first arrived—it was mysterious then, illuminated, charged with possibility. But now it looked like a bar at midday, when the lights are turned on or when someone opens a window.

It was a small airport. A border patrol agent stood near the TSA gate, randomly checking people as they entered. I approached TSA, where I was asked to see my green card on top of my driver's license, but I refused. I didn't want them to see my green card. Why should they? We were already in the U.S., weren't we? Never in any other airport had I ever needed to show my green card, so why should I now? The TSA official waved over the border patrol agent, who was tall, white, and clean-shaven in his green fatigues. I didn't feel like talking, and I didn't want anyone to talk to me. The agent signaled me forward and said in broken Spanish, "Documentos por favor." I handed him only my ID with my ticket. He looked at it and asked me to step aside.

All I wanted was to feel like there was nothing in front of me. Why couldn't they just let me go on with my day?

"Can I see your green card or visa?" he asked me again, this time more forcefully.

I wanted to throw it in his face. Or, better yet, I wanted to throw it on the floor and make him pick it up—to lean down and have to look for it. Nothing said that was against the law, nowhere did it say

I needed to be courteous, but I knew I had no choice. I wasn't yet a citizen, so I didn't want to risk anything. I took out my green card and handed it to him.

He handed my green card back and motioned for me to move along. He was done with me. There would be nothing further to discuss. I couldn't tell if he was disappointed or relieved that nothing became of our interaction. Maybe he wanted a little excitement in his day. Maybe he was hoping to score some points with his boss.

Rubi was already waiting for me by the arrival/departure monitors, and she looked annoyed that I was being so stubborn. All around me, I saw people going on with their day as if nothing had happened. They were smiling, telling jokes, looking at their phones, adjusting their belts, stuffing their faces with a burger. The world was still moving. To them, indeed nothing *had* happened. But it felt like they were rubbing their quotidian liesure in my face. It wasn't their fault that my father had been denied, and yet it bothered me to hear everyone talking around me.

We found our gate, and I left my luggage with Rubi. "I'll be right back," I told her.

"Where are you going?"

"I can't be here right now, I need to go somewhere," I said in a frantic voice.

I went into the bathroom and locked myself inside a stall. It was the first time I'd cried *for* my father and not because of him. I could hear people outside, but no one seemed to mind, or no one dared intervene. They figured it was best to let me dice it out by myself.

It felt like a mathematical equation. Everything on one side needed to equal everything on the other. So, then, what was the equivalent of my father? What was the equivalent of me?

I sat on the toilet for a long time and let my phone ring on and on as Rubi tried to reach me. Then Amá tried to reach me because Rubi had called Amá. I turned off my phone and pinched myself, and slapped myself, and pulled my hair. It felt like it was my fault, like it was all my fault.

On the plane, I tried reading a book, but it didn't make much sense. I couldn't read the words. They didn't feel like words. Instead, they felt like they were stones, like they were heavy and difficult to pick up. It was a long flight back to Detroit. I took a few sleeping pills because the drinks were too expensive on the flight, fell asleep on Rubi's shoulder and never bothered looking out the window to see the landscape below.

[Third Movement as Migration and High Baroque]

——

We crossed the border on a Thursday. The grass was wet. Maybe it wasn't grass. Maybe it wasn't even dirt. Whatever was below us was moving—snakes? I counted to three and stopped. One, two, three, stop. One, two, three, stop. Everything we did was a kind of running. Even when we were just lying there, it still felt like we were running.

In the distance, it looked like the rings of light around a distant planet. I wanted honey, something sweet. But most of all, I wanted to stop and sleep, right there in that field of cucumbers. I wanted my dreams to be of honey, the dark kind that comes from the brightest flowers, from the most bitter of plants, plants that not even beetles touch, plants that at least are good for shade.

What good was shade anyway? What good were our feet, if they could only run so fast?

We probably would have stepped on the snakes if it weren't for the music and our graceful dancing. *There was music?* Yes. It started slow, but then picked up, and then slowed back down again. It was a waltz, it was a polka, it was the boogie-woogie jump swing, bebop. We were in a grand ballroom. Amá was in a gown. *She was in a gown?* Yes. Amá turned and turned as the hems of her dress blossomed toward the edges of the room. We all blossomed like bitter fruit.

We turned to each other and danced. It was High Baroque, it was neoclassical. We wore long gowns, and the men held their hands behind their backs. We bowed to each other and spun in circles. It was a game in which the children played adults and the adults played children. The border agents were the grooms. The border agents were the smoke outside, because everything was burning. *It was burning?* Yes. I put on my father's boots and his hat. I took out a small toy pistol and told him to put his arms up. "Stick 'em up, partner." We spoke English already. "Bang." We were accustomed to the new way of life even before we arrived. We tidied up the place. We baked every fucking pie we saw in the movies.

Yes. It was snakes. But they didn't bite us. They were looking for their own music, they were trying to make it stop. My baby brother in the womb had his own problems, so we left him alone. We didn't ask any questions; we held our heads down and gestured with our hands to each other. We hid in the dark beneath a tractor, and I was told to shut . . . the . . . fuck . . . up. I hummed and hummed a song and kept my eyes closed, and pressed my hands over my ears.

23.

The Midwest was still cold and gray, but I was relieved to be away from El Paso and Juárez. We landed in the afternoon, and I wondered if that cerulean blue of the evening had already arrived and left. The day carried on, but there was no sign of it. It had rained while we were away, and the snow had melted. Maybe the blue came and went with the snow.

There was a reading at the bookstore in town by a poet I admired that same afternoon we landed. I should have rested, but I didn't want to stop moving, to stop doing something and have to think about what the Juárez decision meant now.

"I'm going out, I'll be right back, okay?" I told Rubi as I got dressed and headed out the door. I hadn't called Apá to see if he had made it home safe. I figured he would.

The reading was in a cramped room that felt smaller with everyone's large winter coats still hanging on them. I felt like I couldn't breathe, so I decided not to sit and instead stood near the door in the back, where I could feel the cool breeze as people came and went from the bookstore.

I guess I was supposed to smile too. I was supposed to pretend like nothing had happened. Or perhaps I was supposed to pretend that this was normal, that it happened to everyone. I saw a friend walk in, and we stood quietly next to each other. We hugged and let our thick coats deflate into themselves, pushing the down feathers tight. I didn't need to tell my friend not to let go for them to not let go.

*

I told a few close friends what had happened but immediately regretted it. At first it felt good to release it from my breath, but at the same time, I wished I could keep it all inside me and never let it out, because once it was out, it was no longer mine. I felt like I could somehow still change the outcome if I was the only one who knew about it.

Later that semester, on the first warm day of the year, my friends and I went out to a green meadow for a picnic. We took blankets, gin, wine, some snacks, and books. It was a perfect day to lounge in the sun. I drank gin like it was water. Our other two friends laughed at the sheer joy of each other's company, and for once, I seemed to have forgotten what had happened in winter. There was a group of shirtless boys playing a game of football. They were all frat brothers. Their bodies glistened with sweat in the afternoon sun.

Already drunk, I looked over at Derrick and said, "I want to go play with them . . . look at them, they're beautiful."

"No, honey, you're drunk," Derrick said.

I wanted them to tackle me, so I too could glisten in the sun. But I would glisten like they never could. My dark, golden skin would catch the light and release it as something new and angled. I was beautiful and sad and drunk.

The last time I played football was in the eighth grade, when a boy jumped on top of me and broke my leg at the shin. It split in half. I was small, so it didn't take much weight to break it.

I wanted to go over there with the frat brothers and tell them what had happened. I wanted to tell them about the border officers who were talking about football as if it was just football. *Wasn't it just football? Wasn't it just a piece of paper? Wasn't it just ten years? Ten, ten, ten, ten.*

Instead I ran up and over a hill. I was barefoot, and the grass felt cool to the touch. It was no longer wet, but it was damp where the shade was heaviest. I was sweaty and I glistened either way. I yelled at Derrick and everyone else lying on the blanket to look at me, but they didn't hear.

"Look at me, goddammit," I yelled.

I ran down the hill as fast as I could and tripped, but I was drunk already so I didn't really feel it. I just felt a warmth creep into my foot.

*

Ten years. My mother, too, had been waiting those ten years for my father's return. I knew what his rejection meant. It meant Amá would finally have to decide whether to leave him for good, abandon the charade of waiting, or finally join him in Mexico and never come back.

I called her but she didn't answer, so I left a voice mail. I said I was tired, and I said she was right, it was the same kind of tired.

1.

The fact that I was still in the Midwest, Apá was forced to stay in Mexico, and the rest of the family was in California made us long for each other's company in ways we hadn't known. Something changed. My father's rejection in Juárez made us ask "What now?" All we had known to do with him up until then was wait, but we had reached the end of the road, and ahead of us was a fork. There was no longer a solid something to look forward to, something tangible that we could see in our heads. Instead it was now right in front of us, all too real, a living thing that we did not know how to care for and which was growing beyond control. It was as if something that we were trying to avoid for over a decade finally grabbed our face in its palms, opened our eyes, and said, "Look at me!"

I didn't know if Amá would decide it was time for her to leave. She had done as much as she could have ever done for herself, and for her children, now all adults. Was she happy with what we had done with our lives—with hers? If she did decide to leave, it wouldn't feel like defeat but pride, because it meant that she had made the right decision by not leaving when Apá was deported in 2003, when his incessant pull was strongest. If she did leave, it would be a way of announcing to everyone else that she had had a plan all along, and that that plan had come to fruition.

Every time I spoke to her on the phone while walking through campus, or in my small apartment, back from one of my evening walks, I always braced myself, hoping it wasn't the moment she would finally tell me what was on all of our minds. Sometimes I avoided calling her, stalling myself as well. But I was only lying to myself because I could feel it coming.

At the same time, with each lament of her possible departure, deep inside me was an innocuous and hardly visible trace of elation that she would finally get rest, finally return home and give up the toil she'd led to give us a better life. I wanted her to retire and live a peaceful life, growing a garden in Mexico, but I couldn't tell anyone this, not even myself. I couldn't bring myself to ever say it out loud.

I knew what labor had done to her body after so many years. She hardly had any fingerprints left, each ridge softened away by years of heat and steam from the plum factory, the way a river rubs off the parts of a boulder that can cut you. Her fingers were so sensitive that she needed to wear layers of gloves when she worked. The heat dug closer and closer to her nerves until it hardly needed to touch her hands before she could feel it. Two gloves turned to three—rubber, then cloth, then rubber again.

After Juárez, I was trying to convince myself that Apá had changed. I would close my eyes to try and remember the times I was with him in Tepechitlán and then later in Juárez—how he gripped things, how he talked to other people, how he swatted at flies. I hoped that it was only the residue of violence and not actually violence that lingered in his hands, like the sweet sugar on my palms after cutting open an orange. If Amá went back to Mexico, essentially self-deporting herself, she would be alone with Apá, without ever being able to return, and with no one to help her.

I thought love could have come out of his anger—bitter plants that make the sweetest honey. I confused each of his flowers with a small act of tenderness. There is a tender way we can confuse violence with love, trying to convince ourselves that it wasn't so bad. When a vaquero shoots an injured horse not out of cruelty but because he loves him, there is still blood, there is still a bullet hole, and maybe another hole where the bullet escaped depending on the caliber of the vaquero's mercy, which is to say, it's still violent nonetheless. How vigilant my life had become to temper his anger, to look for it and say "hush," as I would to a beast who only knows two tones of voices. And it was the repetition of his anger that made it so normal—the same song I thought I knew the words to, but I didn't. *He's changed, it's not so bad over there.*

This new thing, this new nothing that was building after the Juárez rejection, that was getting bigger and bigger, made Amá look at her life, made her stop and see what it was that she had built in all her years in the United States. After a total of thirty-five years on and off in the country, she didn't have any money to her name, she didn't own any property, she didn't know the language, but she had all of her grown children, who had finished at least high school and had decent jobs, as testament, as fruits of her labor.

*

She called me one day and was silent for a moment. She could have hung up because I already knew what she was going to say, and she knew I knew, but it's normal and polite to continue with the parts that hurt the most in conversation, even though they can be avoided altogether.

"Mijo . . . mijo . . . mijo . . ."

"My son . . . my son . . . my son.

I'm leaving, my son, I've done everything that I can. You have your wife, you have your school, and soon you will have your own children, and when you do, you will understand. I'm proud of you, mijo. I'm tired. I'm so very tired."

My son. My son. My son.

I hung up and sat there, staring at a wall, for a long time. I called my friend Lauren. We didn't say anything over the phone. It was usually like that with Lauren, who knew that I didn't have to explain why I was calling, crying. So we just listened to each other breathing until my sobs started to wind down and my heartbeats settled, and at last, when it was more or less silent, I said hi. But it was a kind of hi that didn't feel like it broke the silence between us, rather, it felt like it was part of that silence.

We, the children, had always been the ones in the middle. Amá always chose us over Apá, and now she was choosing him. But in choosing him, she still wasn't choosing herself, like always.

*

Amá came to the U.S. for us, her children, and she stayed behind in 2003 even when Apá demanded she return. She lived by her sister's words—"What were you thinking, getting pregnant, you can hardly feed the kids you have."

Amá said the one time she felt strongest and most invincible in her life was precisely in 2003 when Apá was deported. Refusing his orders gave her chills and a crushing resolve that she would pull ahead. She said she felt like a lion, even though as soon as he was gone they laid her off at her job.

Apá wanted to start a new life in Mexico after his deportation, but how many fresh starts can you have in life? How many times can you actually start over? It seems that's all my father was ever good at: dropping everything and starting new somewhere else. It was a way to say, "let's try again," but each time we tried again, we ended in the same spot: in debt, in hiding, sometimes hungry.

When Apá saw that nothing was working to convince her, his pleas for her to join him turned to orders, then to shouting, and after a few years, by the time I'd graduated from high school, it simmered to quiet supplications. As much as he shouted, and screamed, and cursed her, at the end of the day he was only a fizzle of a voice at the other end of the phone that she set down on her lap when the ranting would start. Maybe that's when he began taking baths in a large tub in the sun, when he started caring for his garden, because he realized that his shouting was useless, that he had lost his power over Amá, and so he needed something else to depend on him. Unlike Amá, the plants would die without him.

Amá knew there was no such thing as a fresh start; she knew nothing really changed when you moved from one place to another, you were still the same person, and it was still the same luck and the same life that would lead you to that same dead end.

We got used to his badgering, and it became something like white noise in the background of our lives. It seemed like each year, at any significant event like Christmas, Apá would call and say "It's time," but Amá would say the youngest still needed her. By which she meant the oldest too, and the middle, as well as the grandkids.

"Let me just be there for him until he finishes college," she would say again, and Apá would go back to his shouting, insulting, and ultimately hanging up. Sometimes, however, having run out of choices, she would hand us the phone in desperation.

"Hijo, try to convince your mother to come back. I'm dying here. I don't eat, I can't do this alone. I'm getting old. Do you want me living like this?" I was young, what could I say to that? Each time he pleaded with me, I would try to find the right words, though they never felt right in Spanish. Had I retreated that far away from my first tongue that even saying no felt impossible, even though it was the same word in both languages? He was planting a small seed two thousand miles away through the phone wires. "Hijo, your mother is doing this to me."

How could I explain to him that I didn't believe him?

I dreaded those phone calls. Amá, always next to me, coaching me on what to say, so that I wouldn't say the wrong thing and make a promise on her behalf by accident. I could see her lips moving silently, mouthing the words "No," or "I'm sleeping," or "Ya, hang up" when she didn't want to talk to him. I cradled the phone to my ear and tried to listen to both of them talking to me at the same time.

She stalled as long as she could.

*

The clock began ticking to my mother's departure, and for the first time, I gave myself permission to write about my life in a way that wasn't cryptic, that didn't hide behind the surreal nature of lyric images.

I wrote a poem about the parts of him that I could briefly touch—his hands, how "they were large and capable of great things." How they flung a belt I named Daisy through the air—"my ass purple with welts, my ass purple with love. And I said hello, Daisy, and she said hello," as he wiped his face with his kerchief.

I said my father "would love a man at the first sign of weakness. I was weak, therefore, I gathered that he loved me. That was how we both became men—him for the beating, and me for taking the beating." The poem ended.

To the animals he slaughtered—"His hands were two doves courting a lamb, which was also a dove in its thrashing." To the mouths he fed—"He always had peaches to put in their mouths." To the objects named—"I love you, Daisy."

[Fourth Movement as Language]

===

I got used to the roaches, I got used to the milk crates we used as chairs as we ate a pot of boiled beans and washed them down with black coffee for dinner. I was five, and we had just moved into our first apartment in the U.S., and though it was small, it still felt larger than our house back in Mexico. It certainly felt larger than the room we all crammed into at our uncle's house when we first arrived, careful not to be too much of a burden, though it was hard not to be when a family of seven suddenly moves in. Amá's belly was large, and she was due to give birth any day. Although our new apartment wasn't much to look at, we could scream, we could jump, and no one could say anything to us because it was ours.

We had one spoon. Or maybe it was one spoon for each person, so it still felt like one spoon. Amá rubbed her large belly and spread her legs as she crouched down to eat off an old bedside table. Everyone argued over what the new baby would be named. "It's my baby, I'm going to name him whatever I want," said Amá. Apá had named every child up until then, but Amá knew this would be her last, and she was determined to name him herself. When she gave birth, she kept the onesie the hospital put on the baby even though she was supposed to give it back because she didn't have a lot of clothes for him yet. She had a joke that the baby was made in Mexico but shipped, assembled, and delivered in the U.S. She came home with her baby in her arms and told us his name was Gilberto.

*

Every night was the same. I didn't like the taste of coffee, but Amá held the cup to my mouth and said to drink, that it would help. Help with what? We each cleaned our respective bowl, cup, and spoon. I took the drying cloth and made small circles with my hand until my bowl was dry and shiny. We were poor, but we were clean. The dishes were placed upside down over a towel so "nothing" would touch them at night.

"Beans again?" I said to Amá as we gathered around our bedside table, sitting on our milk crates in the middle of our small living room.

"Yes, now, don't complain," she said. She wasn't speaking in English, and although I didn't know English at the time, my memories of those days are peppered in English now. My mother handed me a taza, not a cup; she poured café, not "coffee." Amá's loud call to come in from playing outside was Ya vente, not "Come in now." But in my head, I see a "cup," I see her handing me a "cup," and the "cup" is now in English even though no one is speaking.

I have to work to put the Spanish words inside my memories—I have to think hard about each syllable inside them. To this day my mother still does not know English, though she is trying to learn it. Apá understands a little but can't speak it.

*

It was around this time, in kindergarten, when I first became aware of another language, a language I didn't know. There was something twisting in someone's mouth, not the kinds of words I was familiar with. A distance started to grow between me and the world, and I gladly walked toward the torpid shores of its strangeness. As we sat crisscross apple sauce, the music teacher at my first American school sat on a chair in front of us, rattling a steady rhythm with two spoons between his fingers. I understood the music because I clapped, we were all clapping along to his beat, some of us singing, others not.

The spoons vibrated like a rattlesnake's tail in front of me. I knew what music *was* and I liked it, bobbing the small frame of my body from side to side. But the strangest and most arresting sound of all was coming out of his mouth, which was nothing that I had ever heard before. I knew the sounds, I knew the rhythms, and even the gestures on his face that accompanied them as he nodded his head up and down. I could tell all of those things together were meant to produce some kind of happiness. I could make those sounds, but not in that order. I thought he sounded funny, so I let out a small giggle in the middle of his song, which prompted a stern look from the teacher keeping watch over us on the side. She must have thought I was mocking the song or the teacher, but I loved them both because despite not understanding them, I understood them differently. I liked the way that rattler kept shaking right above me, saying what most rattlers say with their thrashing tails, "Don't come near me, I am dangerous, I will bite you."

Maybe one day English *would* be dangerous for me, but not in that moment, tapping my small palms on my lap, looking at the song behind the children's song, the flurry of sounds looming above the spoons saying something that must have been happy, given the expressions on the teacher's face, a kind of joy that felt like home to me, a kind of joy that made sense, that reminded me of home.

I ran home elated, carrying that small pocket of joy like a wild mongoose whose belly was full of snake, whose teeth were smeared with blood.

"Amá, I want to be a musician when I grow up," I said.

"That's wonderful, mijo, now go take off your shirt so I can cut your hair," she said. I wondered if she had heard me. She cut our hair often because she said her children would not go around looking ragged.

"Amá, I said I want to be a musician when I grow up." I said again, that time louder. Still, she didn't seem to pay much attention. Maybe I shouldn't have stressed the music but what carried the music—I should have said I wanted to build violins.

*

I stood on a chair near the window, watching the neighborhood kids playing outside without me as Amá moved the clipper up and down my head. I started rambling to them through the open window in what I thought was my newly acquired English. I wanted to repeat what I had just heard in music class, but I wanted to do it without the music—without the spoons. It wasn't really anything coherent, but Amá says it had the effect of being discursive, as if I was standing at a podium addressing a throng of people below me. I waved my hands in the air, gesticulating, giving them instructions in this new language that I was certain they could understand but that they most certainly couldn't.

They laughed and I laughed with them because we were children and because that was what children did. We took refuge in our misunderstanding. I rambled on, trying to make any kind of sound that wasn't a word that I recognized because anything that wasn't Spanish automatically meant that it was English. English was the "other." Amá finished cutting my hair, not without protest that I was moving too much for her to steady her hand, and I finished my long speech, even though my friends had long since stopped paying attention. I felt like I had done something good.

I bowed politely in my chair and went out to the yard again.

In my head, I knew what I was saying, there was meaning behind my squawk. It was in that very short window of time, when I could speak in that primal language between languages, that I could understand things better—clearer. Perhaps I never really left and was always moving back and forth between languages, reaching for something I would never fully attain.

The afternoon was warm, and the sun wouldn't start making its eventual retreat over the mountains for another few hours. Amá went to the kitchen to put another pot of beans on to boil. Beans were still beans, there was nothing new about that, there was nothing that needed translation, I could move back and forth with relative ease.

*

With time, that innocent wonder at my nonlanguage would slowly start to fade and be replaced by English, which would soon mostly replace Spanish. In no time I would find myself sitting crisscross apple sauce just like the other children, bored at yet another music lesson, sedated, singing along to words that were reduced to one thing and one thing only. Music would again just be music and words just words. I would never again reach that wandering calamity of sound, that cacophonous revelry. I'm sure that wasn't the first time I ever heard English being spoken, but it was the first time I remember being aware of it in any meaningful way.

I loved being bilingual, but there was something special in that moment of utter confusion. The short journey from Spanish to English was a revelry, a reverie that deflated like balloons shortly after the party has ended. It was a path on which I moved, another migration. My body had already reached the U.S., but my tongue was a bit slower getting there, taking its time, hopping from rock to rock like a small mountain cat. I stuck out my skinny tongue and hissed at everyone around me.

*

The path to learning English wasn't like a pig being taken to slaughter. Pigs know what's at the other end of that long walk to the slaughterhouse, and they fight tooth and nail to escape. Their long and deep howls seem to come from somewhere beyond their body, from the very earth itself—almost demonic. I didn't fight;

I didn't know what was at the other end, but I ran toward it with open arms nonetheless.

Amá stirred the pot of beans one more time and announced that they were ready. We grabbed our spoon, and our bowl, and our coffee. How unbearably boring the world would soon be. In that moment, though, I was an oracle, I was enchanted, I was *enchanting*. The bean broth was hot as it slowly went down my throat, as it touched that part of me that had no name yet.

2.

Rubi and I were glad to be back in California for good and out of the Midwest after we graduated. All of California was burning, parched, and expensive, but it was home. The air had the dry smell of rice husks left behind in cracked marshes that stretched for miles around my town. I was used to seeing the Sierra on the east and the coast ranges on the west. I was in the valley, where the sun sat low and blistered everything dry. Rubi and I moved in with Amá, in the same home in Yuba City where I grew up, a home she'd rented for seventeen years, where I held her by the arm the day of the ICE raid.

I often heard people ask me why Amá didn't "just get papers if she had over thirty years combined in the U.S.," as if time alone was the remedy. It was like telling someone, "Just stop being depressed." It was remarkable how little they understood how it worked. Amá had an application pending in immigration, which we froze, because if we allowed it to continue, she would almost certainly receive the ten-year ban as well and never be allowed to return. Her application was in the system for decades, petitioned by a relative, but it was going nowhere because we knew where it would end up. We were waiting for a law to change, hoping for Congress to pass something, anything. Our lawyer tried every single legal maneuver possible, and each was nil.

She was stuck in a catch-22. Her only possible option was for Apá to petition for her, but he needed to be a citizen, and the only possible option for him was for her to petition for him, but she needed to be a citizen, or at least a resident, to do that. They were stuck.

I spent hours on my laptop combing through legal blogs, articles, and official government websites, hoping to find something that our lawyer might have missed. Even though she had already made up her mind to leave, I was hoping I would find a way that would allow her to come back, so that it wouldn't feel so permanent. I scrolled

through a directory of the area's lawyers and called to ask who of-
fered free consultations.

We had spent years looking closely at Amá's case with a magni-
fying glass, trying to inspect every detail for a loophole, and perhaps
that was precisely the problem. Perhaps what we needed was to step
back and look at it from a distance. I scheduled meeting after meet-
ing with lawyers who all had the same-looking diplomas hanging on
their beige walls, and tchotchkes from trips to Cancún or Costa Rica.
Some were fresh out of law school, not yet jaded, and took their time
to get to know my mother and what had brought us to that moment
in time. Others just stared at the clock. I had to repeat my mother's
story so often that it started to sound absurd. Hearing it out loud so
many times made it sound foreign, like it was happening to another
family and I was simply a messenger.

One of the lawyers I saw said she had "committed a felony, that
never goes away." The words themselves already seemed permanent,
irreversible. I had never heard anyone refer to my mother like that.
I thanked him for his time and walked out. His secretary asked if I
would like to schedule a follow-up. "That won't be necessary, thank
you," I said, and headed to the parking lot to sit in my car for a long
time, tuning the radio back and forth.

3.

Back in her house, I brushed my mother's hair, which was soft, and thinning. She'd started dyeing it for the first time. Maybe that's why it felt so light through my fingers. She always loved her gray hairs, said it made her look refined, dignified, but not anymore.

We sat on her couch late at night watching a Spanish-dubbed Steven Seagal movie on Telemundo. Her arms were small, and I could feel her sharp bones angled at the softest parts of her.

I rubbed oil in her hair and kept brushing as we both laughed at Seagal, those quick-action camera angles and the infamous pony-tail whipping back and forth. The explosions in the background, twenty years after the movie had been released, seemed faded and uneventful, as if by now, in our dim room's Telemundo version, they were only pointing at fire, and couldn't actually burn, as if they were only saying *bang* but were muted, and Seagal knew this. He was indifferent, with his emotionless face, perhaps already aware during filming of the dim and fuzzy filter he would be seen through twenty years later in a dark room where a boy who was hardly a boy anymore was brushing his mother's hair. It was as if he knew that his voice would be replaced by the voice of a man speaking in heavy Castilian Spanish who had difficulty express-ing surprise when a bomb exploded in his *oh*s and *ah*s, and which sounded more like soft moans. He didn't bother opening his mouth much to speak.

She never had many knots in her hair, but I continued to brush. It wasn't defeat that was growing in the air with each week, it was exhaustion. It was easier to brush her hair than to tell her I would miss her.

I knew she would never return. Could we be blamed for giving up?

There was an abscess growing on her arm from a car accident. It looked like a golf ball on her wrist, and it forced her to become left-handed. I remembered her being mad at me as a teenager and saying "Don't make me hit you with my good hand"—her left hand. It didn't hurt when she hit me, but I had to pretend that it did. What hurt most was the fact that she hit me, the fact that she couldn't hit me with her right, the fact that she had to adjust her body sideways to hit me with her left, and that I stood there, unfazed, angry that I couldn't go out with friends, the fact that it didn't hurt but I cried nonetheless. She was hit by a drunk driver. Apá was driving, and they were T-boned on the passenger's side, Amá's side. Apá walked away from the crash unharmed. The hood of the car sliced open Amá's neck. The right side of her body was shattered. Apá said he saw the car coming, and just before impact, he swerved left without thinking. I wonder how much time he had to choose which way to turn—his side or Amá's side. It's funny how those things happen, how one person can walk away without a scratch while the other is nearly sliced to pieces.

If the lights were on in the room, and if I were looking at Amá for the first time, I would notice the remnants of that accident, the scars running down her neck and the ones on her shoulder where small pieces of glass were still tucked just beneath the skin and yet lodged too deep to extract, too large to dissolve into the rest of her. The largest scar ran down the length of her forearm, where they opened her and replaced all the bones with metal. The metal would stay there, but the glass would not, at least not all of it. The doctors said the shards would come out by themselves, unexpectedly and years later, with "minimal pain," like a slow bullet traveling out of her, like a bullet in a film with an already outdated actor looking directly into the camera as he recites one-offers—"I'm a bad motherfucker."

I imagined the glass making its uneventful entrance into the world two decades later, as if it were alive, squirming the way snakes do when they come out of the shell. Maybe it would be a lonely affair, no one there to see it, except Amá, who would surely be confused at first, seeing something leave her body. Or maybe I would be there to witness this thing that's been part of my mother's body for so long that it could be mistaken for bone. I wouldn't know how to hold it if it fell in my hands. I would put it to my ear and listen, I would hold it to the light before giving it back to Amá so she could know what it was that hurt her every time she lifted her arm to hit me.

[Fourth Movement as an Abandoned Car]

———

We outgrew our first apartment when the baby came. It was a one-bedroom and there were seven of us, plus another cousin who crossed with us, promising to one day return. We moved into a two-bedroom nearby that had a large empty field in the back with dozens of old abandoned cars fixed into the earth as if they had been planted but bore no fruit. They looked ancient, some without windows, others without doors, some with their motors splayed out beside them. I imagined them to be a congregation of old men, sitting on stones, grumbling quietly to each other about all they had lost.

I spent hours playing in that field, going through the spare car parts scattered beneath the tall grass, wondering what their purpose was, playing swords with a windshield wiper or using a hubcap as a shield. I used to keep a small family of rabbits in one of the cars, and would bring them fresh alfalfa every day that we grew in our garden. A few cats ate them one day, and I avoided that car for a while.

*

I liked to sit alone in one of the cars that wasn't so tattered but still had weeds growing inside. Generations of opossums made their den in the trunk. I still didn't know English well, but I was starting to know my body.

One day, sitting inside that car, I reached into my pants and pulled.

I felt the muscles of me hurt because they had never been used like that before. I felt my skin tear at the new weight of that unseen desire.

My dog left me, and I cried for days. My rabbits were eaten, which was a kind of leaving. We left Mexico, we left the first small room we rented, we left the first small house we rented. We were always leaving, so whatever it was that wanted to leave my body didn't seem out of the ordinary.

*

I didn't know what to call my erection. I didn't know what it was that my body was doing or how I knew that it would feel good if I pulled on myself. Who taught me that lesson of the body? Or did it come to me by mistake, or accident? Did I hold myself too long and suddenly feel that first pang of pleasure? And before long I was back in that hot car with no seats, sitting on the metal floor, rubbing the ends of myself as if I knew what I was doing, as if the instructions were written in me already.

Although it hurt, I tugged harder just as the door swung open.

If I was present in my body, I would be able to say something to Amá standing at the door. I felt like my life was one long sustained breath.

*

A checklist of things I saw that day:

1. The first ice cream truck slowly driving by, blasting its twangy music through the blow horn.

2. The neighbors fixing their cars with their shirts off, a loud racket coming from their engines.

3. The sun not going anywhere.

4. The sun doing exactly what it was always doing.

5. Apá working alone on a piece of leather to make a whip, even though no one had horses anymore.

6. The sun in a different place than last time I saw it.

7. Tires tossed on the side of the road.

8. The second youngest, still two, seemingly forever two, aggressively two, playing in the dirt as always.

9. The neighbors yelling.

10. The neighbors kissing and drinking beer on their porch and then yelling again.

11. The neighbors saying, Baby I'm sorry, and walking away.

12. How the afternoon air felt like a blessing.

"Child, what are you doing?"

*

I took out my hand and zipped up my pants. How did I know that that was something I shouldn't have been doing? How did I know I was supposed to hide, to not tell anyone? How did I know the feeling of shame even before the door swung open?

*

Feelings of Shame:

1. Cold wet clay at the bottom of a jar.

2. Blue bubble gum.

3. I ran and ran home from school, as if something was chasing me.

4. Stick 'em up partner.

5. Morning light.

6. Rabbits chewed as if for fun.[1]

"Child, what are you doing in there?"

*

Years later I will find myself sitting at a desk, wiping myself clean after watching a man enter a woman, a woman enter a man, a man enter another man. Shortly after which I'll write a line in my notebook. That line will read, "I could have been anyone's idea of pity, to name each part of me after the names of my mother's lovers or just hold the shame in my hand."

"Child, get out of there right now."

*

If I was watching the sunset for the first time, I still wouldn't doubt that it would return on the other side of the sky in the morning.

*

Through the kitchen window, I could see the neighbors still kissing like they always did, the man gripping the small woman by her skinny shoulders, looking straight into her, saying "I'm sorry, baby, it won't happen again." Amá didn't hit me, didn't touch me, simply sat me on a chair and asked, "Child, where did you learn that?"

Maybe I had done it before, unknowingly, until it ceased to be a mystery to me and simply a repetition. I didn't know what other kids in the neighborhood were doing at the age of six or seven. We were painting things with our hands and making macaroni necklaces at school.

"Child, go think about what you've done."

*

If I stood still long enough, perhaps no one could see me anymore. I wanted to disappear into the small holes beneath the car, or among the tall grasses in the yard, to lie down and stare up at the sun and, if there was rain, let the rain pour over me.

The car would soon be turned back to soil. I used to collect things in jars and bury them.

4.

I kept looking for lawyers who offered free consultations. Apá didn't know how hard we were still trying to keep Amá back, but he had settled down because he'd finally gotten what he wanted, his answer he had been waiting so many years to hear. When he called, his only question was when would she leave, and it irritated me to hear him say it so casually, as if she was just leaving to the store to buy some groceries.

A friend recommended us to a lawyer who was young and enthusiastic. I had already come across his type before, and they usually clicked their teeth and apologized when they saw there was nothing they could do. Although his consultation wasn't free, we took the risk and paid anyway because he came highly recommended. His office was in a tech business park outside Sacramento, not in an old Victorian home-turned-office in midtown, where most of the other capital lawyers resided. With each visit to a new office, they always asked us who our current lawyer was, but we always refused to give them a name because we were a little ashamed that we were looking elsewhere for other opinions. This new young lawyer, however, didn't ask.

Rubi and I sat down and prepped ourselves to tell him the same story we had told every other lawyer, but he stopped us and began with a question.

"Has your mother ever been a victim of a violent crime? Has she ever called the police on anyone who has hurt her?"

"No, I mean, she never really could. She would never call the police, afraid that she would be deported," I said.

"Has she ever crossed paths with the police for any reason? Any reason at all?" he insisted again, trying to find something to latch on to.

Rubi's eyes lit up. "She was hit by a drunk driver a long time ago—does that count?"

"Was he sentenced? Was there a police report?" the young lawyer asked, leaning forward a little too eagerly into the desk.

"Yeah, he was sentenced, and my mom testified, and the man was sent to prison."

"That's good, that's good, that's real good," he said, which seemed strange because I hadn't caught on to his angle yet.

"You see, your mother might be eligible for a U visa, which would overrule any and all inadmissible crimes [previous deportations]. It would fall under felonious assault. She was a victim of a violent crime, and under that law, any victim of a violent crime who helps law enforcement with the persecution of the perpetrator is eligible for a special visa that would soon allow them permanent resident status.

We had been looking so closely, so meticulously that we failed to see that the answer was right in front of us this entire time. Her accident was in 1996, and for nineteen years, up until that moment in the lawyer's office in the summer of 2015, we had overlooked such a glaring detail. Every day that I held my mother's hand, I felt the large abscess from her accident, every time she made lemonade I placed the sliced lemons on her left hand, knowing it was the good hand. It was right there and we missed it.

Amá's pain from the accident never went away, but her pain was secondary to the burden of survival. As much as she tried to hide it, her body pushed back, growing bulges of what we hoped was benign tissue where she hurt most—glass and metal scraping against bone. We knew. We all knew the pain was there, and yet we didn't know it was also what could have saved her.

It was her pain that held the answer all along, and rather than turn away from it, rather than look away, we all should have run toward it. Had we known, had anyone told us she could have applied on the day of the accident, nineteen years before, we would not have wasted a single day. I couldn't imagine how different our lives would have been, how much grief we would have been spared. We researched the U visa and prepared to file her application immediately.

5.

The U visa was a law that was "enacted to strengthen the ability of law enforcement agencies to investigate and prosecute serious crimes and trafficking in persons, while offering protections to victims of such crimes without the immediate risk of being removed from the country." Congress recognized that "victims without legal status may otherwise be reluctant to help in the investigation or prosecution of criminal activity." A person is eligible for a U visa if the victim:

- Is the direct or indirect victim of qualifying criminal activity;

- Has suffered substantial physical or mental abuse as a result of having been a victim of criminal activity;

- Has information about the criminal activity; and

- Was helpful, is being helpful, or is likely to be helpful to law enforcement, prosecutors, judges, or other officials in the detection, investigation, prosecution, conviction, or sentencing of the criminal activity.[2]

Some of the eligible crimes include sexual assault, incest, domestic violence, felonious assault, involuntary servitude, "and other related criminal activity." The process was fairly straightforward: if a person was a victim of a qualifying violent crime and they helped law enforcement in their investigation, regardless if their help led to a conviction, they could petition for this special protection. At any process during the investigation, either during the trial, before, or years after, the victim could begin their motion, and there was no statute of limitations for filing. The first step, however, before anything could be done, was to have a local law enforcement agency[3] sign a certification testifying that a crime indeed had taken place and stating the role that the victim played in helping with the investigation of the case. However, if a victim failed to secure this certification, they could not advance their application, which would essentially kill it before ever reaching immigration—"Without a certification, a U visa petition will be denied."

In early 2015, when we were filing, the law enforcement agency was endowed with complete discretion in their decision.[4] And so even if a person met all the basic requirements, and even if everything they said was true, backed up by court documents, and police records, they also had to meet the subjective requirements and whims of the local law enforcement agency, who decided for themselves if someone like my mother had "suffered enough." There were no statewide standards in place as to what was meant by "enough suffering"; it was simply relegated to each department on a case-by-case basis. And the certifying agencies were not "required to have an internal policy or procedure [of eligibility] before they can sign U visa certifications."

Decisions depended on the department. Our lawyer explained to us that the Yolo County agencies were particularly conservative and were known to deny most petitions for U visa certifications, so it was our job to try to convince them that Amá had suffered enough.

6.

Highway 113 passes through the rural back roads of Yolo County in California without bending for many miles, with rice fields on either side and ditches along the shoulder. It is a two-lane road, and sometimes a long line of cars will back up when a large tractor combine barreles slowly down the middle of the road, taking up both lanes. The road is notorious for the amount of lives it takes because of how straight it is, and because so many drive into oncoming traffic trying to pass other drivers. The road is so straight that it is dizzying, and it is easy to begin swerving, especially in the warm afternoon, after a long day's work. The county tried to remedy this by perforating the asphalt along the middle to stir drivers awake if they began to swerve, but the deaths continue.

That was the road where Amá and Apá were hit by the drunk driver twenty minutes away from home, and the same road Rubi, Amá, and I drove down as we made our way to the Yolo County Courthouse. We were going to recover the court documents from the accident and the later conviction of the man who hit them, in order to begin Amá's U visa process. We were banking on using the government's own legitimacy against itself by gathering as much of its own information about my mother as possible to give us credibility. I could write an eloquent letter stating in a well-thought-out argument that Amá had indeed sustained, and continued to sustain, significant emotional and physical pain from the accident that happened nineteen years before, but I knew their words were worth more than mine. If it wasn't me who was speaking, but rather the government documents themselves, in a detailed account of her wounds, perhaps they would be more compelled to believe them.

We could see the dark outlines of people in the distant fields, hunched over the crops with hoes in their hands, moving slowly and methodically. So much had changed since the years Amá had worked in those fields. They had water stations at both ends of the fields now, as well as in the middle; they had tents for shade, and places to sit. Amá looked out into the fields and let out a deep sigh, because she knew that at the same time, very little had changed. It was still very hard work, but even so, she missed it. She missed the smell of the dirt, and the communion of voices gathered to work for a better life. She said she oddly missed working so hard and so mind-numbingly fast that there was no other room in her head to think about anything else. In that moment, all that mattered was getting as many strawberries into her basket as possible, as many peaches, apples, pears, plums. She made most of her friends working in the fields. They found ways to have fun, like scaring each other with dead snakes mangled by the harvesters.

They learned from each other, they cared for each other, and they grew old with each other. "We could all see the pain when a new young little thing would arrive on the first day on the job, how much she missed her home, but we could also see the courage and hardened resolve in her eyes to work," Amá said as we made our way along the endless road. "We, the older ones who knew, made sure to make them feel at home and welcome. While hoeing weeds, we would make sure to get near a new girl and ease her load. Or sometimes, if it was the peach harvesting season, we would sometimes each drop one of our own bags filled with peaches into her bin to help her a little. It wasn't much, but it made her feel like things would be okay."

Amá liked to work. She liked to earn her own money. But her tales of the camaraderie of the women in the fields made me realize that she also liked having a life of her own, away from Apá, away from us, something no one else could claim.

*

The Yolo County Clerk-Recorder's building rose where the old courthouse once stood. It was a stately, large stone building, with typical Corinthian columns along the front. It reminded me of the

English-department building back at school. The style was neo-classical revival, harkening back to the origins of democracy, from which it was so far removed that only the distinctive columns remained.

We took off our belts and keys and placed everything in a small tray before walking through a metal detector. Amá passed, and it rang. She lifted her arm for the guard to see, and he waved her on without ever really looking at her, his hand slowly making circles in the air.

I passed through the detector next, followed by Rubi, and heard no buzz. The guard seemed to be there more for show and inconvenience. We showed him our IDs, and Amá showed him her Mexican passport.

We took a flight of stairs down to the basement, which renovation had forgotten. The walls still had that thick layer of smoke residue from decades past. The main floor had its handblown glass art deco chandelier and its granite rotunda, but the basement had only the dreariness of the 1970s that no one really liked to remember. The signs led us to a small office with a waiting room lined with receiving windows, small holes drilled into their glass.

"I'm looking for a police record of an incident," I said through the glass. Nineteen years had passed. I had no idea what they would say or find, but technically, it didn't matter that so much time had passed, since the U visa rules stated that there was no statute of limitations on signing the certification. We were simply doing some of the in-vestigative work ourselves that the certifying agency (the sheriff's department, who'd arrived on scene at the accident and written the original report) would need to do, but which we feared would not. Their only job was to determine that a crime had indeed happened and sign off on it, but if we left the search to them, with such an old case, we feared they might come up empty-handed. We wanted to make sure nothing was left to chance in compiling as much informa-tion as possible that documented Amá's case and injury.

The woman told us to wait and went into a back room for what seemed like hours while we waited on plastic chairs that squeaked every time we adjusted ourselves.

Finally the clerk emerged from her window and called us over. In her hand was a thick stack of papers, freshly printed, because some time ago they had switched all of their records to digital archives. "This is all we've got, and it's pretty much everything from that case," she said, flipping through the stack. She didn't ask what we needed them for, but the mere fact that we needed them nineteen years after the date must have meant something to her, must have meant that something new had happened.

They charged thirty-eight cents per page, and I asked her if they accepted cards. She smiled and nodded. It wasn't cheap. I quickly flipped through a few hundred pages and noticed that many sections were redacted in thick black strokes of permanent marker, which I still paid for. The clerk said it was information we weren't allowed to access, but she couldn't specify why. We took whatever we could and thanked her.

The court documents had diagrams of the position of the cars, the angles at which they collided, descriptions of materials, blood alcohol levels, and speeds. The language was clinical and dry, but Amá, sitting quietly next to us in the car as we passed the fields of corn and rice on Highway 113, was the living translation of what the documents couldn't quite completely say. We learned the man's name, and that he'd served three years. It wasn't his first DUI. He too, like Apá, like every other man on the crime scene, had walked away uninjured.

*

Before we could ask the sheriff's department to sign the certification that we needed in order to begin the U visa application, we decided that we needed more proof of Amá's injuries and how they continued into the present day. The court documents alone were probably enough, but we wanted to be extra thorough.

I knew we needed to move quickly; time was against us, and Apá was growing impatient. He still didn't know what we were up to. The next day, after visiting the Yolo County Courthouse, we went to the hospital that Amá was airlifted to on the day of her accident. They too had switched to digital archives. They too accepted Visa, Mastercard, or Discover.

The attendant at the medical records office said she was doubtful that they would have any records dating that far back. "Please, can you check?" I asked. She came back with a small stack of papers with Amá's name on them. Her medical records showed what the police report couldn't—what happened on the inside. It described Amá's injuries in clinical specificity. It said how many plates, how many bones, how much glass could not be removed, and also provided her lab results, which would explain why she lost so much weight in the following years. Her medical records quantified an otherwise unquantifiable characteristic—pain. Amá could say she hurt, but forty-two metal staples on her forearm hiding metal plates where bone should have been was a specificity well understood by bureaucrats in suits.

Her medical records completed the narrative we were trying to build: that her accident wasn't just a single event, but rather the beginning of a lifetime of complications. Each detail on her chart was like a small flag sticking out of the snow in a slow avalanche that was taking the course of her entire life to roll down. We left the clean, air-conditioned hospital office in search of more evidence of Amá's pain.

I was nervous about taking her to the doctor to get X-rays, because I knew they would also want to check whether the abscess growing on her wrist was benign, but it was necessary; it wasn't the same thing to tell them what was inside her as it was to show them a picture. At the doctor's office, I tried to explain what we were trying to accomplish, because there wasn't anything illicit about it, and I asked her if she could write a letter explaining Amá's condition and the years of pain she had continued to endure. By now, we thought all of the evidence we gathered was certainly overkill, more than enough not only to convince the certifying agency to sign off but also, once we sent off their certification, to have her approved by USCIS.

We thought we had made a significant bridge between past and present, and would never have to speak ourselves. We knew our stories would not hold up, so we presented hard evidence in the form of these official documents that could better speak for us. None of our evidence was subjective or biased; we only provided the language and materials that the state had come up with. The last thing I did was take a close-up picture of Amá, so they could see the scars and the size of the bulge on her wrist. But it wasn't too close; I wanted them to see her face, hoping that would help.

We took our packet to the sheriff's department. Surely they would see that, although the accident happened nearly two decades before, she was still living with a constant reminder of that day.

*

I was the one who opened the letter wherein they regretted to inform us that, given the significant time that had elapsed since the "incident," they would be unable to fulfill our request to sign a certification authorizing that a violent crime had been committed.

The decision whether to sign a certification is at the certifying agency's discretion. Each certifying agency should exercise its discretion on a case-by-case basis.

The lump on her wrist didn't get there overnight. It took years to form, because she worked so soon after the accident and thereafter. The glass didn't all come out at once; it was still making its way out. It moved too slow for them to notice.

*

In the course of finding the evidence, filing the papers, and (what I can only imagine) a sergeant or captain in their office looking over at pictures of Amá, her X-rays, descriptions two decades old, and schematics, Amá's body was being examined, carefully scrutinized for signs of a specific kind of trauma, one that might always evade her. They wanted to see a spectacle, something quantifiably violent. But not everything happens like it does on TV. There isn't always a musical accompaniment to underscore the emotional landscape of tragedies. There is pain that isn't instantaneous, that is difficult to see, that spreads multiple generations, that doesn't always have a clear cause, that can't be measured but is nonetheless real. Sometimes it is more real because it is hidden, because you have to go through your life keeping it to yourself, unable to tell anyone the depths of your suffering.

Though we were devastated, we knew we could take the same evidence to two other agencies and try again; to the presiding judge who oversaw the original trial, and to the DA's office.

So back through Highway 113 we drove, and again Amá sighed with heavy nostalgia. The DA's office was across the street from the clerk's office, but the building was midcentury modern, perhaps built even later, in the 1980s, when the new criminal justice laws under Reagan made locking up poor brown and black people a blood sport for district attorneys and public prosecutors.

At the DA's office we sat in yet another waiting room, with a few chairs and service windows, and walked up to the window when our names were called. A young man came to the window. After we'd made our request, told our whole story, and slid all of our documentation through a small opening, he asked us to sit down while he spoke to his boss.

He was back in no time, which surprised me. "I've spoken with the DA, and they say they can only attend to incidents that happened within the last seven years because we shred all of our documents after seven years," he said. He had on a plaid shirt with tight khakis, and a nice watch. He was handsome and blond and looked aggressively boring, as if he aspired to own a chocolate-colored Lab in the suburbs.

"Oh, that's okay," I said through the window. "I have all of the documents you need right here because the court keeps them indefinitely."

"I'm sorry, but they need to be original documents from the DA's office, and we shred them after seven years, so the DA can't attend to your mother's case."

"But—I—have—everything—right—here," I said again, slowly, impatiently. He repeated the exact same thing as before. "These are signed documents from that clerk's office right over there, from which this office received the exact same copies," I said, a little more loudly.

Everything was right there in my hands: the speeds of the cars, the directions they were going, the directions in which they finally stopped spinning. It was all right there, but it was as if we were holding something unclean, something he didn't want to touch, even as I nudged them underneath the glass again. "Please," I said, my eyes beginning to tear up. He looked sincerely sorry, and I knew it wasn't his decision to make. I probably could have yelled and made a scene, but by that point defeat had overcome me. I dropped my shoulders and signaled to Amá that we should leave.

We drove home, again passing the same spot where she'd lain eighteen years before, coming apart, unconscious, as the other driver tried to drive away in his car, which also was intact for the most part.

[Fourth Movement in the Shape of a Poltergeist]

=

We each took a turn looking away. I looked at the street, at my ceiling, or at my neighbor's long black hair as he drank from the hose in the summer of 1995, in the dying town of Linda, California, which was Spanish for beautiful, ironic because it was not. Everyone had their favorite thing to look at instead of looking at Amá—a car, a girl, a boy, a tree.

Apá didn't like to look at her either, after he hit her and her face swelled up.

I wanted to look, but sometimes she hid behind doors or makeup. She didn't want us to see what Apá had done. I got home from school to find the door locked. I knocked and yelled for her. I was still looking at trees, so maybe I was in a forest, but Amá opened the door enough for me to see that I was not.

His hands were the only thing in his life that ever really came close to her.

She said, "Go play with your friends, mijo." So I did. I looked at my neighbor still drinking from the hose; I looked at him walking into his house, which was always unlocked.

If Amá, my brothers, and I each looked somewhere else at the same time that wasn't Linda, that was away from Apá, perhaps we could convince ourselves it was possible to go there. And one day we did. Our new apartment was a secret. No one was supposed to see us.

*

Apá raged. He looked for us at church, at friend's houses, even checking the house again just to make sure his eyes weren't playing tricks on him. He looked for Amá like he had never looked for her before.

I didn't know what became of Apá in those months, but I knew he was around. I was always afraid of seeing him on the streets, or of him waiting for me after school. I had the feeling he was always watching, that he had cameras everywhere. But I never saw him. I wished I could be invisible when I played outside.

Then one day the door of our secret apartment was locked again. And again she said, "Go play with your friends, mijo," and I knew what that meant. She said he hadn't given her much of a choice.

*

Between her beauty and his hands were the three of us, the children. He didn't regret hurting her; he regretted that she hurt enough to leave. He knew the limit now. From now on he would only bury his fists as deep as that limit. Nothing more, nothing less. A calibration. A fine tuning, so that no one else would notice.

*

We needed to ease our way back to him, the way you wade into frigid water, slowly letting your body get numb enough from the waist down to take the dive. He spoke a few words, tousled my hair, then left, then stayed a little longer.

Eventually we made our way back to our old house. It looked the same. He didn't buy anything new, as if he knew she would be back, as if they both knew how it would end. She never left him again. She wasn't able to call the police because she was afraid that it would make things worse. She always combed her hair slowly in the mirror.

Apá kept trying to hold us but never could, as if we were ghosts, as if *we* were the ones knocking all of the frames off the wall, shattering in the late hours of the night. I never took my eyes off my mother again.

Our last hope was that the presiding judge might be willing to sign the certification, even though both the sheriff and DA's offices had refused. We couldn't see him in person, so our lawyer mailed all of our materials instead. I accompanied our documents with a letter as well, Something I hadn't thought was necessary the first two times.

To whom it may concern,

My name is Marcelo Hernandez Castillo and I am the son of ██████████████ ████████, who is petitioning for a U visa certification to recognize her as a victim of a violent crime. I write in order to clarify and explain the special circumstances of my mother's case given the time that has elapsed since her incident. As is self-evident from the documents enclosed, on October of 1996, my mother was involved in a head-on collision caused by a Mr. ██████████████████████, who was heavily under the influence. My mother suffered the greatest injury of both parties involved and was airlifted to ███ ████████████████████ immediately thanks to an off-duty officer who witnessed the crash and was able to detain Mr. ████████ before he could attempt to flee the scene. As you can see from the documents, Mr. ████████ was charged with felony DUI with injury and was sentenced to three years. My mother was called to testify against Mr. ████████ and fully cooperated with law enforcement to help in the case against Mr. ████████ and was present during the trial.

Beyond the empirical evidence gathered from the collision and the medical records detailing her injuries, which included extensive internal organ damage, lacerations to her neck, and the most damaging being her broken arm which required immediate and extensive surgery, it is important to highlight the effects and damages procured in the year following the accident up until the present day. The surgery to her right arm was intended to hold her bones together with metal plates and screws but the aftermath of the trauma changed her life. Over the years, a large fragment of bone and muscle tissue has begun protruding from her wrist, which has caused her to lose strength and mobility in her right arm. Being right handed, she has had to adjust and train her left hand to do most of her work.

Given that my mother works in manual labor, which requires her to sort fruit on a conveyor belt for up to twelve hours at a time, the constant motion has caused her immense pain each and every day since the accident. She has refused to take pain medication for fear of dependency and has instead decided to bear the weight of the pain alone. . . . This accident was not something that merely happened in 1996 and was forgotten. Rather it lives with her each and every day. She has never been able to drive a car since the accident because she has developed a phobia of driving due to the psychological trauma associated with the incident, which means she must continually pay other people to give her rides to work and elsewhere. Although her life entirely revolves, either directly or indirectly, around an incident that happened many years ago, she cannot move on. Thank you for your time and understanding.

Sincerely,

Marcelo Hernandez Castillo

8.

What seemed like hope at first turned into almost an embarrassment. How could we be so naive as to think we could fix this?

A few weeks later, we received a letter from the judge's clerk. I didn't even need to open it to know what it said.

They wanted to keep things in the past, to cherry-pick only the things they wanted to usher into the future. To them, the accident happened nineteen years before and stayed there. To them, it never followed her. Amá was not afforded the luxury of forgetting, of thinking of the past as immobile, as static. She carried it with her, and it never aged, it always became a new pain that simply added to an old scar, a new present.

The sheriff, the DA, and the judge applied a narrow definition of suffering onto Amá and made it impossible for her to fit the mold. But it wasn't just them, the whole law was flawed. The U visa law told women like my mother how they should suffer and provided a checklist for correct forms of suffering.

Amá, on the other hand, was forced to remember not by choice but for survival. Meanwhile, I was writing poems to make sense of why it was that I forgot my past, which felt nothing like a luxury, which felt like a curse in fact. And we were holding each other in order to know the difference.

"It's okay, mijo, we tried," Amá said to me as I drove her to church one day.

"Yeah, Amá, we tried," I said, hoping that between each of our admissions, at least one of us would actually believe it was worth it.

*

Even though I showed them pictures and X-rays and measurements, it wasn't spectacular enough. They wanted a show. They wanted this to have happened yesterday because then it would still be fresh. And if it was fresh, it meant it was real. But it was subtle to someone who didn't know her well enough to notice the particular gestures she made when it stung. She carried it every day of her life like a small weight heavy enough to drown you in water.

I almost wished that we hadn't heard about the U visa because then we wouldn't have gotten Amá's hopes up. In a final exasperated attempt to do something, I dialed the number of a congresswoman running for office who was referred to us by that nice lawyer who told us about the U visa in the first place. He said she might be able to help. I explained the situation to her over a brief phone call. She agreed that it might be good for her campaign to take a look at my mother's case. Immigration was *hot*. After a few emails, her assistants stopped responding. We ran out of choices, and the machinery of her departure began rolling back on track again.

Being split open by the hood of a car was not enough; being disabled and still having to work through the pain without medication was not enough; being beaten by her husband and not being able to report it was not enough; being separated from her family was not enough. When would it ever be enough?

To the government, it was our fault. Always our fault. I tried as hard as I could to see if I could read anything beneath the redacted lines in her report. Maybe that's where it said what they needed to hear in order to believe us. Maybe that's why they crossed it out.

9.

I still liked to spend afternoons in her bedroom, except I stopped brushing her hair. We were watching Tarantino's classic *Pulp Fiction*—dubbed in Spanish, of course. The voice actors were from Spain as well, and we laughed quietly at the way they pronounced certain words, at their registers of emotion that were always two notches above or below. She told me to close the door because the draft was hurting her arm.

The abscess on her wrist continued to grow, the glass continued to move through the pathways of her body like small stones on a trail to a murky pond, and the plates holding her bones made her hold her body close together in the winter, as if she was a doll that could come apart with one loose string.

Samuel L. Jackson popped up in flip-flops with his 9mm Star Model B, and John Travolta was squinting at the camera, flipping his ponytail, and Uma Thurman was dancing the twist and accidentally snorted heroin. How many bullets had Samuel L. Jackson fired since the movie started?

Everything in the movie looked like it was about to break open, but it was the moments in which they didn't that seemed most arresting. When you knew something could happen, but it didn't.

Their dialogue in Spanish sounded as if they were taking their time with it, as if they were in no particular rush to their inevitable demise. It was much faster in English—maybe it was the latent signature of Tarantino's anxiety. It felt like everyone died in the movie, even though they didn't. Vincent died, but he didn't really. It ended with him walking away from that diner, which was actually the beginning. I hated it.

It was a movie that began again and again. It wasn't going anywhere. And if someone asked, they would point and say, That, that right there, was what violence looked like, not the scene in the room, where a boy brushes his mother's hair, mapping all the ways an object could leave her.

[Fourth Movement as a Treatise on Love]

———

I was always falling in love, even as a child. As Apá tossed Amá against the wall, I wrote letters to my fourth-grade crushes at Park Avenue Elementary. As she crouched on the floor, I listened to songs of longing, songs that said things I still had yet to understand. Amanda Miguel cooed into my ear from the radio, "Mi buen corazón / Tú eres mi perdición / Me arrastras siempre al dolor / Me matas en cada amor / Ah ah ah . . ."

I drew hearts and the outlines of people on good white paper. As Amá flinched, I passed notes in class and waited nervously for a response. I said "I love you," "I love you so much." I said "Check the box, yes or no" and drew boxes.

As Amá smiled at me, I smiled back. We were both trying to figure out why love wanted nothing to do with us.

*

I never told my mother that I loved her. Never said those actual words. Instead, I held her hand as she sang to me and played with my hair. What did I know of love?

"Your father cares about us, it's just his temper," she would say, moving her fingers through my hair.

*

My father learned about love from his father, who learned it from his father's father. He learned that love was not something that you did, but something that you made sure someone remembered, for better or worse.

*

In Spanish, you don't usually say "Te amo," "I love you," to your mother. Because *amo* has other connotations of desire. Instead you say "Te quiero mucho," "I like you a lot." It's more common for a mother to say "Te amo" to a son or daughter. It's not reciprocal. Sometimes, even just saying the word amor when speaking to someone gets the point across.

"Amor, come with me to the store."

"Amor, it's nothing."

"Amor, tell your father the food is ready."

Amá knew all about the paper hearts in my room, but she didn't care. *Oh amor.* The trouble was that so did Apá; and he did.

*

"La Tragedia de Rosita" was a song that men outside my house would drink to late into the night, a song I had heard my entire life at weddings and Christmas parties and babies' christenings. It said a man loved a woman so much he killed her. "Tragedy and beautiful women make good company / ... 'Rosita, love of my life ... / how I have waited for this day / to tell you that I love you.' / The Rancher mocked Rosita / and threw her in the corn grinder / and the river swept her away."

10.

To our knowledge, there was nothing left we could do to keep Amá in the country; it was only a matter of choosing the date. However, perhaps because we had resigned ourselves to defeat and had stopped looking, too overcome with grief, we missed a crucial development in U visa legislation and we wouldn't find out about it until years later. A year after our U visa rejections, California Senate Assembly Bill 674 went into effect, which mandated all certifying agencies to sign off on U visa certifications in order to standardize the process and eliminate inconsistent protocols between jurisdictions. It ensured that more individuals had an equal opportunity to have their cases heard by USCIS and not be blocked at the local level due to personal bias or discretion from the authorizing agencies like law enforcement or DA's offices. It ensured that USCIS would "make the determination as to whether the victim has met the 'substantial physical or mental abuse' standard on a case-by-case basis during its adjudication of the U visa petition. Certifying agencies and officials do not make this determination." When our final rejection came, we shut down as a family, and perhaps if we would have held out a little longer, we would have caught this detail. Someone should have caught it, but no one did. If only we would have waited. If only we would have bothered to turn on the news.

*

During those months before her departure, we never actually said any word that indicated departure. We never said "leave," we never said "away," or "gone," or "after." At least not when directly speaking to or about her, or when she was in the room. The topic was in the air, and there was no point in repeating what would happen either way. We busied ourselves planning and preparing

Apá's house to accommodate Amá in order to keep our minds away from the clock.

We sent Apá money to renovate his house so she would be as comfortable as possible, as if that would somehow lessen the pain of her leaving. We should have probably left the house as it was; nothing we could have done would have made any difference. Our plan was to make Apá's house look as much like her house in California as possible, to make the transition easier.

Apá was obsessed with the past, and his house was an homage to that time. It was rough and rustic. I remembered clearly how the walls still had exposed cement without any plaster, the steel beams across the ceiling, and all the doors that looked like barn doors, with heavy welded latches instead of door knobs. The bricks lining the courtyard arches should have been plastered as well, and all along the walls were saddles and equestrian tack hanging from large hooks. It was a Brooklyn hipster's wet dream.

It was difficult to imagine Apá holding anything softly in his hands. It was as if his hands didn't know how to bend toward care, his body wasn't built for it. All of the pictures hanging on the walls were covered with fine cement powder from other construction he did to the house. None of them were pictures of Amá.

*

I always had to be careful about comfort whenever I called Apá to tell him our plans for how we wanted his house to change. "Isn't it good enough?" Apá would yell through the phone. One of the worst sins of poor Mexicans was arrogance. To save face, we had to compromise comfort in favor of feigning humility. But I wanted Amá to be comfortable, and I didn't care if people thought she was arrogant. I was determined to make Apá's house, which I assumed was Amá's house too, the biggest and best house in town. I wanted people to know that this wasn't a loss for us, that she was not returning in shame but rather in victory, and her house was a way to announce it. I recognized my father's pride brewing inside me, but I couldn't do anything to stop it because I couldn't understand Apá's ideas about "roughing it."

Why was it a good thing to suffer, according to him? The truth is, it wasn't. Apá only wanted to display suffering but not actually suffer. Amá, on the other hand, actually suffered but didn't let anyone see. There were times, however, when she could no longer hide it.

I was asking a lot from him. I was demanding that he take apart some of the things on his house he'd worked incredibly hard on.

Apá, you have to cut a door to the bathroom. . . . You have to fill in the two doors that lead out of that room and turn them into windows, you have to plaster the whole house, you have to put tile down, and make sure there is warm water. . . . How about we lower the roof, too? Isn't it too high? You have to make sure the sink has a good faucet. . . . Apá, let's divide the living room, let's make it smaller, let's make it look less like a ranch and more like a house.

*

Putting money in Apá's hands to renovate his house felt like throwing money into a well that you knew had no fortune left. Not all wells are lucky, not all wells are meant for receiving money.

Apá's property in fact did have a deep well in front of the house, near the sidewalk. Kids used it as a dump on their way to school. It was filled with broken bottles, and a few raccoons had fallen in and drowned. We gave him money to fix the well, to cover it up with a metal sheet and clean it up. He hoisted himself down with a rope and cleaned it. His hands were torn ragged from all the shattered glass at the bottom.

We knew sending him money would be difficult. We needed to send him enough to make the repairs we demanded, and it wasn't cheap, so we sent him money in small increments, only enough to pay the workers for a particular job.

He would call us to say how the progress was going and try to paint a picture for us in his head because he didn't know how to send picture messages on his phone. I tried my best to dictate exactly what I wanted, but he always put his own little spin on it, because he knew there was nothing I could do from California other than send him money. He called us a few times and said the money we had sent him wasn't enough, so we reluctantly sent him more. "Besides, it's for your mother," he said, and I had no choice other than to trust him.

11.

In the summer of 2015, Rubi and I flew to Zacatecas to see Apá again. Our plan was to help him with the renovations however we could, but really it was to test the waters. It was our last chance to see if he would treat Amá with care, before she left the U.S. to join him for good, or to find any excuse to make her stay with us. Although it was only my second visit to his house, it was starting to feel routine. When we arrived, I waved to the dog on the roof and opened the fridge. He took us through each room just like he had the first time, a proud look on his face for all the work he had done.

It was still the large and barren house I had seen two years before, but the finishing details made it look somewhat homey.

The furniture was thrown out onto the patio into a giant pile in order to tile the floors, and I could tell it had been there a while from the water stains along the bottom.

"It looks so different, doesn't it?" said Apá, with his arms still crossed and looking closely at us as we admired the interior stone-work and plaster. He wanted to show us that he was serious. He pointed to the ceiling. During construction, he'd asked the workers to put a limestone embellishment around each light fixture. It was almost Baroque in its flourishes. All said and done, it almost looked like a church, with the limestone wall surrounding the courtyard, the white plastered walls, and the ornate embellishments on the ceiling. I called Amá in excitement, describing each room to her, and I could imagine her on the other end, nodding away—though, through the phone, I didn't know in which direction she was nodding.

I had seen that kind of plasterwork before when I used to work in construction, building multimillion-dollar homes in the rolling hills of Northern California. It was sleek, not textured. It was a new kind of design that was trendy among homes that claimed a specific kind of Italian country rustic chic. It was minimalist and impossible to keep clean. It wouldn't last long like that. I could already see a few handprints on the walls where Apá had leaned for balance to take off his shoes.

Apá took pride in the fact that he didn't hire locals for the construction; instead, the people he hired were *expensive*. He smiled as he kept looking at us for a sign of approval.

*

After the first week, the excitement of being back in Tepechitlán started to fizzle, and I slowly acclimated to the rhythm, to the slow midafternoons and the raucous evenings in town, with its street food and ice cream parlors, its plaza where all the old men gathered to gossip, including my father. Apá didn't have a job, but he had a routine that kept him regular, and we followed along to the pace of his life.

I carried around a small piece of aloe vera with me to rub over my mosquito bites, which were dreadful and felt hotter than the rest of me in the summer. My aunts made fun of me and exclaimed "You're too dramatic." Which I read as, "You're too delicate—this isn't comfortable enough for you. You're too soft."

It didn't take long for my anxiety to catch up to me. I was dumb enough to think that it was like a jacket, like I could leave it behind in the U.S. I could feel it in my toes, and wherever the sun hit my body in the morning light as I lay naked on my bed, contemplating whether to get up or not. The room was empty except for Rubi and me.

As we tossed on the white linens beneath the tall ceiling, I imagined my mother's mornings. It was insufferably bright, especially with the new paint. I could feel the cold that came with the night still lingering in the air, looking for a dark place to settle. But there was none. I looked at Rubi, who had gone back to sleep, and pushed my head into my pillow.

I got up and walked through the new door Apá had cut into the wall at our request and into the bathroom, which was still a little dusty from the leftover grout. I washed my face with cold water and put on my clothes, shaking them first for scorpions.

*

I wasn't used to doing nothing, even though *nothing* was far from what we were doing. I forced myself to slow down and try to embody the pace of life that Amá would soon be living. Each day I pretended I was my mother, waking up, putting on my slippers, washing my face with cold water, and tried to imagine if she would want that.

I poured myself a coffee and sat on a comfortable chair in the courtyard beneath the morning sun. I took out a book to read, but I couldn't read. I liked the weight of it on my lap. Apá had already left. He always left before we woke up and always came back around noon for his midafternoon nap. There was a lot I should have been doing, but instead I sat in the sun.

If I left my chair I would probably break a window, I would probably throw myself through one. I ran out of my anxiety medication and couldn't get more. It was quiet despite the horns blasting outside. I gripped the armrest, trying to dig small holes with my finger. I couldn't shake the feeling that we were rushing things, that even if it *was* Amá's decision, what we were doing was wrong.

I couldn't bear to look at all of the furniture piled in a large heap in the courtyard. I couldn't stand seeing it get wet with morning dew, so I took a rag, a bucket, and decided to clean.

Good mezcal was cheap, so I uncorked a new fifth, dipped a rag in a bucket, and wiped down every square inch of the furniture. I turned the tables upside down and scrubbed even where no one would see that I had cleaned. By noon, Apá had returned, and he paced back and forth, insisting that it wasn't dirty, that I was wasting my time because it would be dusty again in a few days anyways. I pretended not to hear him.

*

Every morning Rubi and I made breakfast—eggs from the neighbor's hens with fresh handmade cheese, handmade tortillas, red salsa, and a cup of coffee. If it wasn't for my father, and if it wasn't the circumstances as to why we were there, I would say it was paradise. The flowers in the courtyard were in full bloom, the food was good, and I could have all the quiet I longed for. I could write, I could even take up sculpture. I could go find clay at the river and spend the whole summer forming a large piece of mud into a smaller piece. I wouldn't know what it was that I was making, and it wouldn't matter.

But I couldn't even read a book. What good was writing, what good did any of that do, if at the end of the day I knew the reason why I was cleaning?

Drinking made it easier to live with my father and see past all of the chaos he inflicted; it allowed me to see how small he was, how short his gait reached as he walked, and the way he looked down sometimes when he didn't know what to say.

Being among all of his possessions, among the materials that he made his life out of in his solitude made me think of all the times I had sent him ten or twenty dollars out of pity and wondered how many of those things he had bought with my money. I never told anyone how much I was drinking. It made it easier to imagine my mother's presence in her new home.

*

At night, we heard the loud thunder of large trucks speeding by, their lights swinging across the ceiling.

Every now and then, Apá's dog would run up to the edge of the roof, pound his feet, and bark. Apá was not one to name his animals, so I gave him a name—Capitán, the captain. The dog never came down from the roof. His claws were whittled down from running on the cement. He was a beautiful long-haired German shepherd. All night long we would hear him scattering around the roof, nervously listening for horses or people. I wondered if he ever slept. Eventually we got used to him and learned to ignore his long pleading that something or someone was coming.

Rubi and I made love in that room. It made sense to look for each other in the dark, more so than in the bright morning, when we could see from the gestures on our faces the feelings we were keeping from each other, and the pain in our release. But it was never really dark, even at night. The light from a large streetlamp rolled into the room like a steady stream. I knew it was night because it was cold, because the scorpions took their eventual roost in the ceiling, and because the dog kept whimpering at something in the distance.

*

There was still a lot of work to do on the house. But according to Apá, everything was done. He didn't think it was necessary to seal the grout on the tile spanning the entire house, but I insisted because Amá hated dust. Tepechitlán was nothing but dust. Her home needed to be a haven from the outside.

I gathered my tools and got down to work while Apá paced back and forth between the courtyard and the kitchen, looking down with uncertainty. Every so often he would mumble under his breath, "I don't know why you're doing that."

I could see myself in the reflection of the shiny tile. It was the color of Spanish clay, with small designs on the corners that fit together into a circle where four tiles met. I stroked my small brush with resin up and down. The repetition of the brush was soothing. For a moment, I forgot about my mother, about the fact that we hadn't eaten because we ran out of food and no one bothered to go get more. I forgot that the resin would probably chip off with time because I'd bought the wrong kind.

I started to see the house as my house too, even though it wasn't. I put a pillow on the floor to rest my knees and kept dipping the little brush in the bowl. After the second day, the routine became a kind of meditation. I turned on Apá's old stereo, which only played one cassette tape over and over, took a large sip of mezcal, and dipped the little brush.

For a few days I found consistency, which I liked, because I liked predictability. I woke up, made myself a coffee, mixed some liquor in, and found a nice spot in the courtyard where the sun was just starting to shine. I brought a few books with me and sat down with my mug and notebook. I still wasn't sure if I could bring myself to read, so I scribbled a few notes to save for later. I finished my coffee and sat there in silence.

Apá sat down in a chair next to me. Neither of us talked. I didn't know what he expected from me. We passed the silence back and forth like a gift we were reluctant to receive.

*

It rained often during the summer and the water leaked through the windows onto the living room floor, where it gathered in a small pool. As good as the house looked, it was as if it kept wanting to break down again, as if everything we did to fix it was a mistake.

Everything came apart around me. The house, the town, even the dog looked different. Tired. I was determined to make things better. If I could not change Apá, I could at least change his house. I bought five large tubes of caulking to seal the windows, put my music on, grabbed another bottle of mezcal, and got to work.

The rain fell sideways, and another thin trail of water leaked down the wall at each window joint. I realized the house would never be finished completely and that it was too late, that the wheels of this giant machine had already slowly started grinding forward, and I needed to move out of its way. Amá would not change her mind. Nothing I could say or do, or not say and not do, would make any difference. Either way, I squeezed the white latex caulking with as much care as if the leak could have been the difference between her staying or leaving. I rubbed my finger along the edge of the stone until it was soft and pink and tender.

"What are you doing now?" Apá asked, rather annoyed, standing behind me as I hummed along to my music and sipped from my coffee.

He was proud of his windows. He'd designed them himself and had his friend weld the frames together. He didn't like that I kept finding things wrong.

"I'm just sealing the windows, Apá—all the water is leaking into the house."

"That's fine, it's just a little water, don't worry about it," he said.

But I did worry. I was trying to patch up all of the bad, trying to keep the house from crumbling into itself. I poured large globs of caulking where the windows joined. Still the rain was coming in.

Another day. More tubes of caulking. More music. More cheap mezcal. More water.

The caulk took a day to dry. I went back the next day and threw a bucket of water against the window to test it out.

"Did it leak?" I yelled to Rubi, waiting on the other side.

"Yeah, it's all over the floor."

I let out a deep sigh and went inside to seal the windows from the other side. I moved on to other windows. The caulking came out softer from the tube beneath the warm sun, which made it more difficult to pour. People drove by and stared for a long time, and I pretended not to notice them, or the neighbors sweeping the same spot over and over as they stared to see what I was doing. They knew "Don Marcelo" had children and probably suspected I was one of them. My first visit was so short that no one even noticed I came and went. But this time, I had been in Tepechitlán for a month already, and people certainly noticed. They were weary of outsiders because of the violence that outsiders brought with them in the past, so I couldn't blame them for being suspicious of me.

I slathered the goo in every crevice I could find. It got on my hands, and my face, and my hair. The afternoon was hot, which meant the glue would dry quickly, so I waited beneath the shade of a mesquite in the neighboring lot that also belonged to Apá.

When the glue dried, I poured another bucket of water and called to Rubi on the other side.

"Yep," she said, reluctantly.

It was impossible. I bought more tubes of caulking, and instead of cutting just the tip, I cut the entire tube in half with a knife and used a spatula to cake it on with angry strokes, and still it leaked. I couldn't figure out why. The hardware store ran out of tubes, so I went to another one in a nearby town. I called back home for the family to wire more money.

"Just leave it," Apá said, that time with a little more anger in his voice.

But I couldn't. It gripped me. I wanted to do at least one thing right to make up for all of the other mess I felt partly responsible for putting my mother in. I felt that if I fixed the windows, I would some-how also fix everything else, that if I fixed his house, he wouldn't need her comfort as a substitute. Every day at the same time, a thunderous clap of rain would come, and with it, the small pool of water in the living room. I tried not to think about it, but I couldn't let it go. I walked by on my way to the kitchen and stared at it through the corner of my eye and quickly walked away. The windows were faulty by design; it was obvious Apá was not an engineer. No amount of caulking would keep the water out. They were large, they let in all of the sun—too much sun. I wanted to cover them up with brick so they would stop mocking me.

The outside wall on which the three large windows were mounted was made of limestone. By its very nature, limestone is porous. Even if I managed to seal the windows, the wall itself would eventually let all the moisture slowly seep through the plaster, which was already beginning to peel.

I should have known from the beginning that it was hopeless. The house was telling the story I was trying to avoid, the story my father denied—that life was still, after so many years, hard in Mexico, and would be so (again) for Amá. Frustrated, I climbed up to the roof and sat there for a long time. I didn't think of it as my town anymore, as I had when I longed to return for so many years. I played with the dog, who lay down next to me and gently licked my shoe. He was loyal and kind even though he hardly knew me. I decided to take him down. There was no point in having him protect the house if all he could do was bark. I tied a rope around his chest. He was heavy. He kept moving in the air as I lowered him. I was afraid the rope would wrap around his neck and he would choke. When he touched the floor he went straight to the small garden in the middle of the courtyard and sniffed the plants. He touched the dirt with his paws and rolled around in it, his belly raised to the sky.

*

In Tepechitlán, there were no large stores like Walmart where you could get all of your things at once. You went to the market for your meat and vegetables, you went to the cheese person for your cheese, the fish person for your fish, and so on. I got my hair cut by a woman who had been there ever since I was little and remembered cutting my hair as a child. "I can't believe it's you," she said as I sat on her old chair and she began cutting away. Life should have seemed quaint, simple, and stress-free if you had enough money to get by. We would be sure to send them enough money every month so they could live comfortably.

Comfortably.

Even though Apá had his occasional flares of frustration, I could see that he was always aware of how he behaved. We each knew we were being watched by the other, and we were careful.

Sometimes I could see his lips tightening as if to scream, but he wouldn't. I could see his body tensing up, but nothing would follow. It was obvious in how he carried himself; he held the steering wheel tight with both hands, kept looking in the rearview mirror even if there weren't any cars behind us.

I wanted to see the good, although I wasn't sure I was capable of seeing anything else anymore, simply in order to convince myself it was the right thing to do.

When I spoke with Amá on the phone, I spoke about the things she did not have in the U.S. that she would in Mexico. She would have her water brought right into her kitchen every morning in large jugs instead of hauling it herself from the grocery-store vending machines. Tortillas would be steaming hot and delivered daily on the back of a motorcycle, as would propane, as would the cheese— everything was fresh and made only a few miles away. I didn't tell her that sometimes the gas would go out, so you had to wait until the truck came by the next day to cook. I didn't tell her that Apá was using the same stove they bought thirty years ago that wouldn't light, and never cooked the food well. I didn't tell her that the water from the well we used to shower was calcified and would make her hair fall out. Nor did I mention the sad faces on the delivery boys, who looked numb from driving the same route day after day, collecting a few pesos in their outstretched hands and softly saying thank you.

*

As the days rolled on, Rubi and I spent more and more time alone in our room. We stayed longer in the mornings and made love like we had never before. We hardly ever slept with clothes on because it was hot, and even when we woke, I would prance around naked on my toes in that large sunlit room. I opened the windows and let a cool breeze saunter in through the lace curtains that matched the seafoam green of the windows, which still leaked, but I tried not to think about them.

Every morning I went to the windowsill to see a collection of bugs that had died overnight—roaches, centipedes, beetles, spiders, and sometimes a small scorpion. I picked them up and studied them carefully. I didn't know why they died near the window. Maybe they were drawn to the light coming from the streetlamps outside. I imagined that they knew something we didn't. Each night, another little cluster gathered.

I started writing again because I forgave myself and could at last, with a little alcohol, quiet the maddening guilt I had no business in keeping but kept nonetheless. I kept my flask nearby, and sat on my usual chair in the courtyard, where the sun's heat made me switch directions every ten minutes. I had gotten significantly darker, and the afternoon rain every day made my skin supple and tight.

But inside, I was still writhing. I drank to calm myself. I tried to believe that if I carried on with my day peacefully, if I took my coffee up to the roof with a book, that I could make it through summer, that life wasn't so bad there. I wanted to stay as long as I could to finish more work on the house, but also to continue observing Apá.

Apá and I got into fights, then made up, then fought again. Sometimes it wasn't about anything important, we just wanted to be right. We were the same person in different bodies, I feared.

Deep down, I knew that he was still the same person I knew growing up, but I managed to pretend I didn't notice, and perhaps this time I drank in order to keep it to myself, in order to *not* speak. I could see it in him when we went up to the ranch to herd cattle. How he unleashed himself on a scared calf whose hoof was caught on a fence, its large eyes bulging from its head, darting in all directions, its lips curled back to reveal its large crooked teeth, until someone finally told him to stop kicking and whipping the poor animal.

*

A cousin of mine got married during our last month in Tepechitlán. Apá waited outside the church during Mass because he still considered himself a devout Protestant and refused to attend a Catholic service. At the reception, el tamborazo started playing, so we hit the dance floor, and to my surprise, so did Apá. We danced all night. I had never seen him drunk. I took all of my cousins onto the dance floor, all of my aunts. No one knew the real reason I was in Tepechitlán and why I was so insistent on getting everyone off their chairs to dance. For one night I wanted not to have to tell my body what to do and just let something else do it for me. They knew Apá was fixing up his house and that I was helping him, but no one put two and two together that it was in preparation for Amá.

I moved from side to side for a cumbia, I rocked closely with Rubi at my arms during a norteña, and I jumped up and down when a tamborazo or a banda was playing. I was almost never sitting down, and my feet hurt from the new handmade boots Apá and I got fitted for three weeks prior, but I didn't care.

Apá requested a song from the mariachi and pounded his fists on the table when it started playing. "That's a real song right there, not those chingaderas they play today. Arriba Zacatecas!" he said as he cocked his head back and let out a loud yawp. I laughed and slapped him hard on the back, and he slapped me back with a heavy hand as well. The lights were spinning from the disco ball, and my feet kept moving. I remembered a line I had written earlier that day—"neither of us knew what we wanted but would do anything to have it." I didn't know what I wanted anymore.

When it ended, we stumbled out onto the street along with the band. It was a warm summer night, and the town, though small, was still buzzing with activity. Apá didn't know how to hold his liquor as well as me. He kept mentioning his ranch in the mountains, and the cattle, and the proper way to mount a horse. We walked home together like father and son, both drunk, one trying to forget and the other trying to remember.

[Fourth Movement as Swimming Lesson]

My father taught me and my brothers to swim by throwing us into the river.

"Use your hands! Use your feet!" he would scream at the edge of the water, his thick legs bulging out of his jean shorts. I wondered if I would ever have legs as thick and hairy as his.

My brothers and I thrashed in the water like three angry roosters. Roosters that were bred only to fight, who could kill each other with nothing but their bodies aimed toward the exact outline of their death.

I flailed in the water, trying to come up for air. I could see him a few feet away. I knew I wouldn't drown. I knew he wouldn't let me. But he said if I was to learn, I had to come close.

12.

Four months before Amá's departure, we considered everything that she owned.

We slowly started taking things from her. Each of her children kept something when they stopped by. Although she knew what we were doing, we didn't clear out her house all at once, nor did we do it fast. The number of her possessions shrunk in such a way that she hardly noticed they were gone. One day, there was no longer a frame, or a stool, or a couple mugs. It was like a bowl of holy water slowly being emptied over time when people dipped their fingers to make the sign of the cross as they entered.

Sometimes I took things when she wasn't there because I knew she wouldn't want to let them go.

I took her plants. First the small ones, then the large dracaena, which was almost as old as me, and much taller.

We thought that if we did it slowly, it wouldn't hurt as much. Still, no one talked about it directly. We took things as if we were borrowing them and would quickly bring them back; we believed we were doing her a favor.

But it wasn't always so indirect.

"It's fine, you can just buy another one in Mexico," I said, "I'll buy you another one in Mexico," and threw her toaster into a box to be donated. She wanted to keep more than she could take on the plane.

I almost wished that her departure could happen instantaneously, and that we wouldn't have to drag it out so long. That she would be gone from one day to the next, taken back to Mexico sometime in the night. As callous as that sounded, perhaps if it happened like that, we would be sedated by the blow of the impact. Our minds would be in a fog, and we would use other parts of ourselves to function, the parts that made certain things automatic, like eating and breathing, things that run only on adrenaline and not on any kind of thinking. Maybe that way we wouldn't know the difference between being asleep and being awake. That's what we wanted, to be at that place that time had healed without having to go through time.

But in truth, which one was worse: the long, sustained grief of waiting for the day of her departure, or an immediate vanishing? Each day was a new kind of suffering. Time moved fast and slow at once. I held my breath when I hugged her, and sometimes held it a little longer even when our bodies no longer touched. Sometimes it was hard to breathe.

*

Apá kept asking about the actual date she would arrive, but we could never give him a straight answer.

"Sometime in November for sure, Apá. . . . Sometime in January. . . . Sometime in February," I said to him on the phone. He wanted a definite answer. We kept pushing the date back because we needed a little more time, prolonging our small mementos, trying to decide when each of us had had what we needed to prepare for our sustained absence from her.

Everything felt like an ending. We wanted one last time—one more birthday together, one more Thanksgiving, Christmas, New Year's.

It was her birthday in October. She's a Libra. We decorated the backyard to surprise her. I hung bright ribbons above our heads and blew up matching balloons to make a kind of bouquet in the center of it all. Again, another ending, but we never called it that. It was her last birthday together with her children. And I thought, how did we manage this kind of unity, when everything around us was coming apart?

She turned the corner into the backyard, and we yelled "Surprise!" but it wasn't a surprise to anyone. We just pretended that things were still new to us. The food was served, and I sat on her lap to take a picture, even though I was heavy and the days of me on her lap were long over. We took lots of pictures, nobody said why. We ate and washed our plates. We sang happy birthday to you, happy birthday to you, happy birthday to you. She opened her gifts slowly and folded the tissue paper one by one as she always had done, to save for another occasion.

It felt like there wasn't any noise, like we were in a show and someone had hit the mute button. We could see our mouths moving, our heads thrown back in laughter, but nothing came out.

Then out of nowhere, either to change the mood or because Amá saw the moment differently than we did—as one of joy—she threw a fistful of cake across the room. She smeared another piece of cake on her oldest son, who in turn grabbed another piece and ran to smear it on me. We all jumped for the cake and grabbed fistfuls and threw it at each other. We couldn't stop laughing. We ran back and forth through the backyard, darting past each other with cake and ice cream in our hands. Our hair was thick and sticky with frosting. Our faces looked like failed clowns on a Tuesday night, but the difference was that we were laughing. No one was spared, not even the kids. There was cake on the ceiling, frosting on the walls, and ice cream, so much ice cream. Our sides hurt from laughing so much, and as soon as we settled down, we would erupt into raucous laughter again when we saw each other's faces still covered with cake.

When we were done laughing for good, we each took our respective sighs, those deep sighs you take when nothing is left inside of you, the kinds of sighs that come up from the deepest wells of your body. We spent the rest of the night cleaning, chuckling a little here and there as we gawked at all the places cake could hide. We still felt the residue of that primal strumming in the depths of our stomachs that could at any moment tip us to the edge of uncontrolled laughter again, and did. It was like the silence after a single piano key is struck, which isn't really silence but something else—our memory, perhaps, carrying the note long after it's actually ended.

*

I didn't know how we set a date, but eventually we did: February 22, 2016. It almost felt good to see a date to that thing which we couldn't name. I could see it in my head and prepare myself. I could give it a shape, a substance. I remembered a line of a poem I had written years before—"It is possible to only see things that have been given names." When I wrote it, I didn't know how much it would come to mean; I didn't have a container for it. But it finally made sense—it had a name, February 22 took up space. There was a weight to it; a shadow.

*

Her house was a repository. She'd kept everything over the years because she didn't know if one day she would need it for immigration, meaning that one day she might have to prove her presence, prove that she was actually here for all those decades—a utility bill, a rent receipt, a check stub, or a painting I made in the second grade. *Prove her presence*. But none of that was needed anymore.

We sat down in her living room with boxes stacked in the middle and went through them, paper by paper. It got to the point where we had to begin clearing things out. With each cleaning session, her house got bigger and bigger. It started to look empty as soon as the larger furniture was gone. Soon there would be no trace that she was ever there except for the smudges on the doors, the walls, and the grease stains on the stove that no amount of rubbing would erase. Seventeen years we'd lived in that house, paying our rent month after month, and never once was Amá late.

On the day we were to hand over the keys, she sat on the driveway, the spotted sun through the branches speckled over her, while we finished loading the last truck. I did one last walk-through of the house. Before I closed the door, I ran to my old room, and inside the closet I wrote down in a dark corner, with a thick black Sharpie, "We were here." If they painted over it, I wouldn't care. The words would still be there beneath the paint, even if no one could see them.

She reduced everything she owned to four suitcases. That was all she could take on the plane. In them was the inventory of our madness. We spent hours, days, helping her decide what she truly needed, which was a difficult question to ask. In 1993 she came to the U.S. by foot, with nothing but the clothes on her back, and she would leave through the air with a little more than that. What did she have to show for all of it in the end?

"Mis hijos," she said, by which she meant that we, her children, grown, bearded, our own hair beginning to gray, were what she had to show for it all. It was our bodies, the fact that we were breathing, alive, that we were beautiful in whatever kind of sun. It was the fact that she was alive, that she had made it.

We drove to my house, where she would stay for the last three weeks. I thought about my body, how it took up the space around it, how it was here. We had always been *here*, but it wasn't enough.

Prove her presence.

I went to the bathroom and touched the tattoos on my body, and rubbed the piercing on my nose. It was a screw stud. Amethyst. Amá hated my tattoos and piercings. I grabbed the nose ring and tore it off. If I could, I would have torn off my tattoos.

Prove her presence.

Welcome to America.

The blood in the sink was pink, then red, then pink again. Then gone.

13.

The day before her departure, we gathered for a family portrait. We got dressed up as if it was Easter. It helped that it was a Sunday, made it feel like we didn't have to go out of our way just for this, that it was something we happened to stumble upon in our Sunday best. We wanted to do what every picture does, hold things in place.

Still, no one said why we stood together and posed for a picture.

"Okay, now everyone smile," I said as I set the timer on the camera and ran back to get into frame. I never knew if other people hold their breaths when they take a picture, but I always did. I tense up a little, hold my body straight and tall. My ballet teacher once told me to dance as if there was a string on the top of my head pulling the lines of my body upward.

"Say cheese, say whiskey."

Click.

I felt like I was dancing. We squeezed and arranged close in a different order for another picture, and Amá's thick coat brushed against my arm, her weight next to mine, next to everyone else's, was unbearable. We froze and released. Another picture, froze and released. I don't think we ever saw the pictures. I don't think we ever developed them.

We kept taking pictures on our phones and played with an app that swapped our faces. The app let me try on different templates. As a child, then bald, then as an old man. "How would you look old," said the app.

We all tried on our old faces. Was that how our mother would see us the next time we all gathered together? I had never considered the bags under my eyes, the wrinkles starting to branch out from the corners of them like thin trees in early spring. What would blossom from their tips?

Change happens so slowly that I never noticed, for example, when exactly it was that Amá began to hunch over a little, or how much gray hair was powdered at the edges of her temples. Those changes came over us like a slow song that put us to sleep—we never knew when exactly we went from being awake to being asleep. But there we were, dreaming, not knowing that we were dreaming.

*

After the photoshoot, I took Amá back to my house, where she was staying in my guest room, which was crowded with her four suitcases. She sat on her bed and read the Bible, as she did most nights before going to bed.

"Good night, Amá," I said, and kissed her on her cheek.

"Good night, mijo."

The next day I would take her to the airport, where she would board the plane for Guadalajara. I headed upstairs and sat alone for a minute. I was sure this was the right choice. But if it wasn't the right choice, it still wasn't too late. She was still here, she could still say no. I didn't want her to say no. As much as it pained me, I wanted her to leave because I wanted a definite ending to whatever it was we had started twenty-something years ago. This was it, her grand finale. She would collect her prize at the other side.

What was her prize? To return to a man I'm not exactly sure she ever loved? But it was more than just their reunion. Much more. It was about her not having to work any longer. It was about her not having to still fear immigration in old age, to not have that looming sense of surveillance always following her. I didn't want her to be undocumented anymore; I wanted her to feel like she belonged in the country in which she lived. If that couldn't happen in the U.S., then we would make it happen in Mexico.

We were tired of waiting and tired of having the same conversations over and over about social security numbers, about new updates to the immigration law that never came, about raids in the news. I didn't want her to take any part of it anymore. None of us did, and neither did she.

Her prize was peace of mind. But it wasn't free.

In the end it was not our choice to make, but hers. I went back downstairs and walked over to her room, where she was still sitting on her bed, reading her Bible. I came down to make sure she had everything ready, but I really just wanted to talk.

"Are you ready?" I said. She looked up at me through her glasses. Her eyes were red.

"Ya, everything's ready." Her four suitcases were stacked near the door, and her small carry-on was placed carefully on top of them. She'd decided to take pictures, a smoothie blender, clothes, a few porcelain figurines that held sentimental value, shoes, coats, a coffee grinder, dresses for church, some linens, a few pieces of jewelry, soft towels, paper and pens, and other small items.

"Do you have your tickets ready?" I said. I don't know why I said the plural, *tickets*. It was out of instinct. It was the plural: two tickets, one to go and one to come back. She was the singular, a one-way ticket. I wondered if she picked up on my mistake too, if she knew I took a slight pause after saying that final *s?* I kissed her on her cheek and said good night another time.

I couldn't sleep that night, but I knew that would happen, so I took a sleeping pill to help me, and another cup of vodka, and a Xanax just in case because I couldn't stop my fingers from trembling. Soon enough, I could feel the lull slowly creep its way inside me. My body began to tingle at the tips, but it was not soothing. That night, I was conscious of my body leaving consciousness. In those last moments, I thought of the TSA at the airport looking down at Amá's one-way ticket, her Mexican consular card she used as ID shining against their black light.

I fell off the edge. I dreamed I was trying to put on a shoe, but it wasn't the right one, which was my mother's dream. I needed to get onstage for the show, but I still had a missing shoe. The director was waving at me to hurry. I walked out to the middle of the stage and wept. I was blind again. I could hear everyone in the audience applauding, as if that itself was the show, as if they knew that the play was scripted like that—me weeping onstage, still trying to look for my other shoe, kneeling on the ground and tapping the floor gently with my hands.

[Fourth Movement as ESL]

No ghosts ever appeared to me or followed me around, even though I knew they were real. There are just some people who are meant to be haunted, and others are meant to move through the world disbelieving them. I was neither.

"He needs interaction, otherwise he'll have problems later in life," my first-grade teacher, Mrs. Conejo, said to Amá, who looked at her nervously.

"Don't ever tell them anything," Amá said to me, over and over. It was easier to keep quiet than to make up stories about myself. I made imaginary friends from that quiet, which were not ghosts, but kind of. No one would know the difference.

14.

It was the day of her departure, and still no one said the words we were all thinking. What exactly those words were, I wasn't sure, but they were on the tips of all our tongues. We could see them on each other, even if we couldn't see them on ourselves.

"Let me do your hair," said Amá's only daughter, and Amá sat on a small ottoman in front of her, cradled between her thighs. She brushed her hair and curled it. She took her time to make sure Amá looked pretty, and would stop now and again to pick it up and let it slowly fall on her shoulders. Each brushstroke was steady and with purpose. No energy wasted.

Without intending it, we all sat around them in a circle and stared, as if we were staring at a campfire, mesmerized by the light and the heat that would burn us if we came too close. It was their moment, and their moment only.

"There you go, see how pretty you look," she said to Amá.

Still, no one said anything.

We sat silent in my living room, unsure of what to say because no one wanted to initiate any forward movement. Finally someone said "Okay" and patted their palms on their lap quickly, which meant that it was time. That was the first time any of us admitted it. It was the first time we confirmed to each other that indeed it was happening, that it wasn't just something in our heads, even though we could see it all happening in front of us as we cleared her house, as we packed her suitcases, as we posed for a picture. It brought to the surface our collective grief, which we had all kept quietly inside because we knew if one of us broke, we would all break. We did it for each other.

The puzzle in our mouths spilled out, but it wasn't words, it was sound.

No one was hiding anymore. It was as if in the months leading up to that moment, we had been lost in a labyrinth, and we could hear each other but we could not see each other. We knew we were all there from our voices, but we couldn't be sure. And suddenly the walls lowered. We could see each other, and we could see that each of us was weeping. We had always been weeping, but it was easy to hide it when walking alone through the maze, saying to each other, "I'm okay." But it was then that we all saw each other for the first time. We saw how small and wrinkled we had become. We saw how much we had changed because we rarely encountered this side of ourselves. I couldn't remember the last time I saw my brother weep, but I realized that his grief left his body differently than before. He had changed. We had all changed. We greeted each other in our despair and held our faces. *Brother, how much you've changed since we last cried together.*

We loaded the luggage and took separate cars to the airport. We drove slowly. We appreciated every red light. Every stop, every tractor trailer that merged in front of us. For once, how great it would have been to be pulled over, for the cop to lean into our windows and ask for license and registration. What would happen if she missed her flight? Would that give us the courage to state the obvious? That despite her departure seeming inevitable, there was nothing wrong with staying.

We'd booked the latest red-eye we could find so that we could sleep on the plane and not have to see the world as it happened. We arrived at the airport and parked all of our cars near each other. Everyone took a bag, or a suitcase, or held one another; either way everyone was carrying something. Everyone had a hand in the decision, as if each of us was carrying a piece of her. We knew if one of us broke again and said no, don't go, that the rest would probably follow, and if the rest followed, Amá would see our pain and stay. But no one budged. Was it pride? We all swallowed that thick crow and kept moving toward the entrance, looking at each other, hoping the others, even one of the grandchildren, would break.

It was still early, so we waited at some tables. Still, we kept looking at each other to see if anyone would speak out against her decision, but no one did. We bought coffee and talked about how hot the water was. We stayed until we could stay no longer. Finally we broke, but in the wrong direction. Our seams tore through the paths we had never experienced. We hugged. We didn't know if this would be the last time we would all be together like this. Certainly it would be the last time we all looked the way we did together, still young.

Amá was still standing. We were all still standing. None of us had bent from the weight of it all. We were strong. At least four generations had prepared us for moments like these.

We couldn't take all the luggage through the escalator, so we walked over to the elevator to take us to the next floor. I pressed the button to call the elevator down and the small red light lit up. The doors opened and I took my mother inside, holding her by her arm, which dangled limp off her body in pain, just as it always did. She didn't turn around to watch the doors close with everyone else stuck on the other side. The doors closed.

*

It was as if someone had suddenly turned on gravity, as if that entire time we were actually floating in midair, unknowingly. Her body bent in half when the doors shut, and she screamed. I had never heard my mother make those sounds. I didn't know she was capable of them.

It was more of a wail than a scream—sustained. It was a wail in which all of the words were the same even though they weren't. It sounded like she was saying the same thing over and over, "I'm sorry, I'm sorry, I'm sorry." What she actually said was "This is stronger than me."

"I'm sorry, I'm sorry, I'm so sorry. This is stronger than me."

I don't know if she ever got back up, not completely at least. The whole way through the airport, it felt like she was still crouched over.

Both of us were a little closer to the earth, even though in about an hour we would be a few miles above it. Just before going through security, I turned to Amá and said, "Amá, it's not too late to turn around, are you sure?" But I knew it was too late. From that moment, the distance started growing. From that moment forward, her children would live mostly in her memory.

We passed through TSA as if we were floating downstream in a river. There was nothing in our way to snag us, nothing to stop us. The agent waved us on, she raised the metal in her arm and the X-ray machines waved us on, the drug dogs waved us on, even the walls, if they had hands, would have waved us on. That's how easy it was to return.

[Fourth Movement as Velvet]

My younger brother and I pretended to be deer. We held our hands on our foreheads like antlers and charged through the tall grass in the backyard. "Do they run like this?" asked my younger brother, antlers in full velvet, the kind of velvet they tear away by rubbing against a tree. "Yes, like that, just like that," I said to him and hid in a small cave made by the tall grass, where I picked up grasshoppers and squeezed them between my fingers until they vomited a little black bead of tar from their mouth and eyes. I watched them squirm even long after being dead. There were so many grasshoppers I could hardly take a step without crunching them beneath my shoe. And all of their legs kept jittering even without their bodies, like a silent prom dance in the daylight. "And do they drink like this?" asked my brother, bending his small body to drink from an invisible river. "Yes, just like that." I said as I lay there, in the field where grasshoppers jumped all over me, burying myself in imaginary velvet, squeezing all those little thoraxes until they popped and wiping them off on my shirt.

15.

We landed at the Guadalajara airport in the morning. So far it was my third trip to Mexico, and the changes in my body and mind that I experienced the first time felt like they happened without me, automatic. I had new things to worry about other than myself. Amá held up her bad arm with her good arm as we exited the plane, the same smell of wet earth mixed with diesel wafted in.

"Are you okay, Amá?" I asked her.

"Yes, mijo, I'm fine," she said, her eyes still bloodshot from the night before.

I looked ahead and saw the good that would come out of this. I saw her at her home in Tepechitlán, a home which she owned and would never pay rent. I saw her getting a real ID from a country that claimed her as a citizen. I saw her walking to the mercado in the morning, sifting through ripe tomatoes and jars of fresh honey and bananas for her morning shakes with the blender she carried in her suitcase. I saw her taking her afternoon strolls and watering her plants in her garden and going to the bank to pick up the money we sent her for the week. I saw her waking up late and grinding her own coffee to drink outside in the sun, just like I had when I was there. Nowhere in this vision did I see Apá. I saw her happy.

She handed her passport to the agent, who asked what her purpose was and how long she would be staying in Mexico.

"I'm here to see family, and I don't know how long I'll be staying," she said to the stoic agent, who slammed a stamp of arrival on Amá's passport before she could finish talking.

*

"There, I see him," I said to Amá, who was standing on her tiptoes to see over the people better. It was like déjà vu from my first trip—

Rubi and I landing in Guadalajara, greeted by Apá in a palm sombrero. In the distance was Apá in his usual white palm sombrero. It was the first time they had seen each other in twelve years.

There must have been a time when they loved each other. Maybe he loved her when he first came to the U.S. in the 1970s and left her behind to care for their firstborn, when he would write letters to her, and she in turn would write back. There must have been something more than commitment, or social norms, that held them together for so long, but I couldn't understand it, or I couldn't see it. It was their own distinct language. Whenever they fought, she always reassured us by saying "Don't worry, I know your father."

They drew close and embraced each other. He wrapped his shawl over her and held her in the middle of the aisle. Her arm still dangled to the side. Wrapped together, they looked like one person crouching down, holding their stomach, in laughter, or pain, or both.

The intercom above announced something, but it was muffled. There were small groups just like ours, holding each other closely together, always with one person in the middle letting everyone embrace them. The scene felt familiar, like I knew exactly what would happen next. The small huddles dissipated, soon to be replaced by new ones.

They didn't talk at first, just looked at each other's faces. How much each had changed. They forgot I was there, they forgot they were in the airport and began wandering away toward the door, holding each other still side by side as they walked, her good arm wrapped around his waist and his arm around her shoulder.

It was at that moment that I was somewhat convinced that things would be okay, that this was the right choice. Maybe he *had* changed. I was determined to see it in his face, how he looked at her and how she looked at him. They needed each other the way they did in those first years before the kids arrived, when it was just them in that lonely house on the mountainside with a single room, a dirt floor, and a plastic tarp roof.

With Amá there, Mexico felt like home at last. How long I had waited for that moment. There was no need to go back to that abandoned house in the mountain where she was born and tear off my clothes, to lie on the dirt floor in the sun.

*

Inside the taxi, Amá's bad arm was pressed against Apá, who was still holding his arm over her. He had not let go of her since she arrived. Did he hold her like he cared, like he was afraid she would be lost again?

Amá turned around and smiled at me. It was sincere. I knew she was still thinking about her other children back home and what they were doing. But she smiled because she wanted to show me that everything would be okay, she was reassuring me that it was the right choice. *Don't worry, I know your father.*

On the flight, she said, "I'll tell you everything," by which she meant she would tell us if he hurt her. I was desperate to believe her.

*

Soon enough we were home. *Home.* After the three hours of those winding roads, after stopping at a town halfway for breakfast, after anticipating this moment for years, we arrived at Apá's house, which was now Amá's house too. No more renting, no more landlords, no more "Don't use thumbtacks because we won't get our deposit back." Each brick was hers, and the dirt beneath was hers too.

Amá stepped out of the van. She looked around with dismay. It was the dry season, and on top of that, the government had burned the edges of the roads to prevent fires. The earth was scorched. The air was dry. The vegetation was dead. I could feel it in my throat, and my lips were parched.

I knew there was a dry season and a rainy season, but I had always visited during the rainy season, when the pastures were green, the cows were fat from all the new grass, and the flowers were in abundance.

"Well, this is it, your new home," said Apá, anxiously looking at Amá for any reaction.

"Yeah," was all she said, raising her eyebrows high above her forehead.

We entered the courtyard, which was dirty. Apá lifted up his hands as if he was in church, or making the gesture for a touchdown, and said, "What do you think?"

And Amá said, "It's big," and I nudged her forward.

We entered into the large common area, and I could see Amá staring up at the tall ceiling and shrinking a little from the enormity and emptiness of it all. All of his pleas had finally worked: there we were, showing Amá her new house. *He won.*

We took her room by room and showed her all the work we had done over the summer—the new tiled floor, the plastered walls, the new door between her room and the bathroom, and even the windows Apá had fashioned.

After a while I stopped looking at her face. I didn't want to see what I knew was there deep down, regret.

Her arm was throbbing with pain from the trip. It hung even lower. She couldn't lift her shoulder to take off her coat, so I helped her with it. Apá looked on, unsure of what to do—whether to help or just let me do it. He reached, but I flicked my palm and he eased away. "I got it," I said.

*

Amá hadn't seen her sisters since we left Tepechitlán in 1993. We drove into town, and Amá pointed at all the things that had changed. Things people who never left hardly noticed because it changed gradually.

We had become experts in the language of reunions. Amá's sister Beatrice was out in her garden, watering her dahlias and strawberries.

"Hola, tía, I'm back," I said.

"Hola, mijo, it's so good to see you again. I didn't know you were coming."

"Yeah, tía, and you'll never guess who I brought," I said, pointing to the truck.

Beatrice squinted, but she couldn't make out who was in the passenger seat. The windows were dirty, and there was a glare from the sun. She put on her glasses and walked over.

"No," she repeated over and over. "No, it's not her, it's not her, is it?" she said as her eyes welled up with joy.

Amá stepped out into the clarity of the bright morning. Next to each other, I could tell they had lived different lives. The sun in Mexico felt harsher. Beatrice, though only a few years older than Amá, looked worn down. Her hair was almost completely white, and her hands were spotted with the smudges of old age. Amá's face looked nourished, moisturized, and still had the remnants of her youth. I could hardly believe that they were only two years apart. They'd had similar lives: they'd both worked, they both had husbands who were distant, and they each gave birth to about the same number of children. The difference was that one stayed behind and the other left in 1993. "What were you thinking, getting pregnant. You can hardly feed the kids you have," Beatrice had said, all those years ago. How strange that a small conversation, a single sentence, could change so much. I looked at Beatrice's children, my cousins, and saw myself in them. They were happy, they lived within their means, they were all close, and now that the grandkids had come, they were even closer.

I imagined my life had Amá never left. Maybe I would have married at a much younger age. I would be working at a restaurant, or selling at the market, or as a bricklayer, which is what many of the men in my family did, which was noble and honest work but back-breaking. How strange to think that I would have never known English, that Spanish would be my only tongue. Maybe I would be happier than I ever was now, tending a small flock of sheep and a horse, fixing an old dirt bike on the weekends. I kept thinking, *What if . . . what if . . . what if . . . ?*

Beatrice and Amá held each other for a long time, much longer than Amá had held Apá. She needed her sister. From now on, my siblings and I couldn't provide what her sisters, her new friends, the new grandnieces and nephews could—a touch.

I thought I knew something about distance, something about separation, but it began to dawn on me just how little I knew. Yes, Apá was away, and yes, there were times that I missed him more than others, but his departure and Amá's departure were nothing alike. Watching Amá and Beatrice embrace formed a large knot in my throat and sank deep into my stomach. I would soon learn the real price of distance. I would soon learn exactly what it meant to be away. But for the time being, I brushed it aside. This was a happy occasion.

We went from house to house to see all of her sisters. Each time was the same—disbelief, followed by tears, followed by hugs, and finally laughter. Everything was new, everything was exciting, which also meant that for the moment everything was fine. All of the sisters gathered for a picture. We took so many pictures that you could probably put them together for a movie, and their movements just might make sense together. Her sisters cooked whatever Amá wanted on that first day, and Amá wanted anything that reminded her of the days when she had nothing, of the days that made her leave Tepechitlán in the first place.

*

I wasn't just there to say goodbye. I had a purpose. We saved up in order to buy her all new appliances to make her life a little easier. We went to all the furniture and appliance stores in town as well as the next bigger town over, looking for the right things. We didn't care if people thought we were presumptuous or if they thought my mother was too good for whatever Apá already had in his house. They didn't mean anything to us. Multiple hauling trucks reversed into Amá's driveway to deliver the large shipments of sofas, a stainless-steel fridge shipped from the U.S., a new stove, a bedroom set, other kitchen appliances like a microwave, coffeepot, pans, and other bric-a-brac for the house. The big trucks lumbered back, knocking over a few potted plants, holding up traffic in the narrow streets while the neighbors looked on.

"Are you sure we can afford this?" Amá said at the furniture store, looking at the price tag of another armchair I thought she would like for when she read her Bible.

"Don't worry, Amá," I said.

Buying her things made us feel better—new curtains, frames in which to hang her pictures of us, area rugs, even a new Whirlpool washer and dryer. And again, men came in with their large trucks to the house to drop off the larger appliances. They dollied them in and whistled as they walked through the door, saying, "You got a nice house, ma'am."

"Thank you," she said. And it felt good to hear her speak of it as her house.

Every time I ran out of money, I called back home for another wire and stood at the bank, uneasy, as people pretended not to look at each other. Most of the town ran on U.S. dollars earned by people working up north who would wire it back to their family. It was one of the main reasons Tepechitlán still existed. Every day the line of people would form, waiting for the money earned by distance and sacrifice.

Apá started growing more frustrated with each new purchase. Why now did we suddenly have enough money for a new washing machine, when he had been asking about one for years? Why now did we suddenly have enough money for all the things to make their lives easier?

"We don't need a new washer, what's wrong with the one we have already?" he said as I was hooking up the new washer to the wall.

"Dad, that washer doesn't work, it's coming apart and it spills water all over the floor," I said. It was the one I had shipped to him years before with money I earned over the summer, when I was a teenager.

"There, all done," I said and turned on the new washing machine, but he complained that it didn't wash like the old one and made a rough gesture with his hands, moving them back and forth like an angry bus driver on a winding road, alluding to the violent thrusts his old washer would make on the spin cycle.

"This one hardly makes any noise," he exclaimed, "is it even on?"

"Yes, Dad, that's the point, it's on but it's quiet," I said.

"I don't know, I don't think it works as good as my other one, which would thrash the clothes around like this," he said, and made the same winding gesture with his arms.

"I know, Dad," I said. "But this is for Mom." And with that he was silent.

The last thing we bought her was a cell phone with service to the U.S. I sat with her on a park bench at the town's plaza. We held the phone between us as I showed her how to turn it on, how to call, how to message. I wanted her to be a single button click away, to seem like she was right there next to me. It was our lifeline.

"Do you understand, Amá?" I said.

She nodded. "Yes, mijo, I get it."

We sat there going over the phone's other features as we ate a mango with lime and chili powder sprinkled on top. The kiosk in the center of the plaza was made of lime and volcanic stone, the same stones Apá used to build his house. It was pretty, almost a coral pink, and it aged well.

We made a video call to the U.S. just to try it out. In the little screen her only daughter appeared. The phone came in and out of service, sometimes freezing the image into a collage of disjointed pixels—our faces frozen in a blur. Amá smiled and waved into the camera, and her daughter waved back. She could almost reach out and touch her.

I ended the call and Amá lowered the screen. "This is good," she said.

It wasn't as great as I had hoped it would be, the connection wasn't as strong. They said in a few years they would install more towers for faster service, but that was just a rumor going around town. I knew we probably wouldn't video chat much in the future. We finished our mangoes and drank the sour lemon juice collected at the bottom, puckering our faces, and Amá said we looked like the disjointed pixels on the phone, which made us laugh a little.

"I'll come see you often, Amá," I said.

"I know you will, mijo, I know you will."

I held her hurt arm as we walked around the plaza, gently massaging it as we walked. She was still wearing brand-new clothes; it would take her another week or two before she had to wear the same thing twice. By then things wouldn't be new, things would settle into their normal rhythm, as they had when I spent my summer with Apá. Nothing I saw in that week could be trusted because everything had that newness about it, and that newness could hide what was actually beneath the surface. *Don't worry, I'll tell you everything.*

*

On my last day in Tepechitlán with her, sitting on her couch, looking at old pictures of us, it didn't feel like a beginning or an end. It felt like a middle—worse still, it felt like we were going nowhere, like we were a large engine capable of great speeds but perpetually idle, perpetually shifted into park. But wasn't that what we wanted? For once to stay still?

I knew that if I had a child, she and her grandparents would be strangers to one another. If they ever did meet, my child would cower in the face of her own grandmother, and they would probably not understand each other. Despite my greatest efforts, my child would most likely not know Spanish, and Amá and Apá would not know English. In person, there were other ways to communicate— with your body, with food, with music. But through the small screen in a video message, what other ways of communication existed beyond waving, and saying "Hi" and "Sí" and "No," if that was all the language you had in common? Yes, we would visit, and try to visit often, but my child would always be someone else, someone missing.

To my child, my parents would simply be those people with whom I would spend Sunday afternoons talking on the phone. And I can imagine myself passing the phone over, angrily commanding her to talk with her grandparents, and I can imagine her refusing, just like I did. It would start all over again.

I packed my things and slid my suitcase next to the door. It was a way of announcing something I could not bring myself to say out loud. Amá sat on the edge of the sofa, which was still new and hard. She looked down at the new tile. She looked even smaller in that great room.

"I'll be back to see you often, Amá."

"I know, mijo. Don't worry, I know your father."

In a way, leaving then was harder than when she left the airport. Perhaps because I was still with her, I hadn't officially performed my goodbye, my departure. Everyone else back in the U.S. had already gone through this. I, however, merely witnessed the separation. But now it was my turn. How did the rest of the family do this without breaking in half? How could they find strength in their legs to carry them back to their cars, to drive the hour back home, and to lie down on their beds at night?

I hugged my mother, but she couldn't bring herself to lift up her arms.

"Tell me everything, promise me," I said into her ear.

"I promise, mijo, I'll tell you everything."

She didn't turn around when I stood up. She sat on her couch with her back to the door. I had performed a version of this goodbye with her many times before—the first night I didn't come home from a party, the night I was married, when I left for Michigan. But none of it could have prepared me for how to leave her like this. My family, all we did for generations was leave each other. To depart was in my blood, to live longing in the absence of another was ingrained into me. And yet.

With her arm still dangling to the side, she looked older. What about her would be different the next time I came? Would she shy away from the camera whenever cousins would come over to take pictures to bring back for us? I walked to the door, and she still didn't turn around. I was doing, perhaps, what my body was preparing its entire life for—the gift of its hardest leaving. My mother was better at it than me, or perhaps she'd had harder ones than this. She could do it while sitting still, on the edge of a couch, facing away from me. She could do it without saying a word. She was doing something with her hands, cradling her grief. She held it all in her small body. My leaving was still in its infancy. It made loud noises, it would board a large airplane and pound the walls of a bathroom stall, staining it with a little blood until security was called.

Amá was doing it how my great-grand-father León had done it, how her father Jesús had done it, and how I would one day learn to do it. Apá took my luggage and walked to the truck. As I walked through the door, I turned around one last time to see if she was looking, but she wasn't. I turned and closed the door behind me.

16.

I didn't say anything to Apá on the way back to the airport.

[Fourth Movement as Ethics and Juice]

I used to sell oranges door to door with Apá, and I used to think it was embarrassing. I wasn't ashamed, just embarrassed. There's a difference. He never had a steady job, but you could say he was a hustler of household wares, fruits, and old tools we also sold at flea markets. We drove from town to town, sweeping a hundred miles in a day, hitting all the familiar Mexican neighborhoods down I-5 through Northern California. He always carried a pocketknife to give people a taste—the pulp bursting out as if it was wound up inside like a spring.

He taught me how to hold money, "like a man," as he would say. He licked his large thumb with a stack of singles in his palm, flipping them faster than my eye could keep up. It looked like a small fan spinning in his hand. I licked my skinny thumb just like him and pretended to count. It took a while, but I got pretty good. One day we bought a truckload of sweet corn and sold it all in a day—my pockets were bursting with singles, and I liked to take them out and break change when people paid with a big bill. He bought me a small knife so that I too could spring open an orange. I cut myself, and before the blood had a chance to erupt, he said "Don't you dare cry."

Sometimes, when we spread out to knock on doors, and if I was far enough away from him that he wouldn't notice, I would sell a sack of oranges and keep a few dollars for myself. A finder's fee. I knew what work meant, and I figured I deserved even a little for myself.

"I know what you did. Don't steal from me, you're only stealing from yourself," he said later that day as he winked at me, took a large bite from his Whopper, and held out his hand, demanding the money back.

17.

I stood by myself in a Manhattan ballroom on Park Avenue, and the purple ambient lighting from the large chandeliers rested in midair. The light felt heavy and thick, like I was breathing it, like I was wading through water when I made my way from one end of the room to the other, waving slowly at friends. It had been exactly a month since Amá left.

It was my and Rubi's first time in New York. I had been invited for a literary event. There was an open bar, attendants walking around with trays of small food, and people clustered in groups with drinks in their hands, laughing almost too hard at little things that might not have been funny anywhere else.

I was supposed to walk up to the stage, say some words, and walk back down. Nothing more, nothing less. Everyone was expected to clap. Those were the rules we were expected to follow.

I ordered a whisky, neat, even though I didn't like whisky, but it was free. I chased it with a Corona. I shook people's hands and smiled and thanked them profusely when they remembered my name. Someone grabbed me by the arm and whispered in my ear the names of powerful people. I quickly lost track of Rubi in the crowd.

I was slightly drunk already, but I smiled anyway. If it wasn't for someone leading me by the arm, I would have probably stood there the entire evening, looking up at the crystal chandelier in awe, snatching little trinkets off platters. Everyone was smiling. Indeed, it was a joyous occasion. Everyone's teeth were out in the open, on display, touched by that dazzling light refracted against the crystals.

I tried to be polite and followed the movement of people's heads as they talked to me. I nodded along, smiled again, sometimes demurely, and adjusted my scarf, which had rhinestones and golden threads that sparkled on my chest. I felt glamorous but empty, like a pretty vase with nothing inside. I tossed the tassels of my scarf to the side and let them flutter when I turned.

*

After tossing more hors d'oeuvres in my mouth and washing them down with another whisky, I lost the energy to keep up with everyone else's chuckles and jokes. I couldn't do it anymore. I was tempted to throw away my speech and just scream into the microphone until someone dragged me offstage. Wouldn't that be fun? Or, as I had done at a reading the night before, just say Amá's name until it lost its meaning. I asked everyone in the audience to repeat my mother's name, and they did, which made them uncomfortable.

I was drowning in the purple haze, but no one noticed. It seemed like everyone knew how to swim except me. They all had troubles, but they were better at hiding them than me. I stopped nodding along and just stared blankly at people, which made them cough and turn slightly away to another group. I slipped away from one small circle and wandered into another one before heading to the bar for another drink. The bartender asked what brought me to the party and I pointed to my name on the program. Delighted, he gave me another drink of some top-shelf stuff and raised a glass of water.

"Salud," he said and stared at me with a hint of worry in his eyes.

"Salud," I said and cocked my head back to pour the dark liquor down.

He saw what everyone else was seeing in me, except that he had the courage to tell me, but I couldn't tell him why.

I felt comfortable talking to him. It felt like home, even though our homes were in different places. His home in the Dominican Republic sounded familiar. Since Amá left, I didn't really know what home meant. I had practiced the word for so long that I took for granted its efficiency, its compactness, its ability to fit so much into so little. Most of the waitstaff were people of color, and I could hear some of them talking softly amongst themselves in Spanish. It was like a lullaby coming in and out of earshot—a word here, a phrase there. The lights above signaled for us that the program would be starting soon, so we all looked for our seats with our names on them. Rubi had already found her way to the table but I was too drunk to notice.

*

The host began with some light banter, and people chuckled. Again with the chuckling. I got up and stumbled to the restroom to vomit. It wasn't the alcohol, it was nerves. I didn't vomit, but I also didn't make it all the way to the restroom without weeping. It was slow at first, then it picked up. I didn't recognize myself, or the tears, or the muscles twisting my stomach in all directions, as if I was laughing.

I wondered what my mother was doing at that precise moment. I was one hour ahead. When I was little, and Apá was two hours ahead of West Coast time in Mexico, I actually thought he was talking to us from the future. "What's it like there in the future?," I would ask him, and he would simply laugh.

Maybe she was massaging her arm; maybe she was boiling water for tea in her bright kettle.

All of it was happening at the same time. The host in the ballroom was making another joke, and more liquor was being served, and the waitstaff was hurrying through the double doors with plates in their hands, and my dad was perhaps somewhere up in the Sierra, away from Amá, herding some cows, and my family was back in California, trying to move on.

I washed my face in the bathroom sink and splashed water in my eyes. Nothing in that entire building could bring my mother back— not the recognition I was receiving, not the applause, and certainly not their bright teeth popping out of their mouths when they smiled. There were a thousand powerful people in the audience, and none of them could do anything about it. Worse yet was that they didn't know, and I didn't have the courage to tell them. What good would it be to tell them, what could possibly have come out of that other than pity? "I'm so sorry, I wish there was something I could do." Or, "That sounds terrible, is she okay? Will she be okay?" It surprised me how little people knew about the realities of families like ours, how easy it was for them to move through the world as if everything was fine. And my personal favorite, "She's lived here for more than three decades on and off, why doesn't she just get a green card?"

I walked out, cleaned my eyes, and called Amá.

"Hi, mijo, how are you?"

"I'm okay, Amá, they're about to call my name. I can't talk for long, but I'm having a great time. The food is great, the people are great, and it's all very fancy. I wish you could be here. Can you believe I'm in New York?"

"I'm so proud of you, mijo. I'm doing well, I'm doing really well. Go on and do what you gotta do. I love you, mijo."

"I love you, Ma."

I promise I will tell you everything.

There was nothing else in her voice but sincere joy at the fact that I was calling her from New York. She would have been just as enchanted by the purple light as I was.

Back at my table, I noticed that the entrées had already been served. Lamb with garnish on a large white plate. Everyone at the table looked at me for a moment but quickly looked away and continued with their conversation, except for Rubi, who looked upset that I had ignored her all evening. I was glad to be seated next to a good friend; she smiled, and I knew that she understood. She didn't know, but she understood, and nodded to reassure me that things would be okay. I nodded back and slowly chewed the soft meat off the bone, and swallowed.

*

Up on the stage, together with the others to be recognized, I waited for the room to get quiet and began to read off the paper that we wrote together, which was folded in my pocket. My voice was low; I followed each word carefully, trying to make it sound as deliberate as I could, trying to weigh each word down so that each one sat somewhere deep in everyone's bellies. I said, "Thank you, thank you," but what I really meant to say was, "Please, please." I said, "We're grateful," and I hoped that somehow the words came out as, "Help." But they didn't. I said exactly what was on the paper. I finished and waited for their applause. They applauded.

I wished they could all be silent, that I could have stayed up on the stage to tell them the secret, whisper it into the mic real slow and make them promise not to tell anyone. "Do you think you can do that?" I would say. They would nod their heads, "Yes, I promise," and I would put my mouth real close to the mic and say what I had been carrying inside all evening. But I had been carrying it much longer than that. I had been carrying that secret around for years.

I walked off the stage and could hear everyone around me whispering "Great job" in hushed voices before the program moved on. I finished my drink. The program ended, and everyone went back to the lobby to mingle over more drinks. I would have rather they turned off the lights and left us all reaching around for the exit.

There was a town car waiting outside for us, courtesy of the hosts, and I stumbled away through the large polished bronze doors. There was nothing left there for me.

"Bye, great beam of purple light. Bye, dazzling chandelier. Bye, bright teeth!" I screamed as I slid into the evening.

"That one," I said and pointed to the car, one eye already starting to close.

I was yelling into the street but Rubi quickly pushed me into the car. I didn't know what else it was that I was yelling, but I could feel the reverberations inside my head. Back at my friend Lauren's place on the Lower East Side, where we were staying, the three of us sat quietly in a dimly lit partitioned room. There was a silence between us that didn't feel like silence.

"Thank you," I said to Lauren after what seemed like an eternity in the dark, and went to sleep.

I dreamed that I was blind again, like I was when we crossed the border. I was running away from a lion. I always seemed to be running in my dreams. I could see a little, out of the corner of my eye, some opaque light. It was nothing like my mother's dreams. She always dreamed that she was missing a shoe. That there was a large pile of them, but none of them were hers. I woke up in the middle of the night. I was an hour ahead of Amá. I was in the future. Maybe I could call her in the past and tell her to stay.

[Fourth Movement as the Day Selena Died]

——

I learned how to ride a bike on the exact day that Selena Quintanilla died, which is to say I learned how to balance myself when the queen of cumbia left this earth. I don't think it means anything. That day, the ground was wet from spring rain and oil that lapped on the surface of small dirty puddles where cars were fixed on my street. Things never really stayed fixed for long. Our life was dedicated to the unbreaking of things, and things kept wanting to stay broken.

I always thought the prettiest people died in spring, like Selena.

1.

I called Amá every evening as she went on her daily walks around the neighborhood, carrying a big stick to scare away the dogs. She'd left in February, and it was now April; things would have started to look normal by now—unremarkable. Just as I suspected, it was difficult to get her to video message, so we just talked on the phone. She didn't tell me, but she told my sister that Apá had stopped driving her around, so she had to walk to the market and to church. She said he was in a bad mood all the time for some reason, and generally avoided her. I didn't mention to Amá that I knew this.

"How are you, Amá?" I said in a low voice.

"I'm great, mijo, just getting my exercise running some errands," she said.

"That's good, Amá. That's good. Have you been walking a lot?"

"The fresh air is so good for me."

It didn't take long for Apá to dig up a part of him we hoped he had long since buried.

I promise, mijo, I'll tell you everything.

*

It was noon, and Apá was home for his midafternoon nap. Amá was in another room reading near the window, the same window I'd spent weeks trying to seal with caulking unsuccessfully, when there was a knock at the door to the courtyard. Anytime anyone knocked it was usually for Apá, so Amá never bothered to answer. She didn't know what she had done to upset him, but she was trying to avoid him until he simmered down, so she let the knocking go on and didn't answer. The knocking turned to banging, and Apá yelled to Amá to answer the door, but she pretended not to hear. According to him, anything she did, she did wrong. After a minute or so, he woke up from his nap, put on his hat, and walked to answer the door, muttering things at Amá.

The door had a little window on top about the size of a notebook, which you could open to see who was knocking without having to open the entire door, but Apá never bothered to use it. He opened the door, and two men armed with assault rifles asked, "Are you Marcelo Hernandez?" Calmly, Apá said, "Yes, that's me," and asked them what was their business.

"You need to come with us. Is anyone else in the house?"

And without changing the tone of his voice, without raising his arms, without changing anything about him, Apá calmly and casually said "No" and walked out the door without looking back.

Panicked, Amá called us—Apá had been kidnapped. You hear about it on TV, but you never think it could happen to you. Amá grabbed her purse and nothing else, without bothering to check what was inside, and called a cab. She didn't have time to think—the only thing on her mind was to flee, because she didn't know if they would return. In a matter of minutes she left behind the house that had called to her for over a decade—what had consumed us for so many years. She left behind the four suitcases that made up the entirety of her belongings we decided she would take with her to Mexico. In that house, brought over in Amá's suitcases, were all of our family albums, some of the pictures half a century old—all of our family's memories, gone. She left the dog on the roof, her only companion, and she left Apá, the one who saved her, unsure of his fate or where he might be. In the end, Apá's maniacal insistence that she return, her eventual agonizing return, and the pain of saying goodbye was all for nothing because we would lose it all—the windows I obsessed over, the endless shaking at the tips of my fingers from laughter when there shouldn't have been laughter, the weeping.

She told the cabdriver, "Just drive west, keep driving, keep driving, somebody will pay you at the other end." She had no money.

*

I had prayed for her to one day return, but not like this.

I didn't sleep for two days, and I could hardly eat. If it was up to me, I would have boarded the first plane as soon as I got the call, but we had to work together as a family. I was working with a class of kindergartners when I found out. Amá had managed to escape and was safely tucked away somewhere in a large city. All of the family, her sisters, were calling us, asking where she was, but as much as it pained us, we couldn't tell them. We were paranoid. We didn't know who was watching, if they were tapping our phones, if she had been followed. We couldn't trust anyone. All we could say was "Please, trust us." We didn't know how far the kidnapper's reach was—if they might be outside our houses in the U.S. We didn't know who was involved, so we assumed everyone was. Never in my life had I ever considered owning a gun until then. Besides, I already knew how to use one, thanks to Apá.

We spoke to men who shouted on the phone, who made promises and demanded a lot of money we didn't have. I heard Apá's voice; it still sounded calm and collected, but tinged with an undercurrent of fear. I knew they were telling Apá what to say because I knew those weren't his words. I booked a flight to Mexico to meet Amá where she was hiding, and the rest of the family stayed behind to handle the calls. I made promises to God. I didn't buy a gun.

*

By chance, Amá's Mexican passport was in her purse, which allowed us to buy a plane ticket for her to Tijuana. We met her in an airport. Her eyes were red and sunk deep into her head, like faraway lights floating in water. She too hadn't slept. She had a small borrowed blanket wrapped around her. In her purse were her blood pressure medicine and monitor, cell phone, and a few mints. We held each other for a long, long time, longer still than most people held each other at airports. "Tell me everything that happened," I said.

It seemed like the more I engaged with the border and immigration, the more it ground us into a pulp, as if we were deathly allergic to it. Amá had only been in Tepechitlán for two months. Since we hadn't told anyone that she was returning to Mexico, and she just suddenly appeared one day, if a kidnapping was already planned, Amá's arrival would not have changed its course. It might have been merely an inconvenience, a slight variation of plans. But I feared the worst: that the kidnapping had occurred *because* she returned—that we played a part in it by not being subtle in making her comfortable. Two months was enough time to plan anything. Tepechitlán was not what it used to be; the entire state was being fought for by warring cartels for its convenient central location.

Rubi stepped in and hugged Amá while I continued to make more calls.

*

A chance for Amá's return had been inconceivable before, but now, though under unfortunate circumstances, one was possible. We knew she wasn't safe anywhere in Mexico; we knew that from that point on, Mexico was a thing of the past for our entire family. We would never be able to return. It didn't matter that I had a green card—that was beside the point; there would now be different reasons that I could not cross back. We were afraid for our lives. We knew their eyes were everywhere. In reality there was nowhere you could hide. Even in the airport, sitting on a hard bench, I looked at people walking by and wondered if any of them were involved. I tried to see if anyone was staring at us.

Our only hope was to fly Amá to Tijuana so she could surrender herself to border patrol and ask for asylum. It was a long shot because at the time, we didn't have a lot of information about who the kidnappers were or their motives and Mexican citizens didn't usually qualify for asylum. In April of 2016, the race for the U.S. presidency was picking up steam. More and more, it seemed like the country was making it harder for cases like my mother's to be processed.

It felt like she was in the middle of a tug-of-war, with forces larger than us tugging on each of her arms, or pushing her away. We had just taken her to Mexico, and now we were bringing her back. I called our lawyer because we didn't feel like we could call or trust the police, and he explained to us what we needed to do and the possible options. Suddenly we found ourselves back in the same scenario as before with the U visa: trying to convince others of the scale of Amá's suffering.

My only job was to bring her over. I wasn't supposed to think about Apá, or focus on anything else other than bringing Amá. And was she really better off with us in the States? Could we really protect her more than if she stayed in hiding somewhere in a small hut on a coastal village in the Gulf Coast? Who were we to those people who had Apá? We were insignificant, we were nobody. But we wanted to be together and be nobody. When she left, we promised ourselves that if anything happened, we would do whatever it would take to get her back. And that was what we were doing.

*

Before we boarded our plane, I begged Amá to eat something. We sat down at a Chili's. It tasted like all the food had been prepackaged and cooked in the U.S. I took a picture of her poking at her soggy potatoes just as she looked up at the camera, and sent it to everyone back home so they could see for themselves that she was safe.

2.

Our drive in the taxi to our hotel in Tijuana felt just like the trip to Juárez, except this time, we were trying to cross Amá over. She had no appointment like Apá; she would undergo no biometrics, but simply present herself unannounced. We arrived in Tijuana on Saturday morning and decided we would wait until Monday morning to go to the border, when we would be sure the supervisors were on shift. I knew most people asking for asylum were not staying in hotels, I knew the incredible privileges we were afforded and didn't take them for granted. I was merely doing for Amá what was in my greatest capacity. If I had more money, I would have probably considered flying her over the border in a Cessna. We were doing all that we could to help, to get us through it, however little or much that was.

We arrived and checked into the hotel. Amá lay down on the couch in the lobby with a sweater over her head while we waited for our room to be cleaned.

"Mom, wake up, our room is ready," I said quietly, as if I too believed she was sleeping. Sleep was a faraway thing that receded more the closer we came toward it.

She opened her eyes and stood up. Her movements looked robotic. She was trying her best to look normal, untroubled. We all looked the same, and I wondered if people could tell from the smiles on our faces.

"Finally," she said as she picked up her small purse, her only possession. I thought about all of those days we'd spent arguing over what should go in her four suitcases, how I nearly stormed out of her house when I couldn't convince the others that she didn't need to take a toaster with her, that she could buy one over there. We were starting again from zero. Always starting again.

*

A tall and slender man helped us to our room with our luggage. "Thank you," I said. "My pleasure," he said. He stood at the doorway and smiled at us. I didn't have anything else to say, but he remained there. My mind wandered elsewhere. I didn't get the hint, and he tightened his lips and walked away. Rubi and Amá walked in and plopped themselves on the bed, breathing a heavy sigh of relief.

"You didn't give him a tip?" Rubi asked, lying back on one of the double beds.

"I blanked—do you have some cash? I can go give it to him."

"No, that's fine, we'll catch him on the way out."

Rubi closed her eyes and padded the plush pillows. We were all tired, but she was the one who'd booked the flights, who'd read the reviews of the hotel, who'd kept me calibrated. Without her, I probably would have stormed into Tepechitlán by myself with a death wish. I smiled and nestled against her warm body. For a moment, we felt safe. The blinds were drawn, and the door looked sturdy—the windows were thick and double-paned. It was quiet except for the steady hum of the traffic outside. We felt hidden, but we still couldn't allow ourselves the pleasure of releasing the tightness winding in our bodies. Even lying in the bed felt like uselessly pushing against a wall, and the entire world was on the other side, holding my father perhaps in a dark room somewhere on a mountain.

3.

Amá still didn't talk about Apá, and I didn't want to tell her what I knew. I closed the curtains tighter so that it was completely dark except for the small sliver of light coming from beneath the door. I blocked the gap with a towel and turned on a desk lamp.

Rubi went to sleep immediately, with all her clothes on. I went over to Amá on the other bed. I held her on the edge, neither of us speaking. I wanted her to be mad, to scream, to find a gun and swear vengeance, but instead all I felt was the sharp edges of her bones. It was nice to be completely silent, each of us knowing what the other was thinking.

"Mijo, I want to take a shower," she said as she held my hand.

"Sure, let me turn on the water." I walked over to the bathroom to draw her a bath.

The towels were neatly stacked, and the tile floor was cold on my feet. I turned on the water and adjusted it for her. I let my hands run beneath the faucet, not to clean them but to feel the vibration of running water. The sound of rushing water calmed me. It felt mechanical—predictable. I liked how certain it was: I could turn the lever, and water would always come out. I set a towel on the floor for her to step on and put the toothbrush we bought at the airport near the sink.

"The water's ready, Amá," I said.

"Thank you, mijo."

It was four in the afternoon on a Saturday. She hadn't really slept since they took Apá on Thursday. She and Rubi went to sleep to the vibration of the highway traffic outside. She would not wake until the next day in the afternoon.

*

I couldn't sleep as well as Rubi and Amá, so I spent most of the night watching reruns of HGTV's *House Hunters International* and arguing with the homeowners in the show about their poor taste in kitchens.

The next day, we got dressed and headed downstairs to eat. Our waiter lit the candle on our table and bragged that their kitchen was the finest in the city. It almost felt as if we were just out on another weekend afternoon, eating dinner. We all ordered chicken because the waiter said it was to die for. He said it like that, "to die for," even though we had been speaking Spanish the whole time.

There was an American couple a few tables over from us who weren't so quiet. The husband was wearing a loose medical gown and had an IV stand next to him, with a tube running into his arm. The hotel was a hotspot for American medical tourists who came for cheap procedures. The man looked like he was in recovery. Through a small fold in his robe, I could see that he had bandages around his waist. Hotels catered especially to those Americans, offering free shuttles to and from different clinics, which were mostly conveniently located in the hotel district of the city.

When the food came, we ate quietly. The waiter stopped by our table to ask if everything was fine. We nodded, and he refilled our glasses of water. I thanked him, a reflex. Everything seemed to be a reflex. I grabbed our room keys out of reflex; I looked at the attendant in the eyes and thanked him out of reflex. I felt like my body could function without me, like if my spirit left the room, my body would continue, thanking the waiter, saying "Excuse me" and "Please" and "You're so kind."

I ordered a dirty martini. I had never ordered one before, but I didn't know why I wanted one then. I felt like a dirty martini was supposed to say something for me to the waiter and those around me that I couldn't say myself. I said it loud so everyone around could hear. I asked to make it extra dirty, without knowing what that really meant. I'd heard people liked their dirty martinis extra dirty. I wanted more alcohol, but didn't realize having it dirty meant less.

Amá's eyes were still red. It was difficult to deny the language our bodies spoke without our will or permission.

"How was your chicken?" I asked Rubi.

"It was whatever," she said with a bland look on her face.

I was instructed not to answer, but continued to receive calls from strange men who left voice mails demanding things and what sounded like impersonations of my father. I put the phone away quickly.

"Who was that?" Amá asked.

"Nobody, Amá, it's nobody." I said, but I knew she didn't believe me. After dessert, the waiter brought our check with a broad grin.

*

We finished eating, and I forced the last of my dirty martini down with a bitter look on my face. It wasn't very good—not that I knew the difference anyway, but I wanted more vodka, less olive brine. Amá never liked it when I drank. In my head, I imagined myself calling the waiter over and saying that it was too dirty. In my head, the waiter knew what I meant by "too dirty," and he knew me by name and would ask about my work. But I didn't say anything. We walked back up to our room without leaving a tip.

Our rooms were exactly as we left them. I looked for any signs that anyone might have entered, but I couldn't find any. I felt like everyone around me knew something that I didn't, like I was in an episode of *The Twilight Zone*, or in the movie *The Truman Show*, and everyone around me was playing a role. Everyone was looking at a small invisible camera except for me.

*

Better yet, I felt like I was in the movie *Labyrinth* with David Bowie and Jennifer Connelly. Everyone around Connelly's character, Sarah, knew something that she didn't. Their absurdity was justified by the fact that they had seen everything happen before, they knew how it would all end. Perhaps absurdity was the only remedy and explanation for having seen the future.

There was no real point in trying to make sense of anything. We were back on the border of Tijuana and San Ysidro, just as we were in 1993 trying to do the same thing again and again.

In the *Labyrinth* scene with the Fireys, they removed their limbs according to the whims of their games, which had no specific rules. They tried to remove Sarah's head but didn't understand that hers didn't work like theirs did—you couldn't just saw it off and put it back together. I remembered Sarah's eyes shot with terror. Theirs were two realities that had so much to do with each other, yet so little. And the worst was that the Fireys could not understand why Sarah's head could not be unscrewed off her shoulders like theirs. Perhaps if she stayed a little longer, they would hold her down and laugh unknowingly as they sawed it off, until realizing they couldn't put it back together, that she could not just laugh it off like them.

My phone kept ringing, and the men promised to do the same to Apá, and sometimes they laughed too.

Sarah looked rich in the movie. The white suburban girls always looked rich. If only the Goblin King had wanted money instead of innocence, like the people who had my father, perhaps Sarah could have saved herself all that trouble.

They knew Sarah would reach the palace, and they knew she would return with her kidnapped brother safely in her arms. Sarah was the only one out of the loop, like in *The Truman Show*. All uncertainty was concentrated into one person; for everyone else, it was repetition.

It was the last movie Jim Henson, the creator of the Muppets, directed before his death. I couldn't remember if anyone died in the movie, or if they just disappeared.

And what do you say to someone whose loved one has died? I never knew the right words.

In Spanish, when someone dies, you say to their loved ones, "Mi más sentido pésame." But this had always sounded too artificial to me, or too much of a template for what we should have said but couldn't. It seemed like the easy way out. I thought you should have to struggle a little, even if that meant saying something that you would regret in the future. I didn't know if anything like that existed in English.

I remember the first time I heard someone use the words "Mi más sentido pésame." I was confused. It sounded like something in the phrase was missing. The syntax seemed off. Literally translated, it means "My greatest sentiment, it weighs down on me," or "My sorrow, it is your sorrow too." More appropriately it means "My deepest condolences." But the more I thought about it, the more it seemed like it should mean "Believe me, I know what you are feeling," or "What I am capable of feeling I possess because of this," or "The weight of this, I too am carrying it." It is a template for empathy that people use at a time when sorrow won't allow them to think, when all they can do is move their mouths.

Mi más sentido pésame. Our chicken is to die for.

4.

I went back down to the bar by myself, took out my laptop, and pretended to work on something. "Dirty martini with Bombay Sapphire, please," I said to the bartender, pointing at the bottle.

There was a painting on the wall that I was drawn to. I noticed it when we first arrived. It was a picnic scene. Everyone in it was young and cosmopolitan. They were lying on the grass, drinking wine and eating what looked like bread, or cheese, or both. They all looked like they had just gotten good news, or anticipated getting good news soon. Either way, something good was happening to them, and they were aware of this—they knew their future.

It didn't look like they had any plans to leave. It wasn't clear how long they had been there. I couldn't tell if it was morning or afternoon, but there were shadows from the large branches hanging overhead. It probably wasn't morning. Their brown skin glistened. They were dark-skinned like me, they were beautiful. It was obviously a painting of leisure—one that I've seen many times before but with different actors. They looked like they came from money. They looked as if they all had the last scene of *King Lear* memorized to perfection. They'd read all the French Surrealists and could recite certain lines during sex. You loved to hate them, and they didn't care much about you. Maybe they all made love to each other at one point, often in groups of three. They were tender lovers. It didn't look like any of them would be in bed by midnight.

I wanted to be glamorous like them. I called my friend Derrick and wept over the phone. I had had enough. I didn't want any more of this. I wanted something else, anything but this, this goddamn place, these goddamn papers, these goddamn people leaving voice mails on my phone.

It felt like somehow this had all happened before, and was destined to happen again, so what was the point in being mad? If that was the case, I should have surrendered, I should have stopped fighting, if there was no point in changing the outcome. I kept crying into the phone, and my friend just listened to me weeping softly, silently, at him.

"I'm sorry but I can't tell you where I am," I said.

His voice was calm and reassuring. I didn't expect him to say anything, but I wanted to hear someone breathing, so I kept up the conversation. After a while I hung up and took the last drink of my dirty martini.

*

I couldn't help thinking how far removed I felt from the kind of life the people in the painting lived. It looked like something Joan Didion would write about. I loved being confused by Joan Didion. I loved not knowing the people she made references to in her essays, and I purposefully never looked them up because I wanted them to stay mysterious and never lose their splendor. She said it with so much languor and abandon, not caring if her reader knew who those people were or not. I remembered a passage where she talked about someone named "Axel Heyst in *Victory*, and Milly Theale in *The Wings of the Dove* and Charlotte Rittenmayer in *The Wild Palms*." I had never heard of those people or those works. I didn't know if they were books, or movies, or plays, or all three, but they sounded like something I could never access. They sounded strange and shiny in my mouth. I didn't know what a chiffon dress looked like or how it would feel against my skin, or a frangipani. I adored it all. A distant glamour that was always walking away. I guess that's why I ordered a dirty martini at a hotel bar in Tijuana—because I didn't want to be drinking a dirty martini in a hotel bar in Tijuana.

Our chicken is to die for.

*

I paid my tab and ate the olives that I'd set aside for the end. I could taste the vermouth infused into them. They were still very salty, and they left my lips dry. I hadn't taken a shower since I left Sacramento on Friday, but it didn't bother me until I got to the elevator. When I touched the metal button of my floor, it felt oily. I imagine that it tasted like the inside of a battery, or chewing on a copper wire. I ate a chicken's heart and liver that tasted like that once—all metal in my mouth. Apá forced me to eat it, though I didn't want to. It made him angry. "Eat, it's good for you," he yelled. The taste of iron and the gelatinous texture slid slowly down my throat. I closed my eyes until the door opened on my floor.

I felt guilty that I'd brought my mother to this hotel, thinking this would all make it better, that the food, the martinis, and the fresh linen would make it all go away. I smiled at an employee walking by and struggled to open my door.

In the bathroom, I stripped down and looked at myself naked in the mirror. I had gained a lot of weight in the last few years. Most of it was from the Prozac. I stared at my caramel skin, at all the hair below and around my bellybutton, at the hair on my chest and around my nipples. It looked like ripples in a stagnant pond. My thick black pubic hair looked like an oasis in an empty desert. I opened my mouth and stuck out my tongue as far as I could. I examined myself for a long time. The flat fluorescent light in the room highlighted my scars, cellulite, and stretch marks. I had a strangely shaped body—skinny but round in all the wrong places. I rubbed my beer belly that I'd sworn I would never get and turned on the water. I planned to take a taxi to the border checkpoint in the morning. I knew I needed some sleep.

The next day I had to be patriotic. I needed to tell them that America was the safest place for me and my mother. I didn't know how it would work; if they would detain her, take her away and keep her, make her go back and wait in Mexico, or pass on through. We were going to ask to be paroled into the country on a humanitarian basis, and ask for asylum.

The Universal Declaration of Human Rights passed by the newly formed UN on December 10, 1948, did not foresee our specific situation, but it did foresee our suffering. It had defined our cause half a world away, half a century before. Our pain, again, might have looked different than others, but according to the declaration, we at least needed to be heard. We at least had the right to make our case, though that would change two years later, when a different man would come to occupy the White House.

*

Universal Declaration of Human Rights

Whereas recognition of the inherent dignity and of the equal and inalienable rights of all members of the human family is the foundation of freedom, justice and peace in the world . . .
Now, therefore,
The General Assembly,
Proclaims this Universal Declaration of Human Rights . . .
Article 6: Everyone has the right to recognition everywhere as a person before the law.
Article 13: (1) Everyone has the right to freedom of movement and residence within the borders of each State. (2) Everyone has the right to leave any country, including his own, and to return to his country.
Article 14: (1) Everyone has the right to seek and to enjoy in other countries asylum from persecution. (2) This right may not be invoked in the case of prosecutions genuinely arising from non-political crimes or from acts contrary to the purposes and principles of the United Nations.[1]

*

Was our claim political? Were our bodies and our pain political? I took a shower and went to sleep. In the morning, we packed our bags and said a quick prayer. We got into a taxi and headed one more time to the border, as was our right.

[Fifth Movement as Fracture and Surveillance]

‗‗

Everyone was a possible border agent. Everyone was out to get you with their night-vision goggles, with their floodlights, with their dogs. Everyone you touched could touch you back. You were not an apparition, even though an entire country was scared of you. No one in this story is a ghost. This is not a story.

My dentist was an agent. Each teacher was an agent. Every paper I ever touched was an official paper that would be labeled and filed away for later use against me. Even my pastor was an agent, scanning the congregation with his small eyes. All anyone had to do was pick up the phone and call.

*

I was afraid of the doctor because forms in the hospital were official. They looked official, with their carbon copies and letterheads. They were written in the official language—English. And English could say anything it wanted. English could change its mind on you mid-sentence, and then change back while you weren't looking. English could make you say things you didn't want to, or mean to; it could make you agree to things you didn't know you were agreeing to. English was the language of small print. Even those same forms that were translated into Spanish were still only the same English forms with Spanish masks. I was afraid that one of their questions would lead to another question that couldn't be answered.

No health insurance, no number.

*

When I was run over by a car in high school, I pleaded and mumbled to the EMTs to let me go. "I'm fine, please, I have to make it to school," I said as I lay on the side of the road where the car tossed me. Its hood was dented to the shape of me. The EMT tried to cheer me up by saying "Relax, you're getting out of school today, kid." I moved my fingers in slow circles and gripped the grass tight to keep myself planted to the ground as they stabilized my neck and hoisted me on the gurney into the ambulance, bits of grass clenched in my palm. And still I begged, half conscious.

"Please, I'm fine, I'm not hurt. I can move," I said, and wiggled my toes, but they wouldn't listen.

Amá sat quietly by the side of the hospital bed, startled to her feet each time the door opened. The white woman who hit me with her car brought blueberry muffins. She said she was a devout Christian, and Amá felt compelled to pray for her nerves. We prayed for her together.

"We're Christian too," we said, as if trying to make her happy. We didn't press charges—we didn't think we could—and the woman thanked us profusely. I didn't know why she thanked us, if it was for not pressing charges, for praying for her, or for understanding her predicament. She was very tense and shaken by the whole situation, so Amá kept patting her shoulder, just to make her go away. She left the muffins with the price tag still on—$4.99.

5.

The line wrapped around for about half a mile, past small shops that sold perfume, American clothes, and cell phones. The last time Amá and I were together in Tijuana, I was five, and she was thirty-eight. I didn't remember much of the city itself, but Amá said it didn't change, only the names on the businesses. Everyone else was in a hurry, but no one was really moving much. They looked like they had done this before—a glazed and sedated expression on their faces. There was an air of monotony and fear, even though it is difficult to be afraid and bored at once. We took our spot at the end and began waiting.

The man in front of me was also rolling a large suitcase, and he stepped aside for a minute to see how far the line went on. He shook his head, "chingado." Neither of us could see the front. I could sense the frustration in him, but like me, like all of us in line, he hid it as best he could. We were the ones asking for something—an entrance. If the line took two days, a week, a month, for some of us it would still be worth waiting. Our desperation could be measured by how long each of us would be willing to wait. We could probably guess how far any person in line had traveled to get there by how long they were willing to wait.

I noticed that not many other people had luggage, except for a small purse or bag. They looked like they were going to work. Those fortunate enough to have a SENTRI visa came and went almost daily. The checkpoint was just another small burden, an inconvenience, their morning commute to work. They would be the first to leave if the line stopped for good.

Rubi and Amá had a worried look on their faces. "Everything will be fine, don't worry," Rubi said to Amá as she massaged her shoulder. I tried to look calm, but I knew I was a nervous wreck. Border agents were trained to spot that kind of behavior. They would ask the same questions over and over to see if they could trip anyone up. They looked for eye contact, tenseness, and they paid close attention to what people did with their hands, always the hands.

Amá practiced what she would say so that her nervousness and incipient shock from the whole experience wouldn't be misinterpreted for fraud. Just as in my immigration interview, it was the border agent's job to assume that everything was a lie. I didn't know how these agents could wake up in the morning and prepare themselves to deny any truth. To them, everyone was lying, everyone was trying to sneak in drugs or people to the other side. Everything we said needed to be perfect.

I didn't want to, but I asked her again.

"Amá, do you remember your facts?"

I quizzed her, I interviewed her, just like I did with Apá. Perhaps I was making her more nervous than if I just kept quiet and let things go on as fate intended. I still thought I could control the outcome of our lot; I still had the gall to think that anything I said or did could make a difference. Her eyes began to water a bit, and she looked away as she spoke. I stopped asking questions.

6.

While still waiting in line, I heard someone singing. An elderly woman behind us was pushing herself alongside the line of people in a wheelchair. On her lap was a child who looked like he could be her grandson. Every few feet she reached out her hand with her palm up. She pointed to the child on her lap, with his beautiful brown eyes and curly black hair. She stopped beside us and continued singing.

I had heard the song many times before; it was called "El Bayo Cara Blanca." It was about a famous racehorse who never lost a race, and was praised like a god for making some rich while leaving many more in ruin and misery for betting against him. The song said that the horse eventually went blind, unable to race anymore, unable even to wander the fields by himself. His owner thought the only solution was to shoot him. What was the point of running, if he didn't know when to stop running? The moral of the song, because it was one of those kinds of corridos that needed to end on a moral, was that fate was cruel, and that no one could escape what was already written in the stars for them.

The woman on the wheelchair had no instruments, and the child was too young to sing along. I was surprised by the strength of her voice. She sounded like Chavela Vargas, with that distinctive rasp of pain at the end of each breath, making her almost break into laughter. It didn't seem like that voice could come from such a small body, but it did.

"Do you have any change, or anything?" I said to Rubi.

She scrambled through her purse for some change. Everyone in line knew the song. Everyone could have sung along if they wanted to, but most of them tried to avoid her sharp glances. She looked to the crowd for anyone paying attention, for her audience. Her stare was piercing. Unlike the rest of us, she was unwaveringly present. She didn't look bored or glazed over; she wasn't afraid of looking

straight into people's eyes, and holding them. She wasn't the one try-
ing to cross.

"I have a hundred- and a five-hundred-peso bill," Rubi said.

"Give her the hundred, not the five hundred," I said.

We knew the pesos weren't worth much if we traded them on the
other side, but out of reflex I gave her the smaller bill, worth roughly
seven dollars at the time. I could have given her more, but I didn't,
unsure if we would need to stay longer in Tijuana. Rubi gave me the
rolled-up bill, and I placed it on her palm. She didn't stop her song,
just nodded at me, rubbing the bill with her fingers, feeling the edges
and grooves, and putting it in a small pouch around her neck.

*

"Ay qué rechulo animal / No mas hablar le faltaba . . ." went the
song.

Hers was an implied contract—if you stared or mouthed the lyrics
to the song, you were confirming that you could see her, that you
could hear her. You were doing what most people didn't do for
beggars, admit they were there. But she wasn't a beggar; she was giv-
ing you something in return, it was a transaction. You entered an
exchange in which she offered her voice for your money.

And you validated her plea. In this way, theft was a common
thing. If you heard her and sang along, either out loud or in your
head, but didn't give anything, you were stealing what wasn't yours
to keep. Temporarily—the sound. Permanently—the memory. It's
a lie we tell ourselves—that our emotions are ours, and of our making.
In truth, they are given to us like small gifts wrapped inside a word.
Her song would be over in minutes, but the memory wouldn't. Hearing
her meant that you entered the contract, and you would either keep
it or break it. If you kept it, it was because the song she was singing
brought it out of you—it was because you couldn't deny her gift. She
rescued those emotions and memories from the depths you worked

so hard to bury them beneath. She knew which songs dug the deepest. "How beautifully she sings," said my mom. "Pobre mujer, mujer sufrida."

Her product was nostalgia. Everyone in the line was already hurting in one way or another, and hearing that song only made it worse. For a moment, we held something inside us that was not part of that border line we were in, something outside the distance between us and the people on the other side, not part of the green-and-white immigration trucks we saw driving alongside the wall.

"I remember that song from when I was a little girl," Amá said with a slight smile.

"I knew a horse like that, it never lost, until one day it did," she said.

Amá knew the song well, and she knew a lot about horses.

"Amá, what's a 'caballo de siete cuartas de alzada'?" I asked her, hearing the words in the song.

"It's a kind of horse, like a quarter horse." She looked directly at the woman, who in turn looked back.

The line wasn't moving—I wanted to get there already. But the woman continued her song, not caring if the line moved or not.

It was as if her song was telling me to leave that place. To never come back. She was making me remember something that I had lost, something that I was sure to never forget again—the horse in my childhood, she was a quarter horse, she was a racing horse, she did what she naturally was born to do, despite having a small child on top of her. She wasn't racing against anything, because she didn't need to. We only put two horses against each other to make us think we're the ones that make them run, that we have anything to do with their insatiable desire to get away. Apá ran after me because he had to, not because he was born to do that. He was born to run the other way.

*

Maybe there was pleasure in the small wound made by that woman's cries at the same time as grief—Chavela Vargas back from the dead. The wound was not so much because we hurt for her, though we did, but because at least once we also wanted someone to hurt for us.

The merchants stood outside their stores alongside the line, occasionally looking up uninterestedly, and back down at phones in their hands. The noise and the traffic lifted a cloud of dirt into the air.

For everyone in the line, there were two outcomes: they made it to the other side, or they didn't. It was as simple as that. But the old woman on the wheelchair wasn't looking to cross. She would move up and down the line for the rest of the day, hoping that someone remembered her song. How freeing it must have been, to walk up to the line and have no intention of crossing.

The woman's left eye was cloudy with cataracts. Maybe she would soon be blind. Maybe people would be less compelled to give, if they knew she couldn't tell who was listening, making eye contact, mouthing the words to her songs—who was hurting most on the inside.

*

In the face of the border agent at the front, I couldn't just be the son of a farmer, the grandson of a farmer, the great-grandson of a farmer. I had to put forward what being the son of a farmer had allowed me to become—not in spite of, but because of. A code-switch, moving back and forth between languages. I needed to exercise my best English, my courteous manners, my "yes, sirs" and "no, sirs," "yes, ma'am, no, ma'am." I had to get them to see themselves in me. To enter into our own contract.

It wasn't so much a matter of conveying the grief Amá was carrying all the way from Tepechitlán. Anyone who looked at her could see something terrible had happened. It was again, as with the U visa, a matter of empathy. How easy it was to say "I am suffering," and how much harder it was to get other people to believe her.

Since I would initiate the conversation, I needed to strike just the right balance of casualness and respect. Maybe I would talk about "the game," whichever game that may have been. Didn't someone usually play on Sunday night? Maybe I would talk about how it was Monday morning, and chuckle about things that felt particularly American—say I hadn't had my coffee either, or ask how the traffic was, coming in. These were American things to worry about. So many years I had spent trying to decipher and mimic what it was to be American. I washed it on and off my body like water, so that I wouldn't feel dirty when someone called me a wetback.

How do you like your steak?

Rare. Extra rare. I like my beef still moo-ing.

The chicken is to die for.

Part of me hated the U.S. I hated what it had done to my family. But maybe Mexico would have done the same thing. I hated the suburbs, the college frat brothers who demanded an A for their C work in my class; I hated the evenly squared tiles in the grocery store, the way people looked at me when I left a building. And yet where else was there for me to go, for us to go? What other choice did we have, when America forced us to come, and a return to Mexico was no longer an option? I hated the beauty, but nonetheless there was beauty.

There was something different about Amá, something I hadn't seen in her before. It was as if being back on the line woke up the instincts that had allowed her to survive her crossing, five months pregnant, in 1993. Up until that point I had been leading her, telling her where we should go and what we should do, but now I realized just how different a life she'd had before me—how much more normal what we were doing had been to them back then, and how much more she knew. She had done this many times before—crossing, that is—each time unique in its own way.

She had a dogged look on her face, her eyebrows stayed a little furrowed without breaking, and she gripped my hand a little harder. Amá was the kind of woman who would say, "Well, life is what it is" whenever I told her something tragic, but it was strange to hear her say that when it was happening to us, in that moment. Life was what it was, and she tapped into a part of her that she left behind on the border in order to keep on moving forward.

*

I could still hear the old woman in her wheelchair singing up ahead with her thundering voice. She began singing "Los Dos Amigos" by Los Cadetes de Linares. That song made my skin shiver every time I heard it. It was a corrido about two men robbing a train, and one of them getting caught. It was about a mother praying for her son, and her prayers being answered. It asked the basic question—was prayer even necessary, if what was going to happen would happen either way?

More people were now walking up and down the line, selling food, novelties, and newspapers. They wore badges slung over their chest, with their picture on them, an official-looking seal stamped over their faces. The badges made it seem like there was control, like there was a vetting process for who could sell, advertise, and function at the border. It was supposed to provide some comfort to tourists, especially white tourists.

I still could not reconcile whether I was a tourist or not. However hard I tried, everything about me said that I wasn't raised in Mexico. I might have been born there, but I certainly didn't fit the part. My shoes, my clothes, even how I held my body, told a different story. I tried to look bored. I tried to hide the fact that I couldn't stop my heart from beating as fast as it did. I was still unsure whether they would let me stay with Amá or separate us once we went into the compound, and that made my heart race faster.

The line, after what felt like hours, finally began to move a little ahead, but then suddenly it halted again. They were letting in one group of people at time. Amá grabbed one of the suitcases and nudged me forward. Rubi was struggling with her luggage, and I could tell it was beginning to annoy her. The sun was starting to feel uncomfortably hot. "I'm tired of rolling these suitcases," she said. We took off our jackets and used them for shade above our heads. They opened the door for the next group of people, and we scooted a little ahead.

I knew Amá didn't want to tell me everything she knew, just as I wasn't telling her everything I knew. Every time I got a phone call, I walked away from her and looked back to make sure she wasn't listening.

The line moved a little more, and I could finally see the gates of the compound—the most trafficked border checkpoint in the western hemisphere. This was the case even before the caravans, before the humanitarian crisis and the new president's policy of separating children from their parents. Soon the streets would be lined with migrants waiting months to enter with little to no food or resources; to simply be seen and hear their numbers called. Soon many of the privileges associated with asylum cases we hoped Amá would be granted would be repealed.

I could see the line of cars stretching across, ten lanes thick. It looked like a college campus. How normal everything looked in there; how manicured the hedges.

7.

A guard waved us into the compound, which was clean and tidy. You couldn't see into the windows, but they could see out. Everything we did was being watched on a TV screen somewhere in a dark room; perhaps someone was jotting down notes with a small pencil on a notepad about how I lifted my bag, my phone. A guard came up to us and yelled into my face because I was using my phone. I read his name tag—Rodriguez. I hung up with my lawyer and walked inside, Amá and Rubi ahead of me.

It wasn't until we were inside that I realized we didn't really have a plan. We were just going to surrender ourselves and say, "My mother is seeking asylum because she fears for her life." It was odd to think of it as a surrender, as if she was, after so many years, finally coming out of hiding—"Here we are, take us."

The line moved ahead, and suddenly it felt like it was moving too fast, like it wouldn't give us enough time to think. In my head, I knew what I would say, but it wasn't until then that I mouthed the words beneath my breath. Once they became breath, air, and vibration, they seemed strange, different in my head, not how I wanted them to sound at all.

The line moved even faster as we got closer to the guard's window, which looked like a TSA queue. I really only needed to say one word, and the machinery of that agreement written up half a century ago in Europe would go into effect.

Asylum.

*

It was like waiting at the supermarket once we got to the very end, with one line breaking off into a few. At last it was our turn, and an agent waved us over to him. He had his rote routine and went straight into it, but we weren't part of that routine. We hadn't come to be part of the show; we couldn't just show him Amá's papers because there weren't any. I didn't know how to begin speaking: "Okay, so here's the thing," or "There's this thing that happened, sir," or "What I'm trying to tell you . . ." How do you walk up to a person and tell him you are running for your life? Wouldn't it make sense to just start from the beginning? But when exactly did all of this start?

"So then what are you doing here?" he barked after I said Amá didn't have "the proper documents," as if he couldn't fathom our presence before him, as if we should have been out there instead, trying to cross through the mountain or desert like everyone else. Once I got going, I couldn't stop. I told him each detail of events. Amá's eyes began to water, and he looked at us for a long time with clinical precision.

In my head, our conversation had gone very differently. I didn't say half of what I was supposed to say. Maybe he was taken aback by our boldness, our gall at having walked right up to him with no plan in sight and asking to enter, to be paroled in on a humanitarian basis. He ran each of our passports, asked us to place our fingers on a small screen to scan our fingerprints, and looked at his computer for a long time, his glasses nearly falling off the tip of his nose as he studied the screen.

I didn't want them to separate us; I would do anything to stay with Amá. I couldn't afford to lose her again.

"Follow me" he said, and walked out of his booth.

"C'mon!" he urged, because we hadn't started moving. We were locked in place, frozen with fear. We didn't know what would happen next. It was too late now to turn around and walk back; our intent to enter had been made. We weren't in the mountains, where we could see the U.S. ahead in the distance, where all you had to be certain of was that the sun was on your right in the morning and on your left in the evening. We were inside a building with no windows, and there were rooms where you could perhaps spend weeks and never know if it was night or day.

"Follow me," he said again, and gestured toward a sitting area, where we took our seats. "Wait here." And then he went back to his booth to help the next person in line, back to his routine, his everyday business, as if nothing out of the ordinary had happened. We'd wasted our energy on him; he was a nobody with no real power to decide our case, which was now officially in the system, making its way, slowly, to an immigration judge five years in the future.

*

Down a corridor, I could see the automatic double doors swinging open as people left the building. That was it, the U.S., right there, just a few dozen feet away, but it might as well have been as far away as the moon. We sat quietly in our small chairs inside what looked like a corral, surrounded by a waist-high wall. A few other people were inside already, looking down, avoiding eye contact with each other. I saw people filing by on their way out of the double doors, which let in a slight breeze each time they opened. It was right there.

It was chaotic in there, but no one seemed lost. Everyone knew where they were going except us and the others detained; lost yet locked in place. Another guard came up to us and said Rubi and I had to leave. We couldn't stay with Amá. I pleaded with him. I tried to say anything I could, but nothing seemed to register with him. My voice got louder as a growing frustration welled within me. There was nothing else I could say to make him understand, to convince him.

I quickly took out a pen and scribbled my number on her arm, and a few other important numbers she might need. The pen wasn't working well, so I dug it deep into her arm, and she winced a little from the prick. I told her to memorize the numbers in case the ink washed off, or in case they made her wash it off.

Amá sat between us and the guard. Looking ahead, her hands on her lap, resolute.

"You have to leave now," the guard said, "or else."

Or else what? I thought. It was ironic that he was forcing us to enter the U.S. He was forcing us to do the only thing we wished my mother could do, and what I myself hadn't been able to do for over two decades. I looked at Amá and told her everything would be okay. I repeated my phone number again. She shook her head, tears running down her face.

"Now," the agent said one last time, in a tone he hadn't used before. We picked up our things and walked away from Amá again. Again she sat there with her hands in her lap, staring away from me.

"I won't leave, I'll be right on the other side waiting, Amá," I said to her as I left.

We headed in the direction of the double doors. I looked back to make sure she was there, to make sure all of this was real. She was, and it was. She was on her own.

My leaving looked nothing like hers.

[Fifth Movement as Simulacra, 2005]

———

I sat at the dinner table with a razor in my hand. It was one of the thin straight razors my father used to shave with. Even though I was already in high school, I still couldn't grow a mustache or beard, but his razors were still around. It wasn't that long since he'd been deported. On the paper on the table, my name was printed in every font I thought was at least close to the real thing; every ligature, type style, and size. It was my first lesson in typesetting, my first lesson in form, in composition by field.

I needed to make my own social security card to show an employer for a new job. I also needed a "mica," a green card. Up until then, I'd been young enough that any job I took I could be paid under the table, but not anymore; I would have to be put on the books. I needed my name printed on that good cloth paper, the kind of paper with the small filaments of colored cotton like you see on money. But a real social security card was worth more than money. It was worth more than gold.

*

Courier New was the typeface that looked almost right. And yet, as I squinted at it beneath the desk lamp, no matter how I tried to align my name and glue it on, there was something different about the original. The ligatures between the graphemes felt like a secret code that couldn't be replicated or cracked. I cut around each letter of my name with a razor, going around each serif, each foot, and each joint with precision. I had to do it by myself. It was something we all had to learn at one point or another, like learning to drive or tying your shoes: the big loop over the little loop, under and over. I couldn't get my license, either, but this felt more important, made me feel like more of an adult. I could do things my friends couldn't.

At a certain point, cutting closer and closer to the ink, along the edges of the letters, I couldn't tell what was my name and what wasn't. It drew away from me and back again. It felt like I was playing tag between what was familiar and what was not.

Marcelo, Marcelo, Marcelo, Marcelo, Marcelo, Marcelo, Marcelo, Marcelo, Marcelo.

I'd taken for granted the consistency of machines, how they could place things in symmetrical longitudes and latitudes, how easy it was for them to form a straight line.

*

My mother watched me do things she wished I didn't have to do. I had to do them alone.

*

No one really left my town after high school, so the idea of going into a Walgreens to get a passport photo made me feel famous. I wanted to tell the photo clerk I was going to Europe, or Buenos Aires, or that I had a stint in Marrakesh. I wanted to say the word *Marrakesh* very slowly. But I wasn't getting a passport; I wasn't going anywhere. I couldn't tell her that. The camera clicked, and a single flash popped out like a wet firework. Stevie Wonder was crooning through the speakers above me.

*

I wondered what it took for something to be believable. To pass. At the tip of my razor was a question: Was it good enough, was *I* good enough? I always wanted to be the real thing, to move through the streets completely as myself. I wasn't using anyone else's name, but the fact that the card wasn't real made it feel like it wasn't my name printed there. Each name printed in small variations of Courier New carried its own weight, as if it were a congregation of Marcelos on the page, and we had all jumped into this body at one point or another.

I kept cutting parts of me that I thought would never come back, as if they were ever mine to begin with. I messed up on one name, cut across an *a*, and started again on another. I had plenty to choose from. I thought of all of those lost years pretending I was someone who I was not. Perhaps this was just the same. I was always aware of each of the twenty-four letters that made up the entirety of my name. It always took too long to say out loud, and I had to say it slowly to people. Even spelling it out was difficult for some; everyone always spelled it the Italian way, with two *l*'s. Sometimes I never corrected them, to avoid any tense moments.

It wasn't so far-fetched or paranoid to believe that everything I did gave me away as undocumented. I policed my body to the point that I could do nothing without consulting the voice in my head first—"Is this a good idea? Have you said too much?" It was exhausting just to live like that.

Everything I did was first filtered, scrutinized, and assessed before it left my body. If I said "please," it was a kind of "please" that was precise, that meant exactly what I wanted it to mean. If I was quiet, it was a deliberate silence. *Laugh now, laugh hard, spit out your food*. But I had no control over my name. Each time someone said my name, it said things back to them without me, before I could respond. And it was my job to put out all the small fires it sparked in people's imaginations.

*

The border security apparatus is mobile and ready to be deployed anywhere in the country should it be needed.

*

I knew a guy who knew a guy who knew a guy. He stopped by my house and placed in my palm my freshly printed green card, tucked inside the smallest manila envelope I had ever seen. Whoever made it cut crudely around the edges of my skin and hair and made my head look blockish. The laminate was too thick, made thicker by the cutout of my face, glued onto the card from my Walgreens passport picture rather than digitally transferred. It was a joke. I laughed a little when I saw it and paid the other half I promised, and said "Thanks man, I owe you," still chuckling. And he laughed, too, because he couldn't deny how bad it was either.

The most glaring marker of inauthenticity was my thumbprint. It wasn't really my thumbprint. I didn't know who it belonged to. Maybe it wasn't even a thumbprint, because there were hardly any ridges and grooves. It was just a large black smudge at the bottom right of the card. But it must have belonged to someone. I desperately wanted to know who.

Maybe it was a person who actually got their green card but stopped caring long ago about being found, and the prints were nearly wiped out because they were rubbed down to the bone from working, or from being copied over and over again.

*

I imagine the scene in the house where the mica was made—a kitchen table, much like my own. Someone is cooking in the kitchen, and the scent of poblano peppers roasting on the stove in the midafternoon of summer lingers in the throat. A child is doing her homework on the sofa. It is hot. A mother sits at the table, which is strewn with small pieces of paper, a laminating machine, and tiny envelopes. There is laughter coming from the TV, though no one is laughing in the room because the child is busy studying for a test, and the father is cleaning his work shoes, and the mother—the mother is steadying her good hand. There's a calendar hanging next to her with her children's soccer game schedule. She asks her kids to help because they have small hands, which don't shake and are better at cutting out the silhouette of the people who have paid two hundred dollars for a green card.

The child obliges. Maybe she will use this as a basis for her art when she grows up. She will become a famous sculptor and entertain rich patrons by explaining the labor of forgery in late capitalism. Her brother is a little more resistant to the work because he is embarrassed, maybe ashamed. In any respect, this is a family business, just like their neighbors who sell Avon. They're trying to be good people.

In a previous century, had they come from another country of fairer-skinned people, this family would have been called industrious, even entrepreneurs. They would be lauded for their creativity, and how they answered the demand of the market. In a previous century the children would have gone on to Ivy League business schools to start their own companies or carry on the tradition of the family.

The scene is peaceful. I imagine the courier who hands over the client's raw materials having a charming conversation with the father or mother—about the weather, about their children's school, about a PTA meeting where they were promised a Spanish translator but got none.

Present are the tools of the trade: fine drafting blades, rulers, glue, and of course, someone's sample green card as a guide, someone's thumbprint. Perhaps the thumbprint belongs to the father, and he copies it over and over again until it is unrecognizable and can't be traced back to him. He presses down on the ink pad, sending himself out for the world to see.

*

The card is a copy of a copy of a copy. It's like a VCR tape that slows down a little each time it gets played, gets a little more distorted, a little less recognizable. The change is gradual, but even the faces on the screen are stretched. In this scenario, let's play telephone: Start with the words on the green card, spread the word down the line, and giggle when the last person repeats their story to you like a confession. "I did nothing wrong, I was only trying to make an honest living."

8.

Our luggage clamored against the tiled floor, but Rubi and I, holding Amá's blanket, stopped right before the double doors opening into the U.S. Weeping must have been common there, because no one seemed too concerned that we were doubled over, with our hands on our knees. After a minute or so, the private security guard (clearly not an agent) posted at the door walked up to us and asked what was wrong. It was as if he was there by mistake, dropped from the sky like Dorothy in *The Wizard of Oz*. Unlike the other guards, he seemed confused at our grief but also told us we couldn't stay there, that we had to leave.

I'm leaving, my son, you don't need me anymore.

We felt all of that chaos pushing us forward. We tried to lock our heels in the ground like stubborn mules, but it was no use; the push was greater than us, and we inched forward into the country of opportunity, the country of promise. I could no longer see Amá around the corner.

We emerged from the double doors to an unbearable brightness. There were no longer any lines. Everyone was scattered about, hopping on the bright-red light-rail train headed to San Diego. Everything looked authentically American—the shops, the sidewalks, the gait of the passersby going wherever it was that they had to be in a hurry.

Rubi and I sat down on the cement in the middle of the plaza and cried. We held each other, but we couldn't feel our bodies. We wailed beneath the bright sun reflected in the polished floor below us. Everyone around us kept moving, nobody stopped. It was as if they were water, moving around and away from us, and we had become two large boulders in the middle of a river. We grew still and hunkered toward the earth we had become.

We couldn't breathe, unable to hold our bodies together any

longer. At least when I left Amá in Tepechitlán, I'd been able to walk away, I had enough strength to carry my bags.

I wanted my green card to be something I could give away, something I could trade legitimately for. I would give it to my mother. If that was an option, I would gladly have stayed in Mexico for the rest of my life in hiding, if it meant she was safe on the other side.

Trade me. Take me.

A woman who was standing beside us finally had the nerve to come up and ask if we were okay. What kind of question was that? I don't know why I entertained her with an answer. Reflex. In between any breaths I could manage, I told her my mother was in there and pointed back at the compound. She looked at us with a puzzled and worried face, as if "in there" was nowhere exactly, a nonplace, as if it had no bearing on what was out here. But at the same time she kept shaking her head as if to say, "What a shame, what an absolute shame." She apologized and walked away.

My leaving was loud, it could never hold still.

I held Rubi, and she held me. We took some pills to calm us down and looked into each other's eyes for a long time, until our breathing began to settle. Holding Rubi's hands, I could feel her pulse, and I tried to see if I could match it. We breathed and nodded to each other before getting back up.

*

We wandered through the town of San Ysidro, rolling our luggage behind us like a pair of dead dogs by the tail. We didn't know what we were looking for, so we just kept walking. I didn't have the energy to call back home just yet to tell the rest of the family what had happened. I didn't want to stray too far from the compound. I wanted to stay close to Amá, even if she didn't know I was there. She knew we wouldn't leave.

We booked a hotel nearby. I was tired of hotels. I was tired of the same continental breakfasts, the same musky odor of the beds, the same towels, and the same mirrors, which told a different story about me every time—I was too fat, I was too skinny, I was too dark, I was too light, I was too bony. I was never just enough of anything.

We checked in and headed to our room. It was the same procedure. Open the door, close the windows, lock the door, roll up a towel beneath the door, unplug the phone, check the bathroom, check beneath the door, open all of the drawers, lie down and stare at the ceiling.

I had to take sleeping pills, even though the only thing my body wanted to do was sleep. I took another hot shower, too tired to care about the water shortage, even though my guilt didn't drain as easy as the water. I thought I would make up for it later by not washing my jeans for a month. My skin was tender and red, my fingers started to wrinkle. I opened my mouth against the shower head and let it fill with water.

I lost track of time. Everything I ate tasted like almonds. Still the same hot shower, still my mouth wide open, still the curtains drawn, still the Do Not Disturb sign purposefully hanging on the door, still my dirty clothes piled on the floor, and the same goddamn home-improvement channel drumming about a chic midcentury remodel and young couples who didn't deserve to be happy. I grew resentful of the other guests who smiled at me at the breakfast bar in the morning. I either didn't return their smile or snarled beneath my breath and walked away. I started bringing my breakfast up to my room.

My paranoia was growing, and not being able to sleep didn't help. I thought cars were following us and our phones were tapped. I kept changing my clothes at all hours of the day and peeking through the window. I was awake even when I slept, just waiting for my phone to ring, obsessing over its battery life.

9.

It was a Wednesday when I got the call.

"Your mother will be released at the McDonald's near the San Ysidro Port of Entry," said a stern man.

McDonald's?

It didn't sound real. I didn't know who to trust anymore, and my phone grew strange in my hand. I looked at Rubi, and she knew exactly what the phone call meant. We threw everything into our suitcases and took a taxi back to the port of entry.

Going back to the port, I thought about my jagged numbers etched on Amá's arm, her map to find her way home. There was doubt in the man's voice over the phone, almost as if he didn't want to give us a guarantee that she was actually getting out, but only hold out the possibility. We returned to that bright plaza where everyone walked in different directions, where they hopped so casually onto the bright-red light-rail trains with the word METRO printed on their sides in large white letters, edging to the very tip of the border before whisking away to the north.

I waited inside the McDonald's, and Rubi waited outside, in case she was released elsewhere. Every woman in the restaurant looked like Amá, and I had to stare closer and longer to convince myself that it wasn't her. The smell of processed meat and oil from the deep fryer made my stomach turn. Families went about their business, eating their large burgers, dipping their fries into ketchup, and belching after taking long drags from their Cokes. It was difficult to concentrate.

There was too much noise, too many wrappers, too much color. I still hadn't slept well, and I got nervous when people edged too close to me. I remembered begging my father to take us to McDonald's as a child, refusing to eat what Amá had spent all afternoon cooking unless he took us to those golden arches.

*

I held myself at the edge of a table facing the street for a couple of hours. My eyes began to strain. I was suspended in a tightness that wouldn't let me relax, and with each hour that went by I wound myself up tighter and tighter, scanning the busy bodies ahead. I was afraid anything would make me spring open. Worse, that I would slowly start to lose hope with each hour—the gentle weight of defeat pressing on my shoulders, unwinding, easing me down into a loose wire tossed on the floor.

None of the faces, none of the bodies, none of the shadows along that bright plaza were my mother's.

Out of the corner of my eye I saw a small woman with disheveled hair and a small plastic bag hanging off her arm. A large American border guard walked her up and left, patting her back as he turned away. She wasn't moving; she was looking cautiously around her, hands folded at her stomach.

It was her.

I jumped out of my seat and ran toward the door, yelling "Amá!" It felt like I was holding her for the first time. She looked thin and like she hadn't slept or eaten in days. I couldn't believe she was there, in front of me, holding a plastic bag with "Department of Homeland Security" printed on it.

And again we stood there in the middle of the flow of foot traffic, motionless, with everyone walking around us, barely noticing or caring to notice the miracle that had happened before their eyes. She was wearing the same thin fleece jacket and gray sweatpants that she'd been wearing the day we left her. We walked away from the port, and I held her hand tight but not too tight, and Rubi held her other hand. We didn't know who was keeping the other from falling.

"Don't tell me anything right now, we'll talk about it as soon as we leave here," I said, still holding her arm, looking around suspiciously while Rubi hailed a cab. We wanted nothing more than to leave that place. It made our stomachs turn to think of staying there any longer. Part of me wanted to burn all of it to the ground, leave in my wake nothing but ashes, but instead I turned to my mother and smiled.

*

As we waited for our taxi, Amá pointed to her shoe and lifted her pant leg a little, revealing a large black box wrapped around her ankle with a black band. She had a GPS tracking device placed on her as a condition of her release while she waited for her court date in the U.S. A small green light flickered on and off, sending a signal to a computer somewhere about her every movement.

Her options were to either wait six months in ICE detention or wear the ankle monitor, which was an obvious choice. And she only had a choice because they allowed her case to move past the next step: to go through a credible fear interview. They wanted to make sure that my mother's fear was legitimate, that there was a reason why she was running, why any of us were running. She rolled her sweatpants back down over the device and smiled, but her eyes were dark and tired. We hopped in the taxi and headed toward a car rental company outside town. With each mile we headed north, Amá said she could breathe a little better. With each mile north we felt our bodies unclick their tightness one cog at a time.

Because of the ankle monitor, her prison would be everywhere and everything, surveillance looming everywhere.

They told her she needed to establish a routine so that they could enter her patterns into an algorithm that would determine if there was any suspicious activity. She gave them the address where she would be staying and a list of the places she might frequent. They told her that at any moment, they could show up to ensure that she was abiding by the rules. "This is a privilege," they said as they tightened the monitor around her ankle inside the compound. "You don't want to ruin it."

She was terrified of that device, and as much as she wanted to run away from it, she couldn't. It was as if someone had told her she needed to hold a snake for six months, or else.

Or else what?

It was a long, invisible chain and the person or machine at the other end felt each and every little tug she made. They said it would talk to her if it detected any tampering. A voice from a thousand miles away would come shouting out of the little black box, and an alarm would ring, and agents would be dispatched immediately to find her. She needed to switch out and rotate the two batteries it came with in order to keep the device charged on a daily basis, otherwise it would set off an alarm. She was paranoid (as we all were) that it would unexpectedly die, so she switched batteries much more often than what was required, sometimes three times a day. We were always looking at the green light to see how the battery life was doing. We didn't want anything to go wrong. It was always watching. At least, that's what we were told.

I almost felt a little at ease knowing she had the monitor on. Someone would always be able to see exactly where she was, which meant, by extension, that we would always know where she was at, which meant, hypothetically, that we could never lose her again, that she would never go missing like Apá.

10.

We rented a car and drove away from the border. I drove fast, pushing ninety-five. I wanted to get home as quickly as possible. *Home.* Home to the rest of the family, home to my bed and my own mirror, and my own quiet.

But it was as if something didn't want us to leave. We were still stuck in the labyrinth, and the Goblin King was laughing somewhere in a room, tracking my mother's device. On our way down the summit of Tejon Pass, we got a flat. I screamed at customer service over the phone, I screamed at the tow truck company, who said they wouldn't be able to get there until the next day. We booked a night at yet another hotel nearby. I was almost certain that I had no more credit on my cards, but I tried anyway. Thankfully one of the cards worked.

The hotel belonged to the same chain as the one we'd stayed at in Ciudad Juárez when I took my dad for his appointment. The receptionist asked if I wanted to open a rewards account, since I stayed with them so often.

"No, I'm fine, thank you," I said with a tired smile, even though I knew I would probably be back in another one of their hotels either way. Something always drew us back to the border.

Even though it had been two years since Apá's Juárez appointment, walking into the hotel room made it feel like it was just the day before. It looked identical to the one in Juárez, and I almost expected to see the bustling streets of Juárez if I peeked out the window. It was evening, and the sun was going down over the rolling hills of the valley below. We were tired but didn't really notice while driving up. My lingering paranoia made me shut the blinds, unplug the phones, and stuff another towel under the door crack. I did it very subtly so as to not scare Amá.

It wasn't until we lay down on a bed that we realized just how tired we were. It was the same endless scene we had been performing. We all took a shower and tried to sleep. We would continue in the morning. Things would be better in the morning, we told ourselves. We could start over in a different car.

We were in bed for maybe three hours before we couldn't stand being in one place any longer; the idleness was unbearable. We left in the middle of the night in a taxi, headed toward Bakersfield to catch the next Amtrak headed north.

*

"I love trains, it's been years since I've been in one," said Amá as she adjusted herself on the seat, with a small table in front of her. The sun would be rising in a few hours, and though it was dark outside the window, Amá stayed glued to the glass, looking over at us occasionally and smiling. The train started its heavy groan and trudged forward.

The sun started to rise, and we could see the outlines of the mountains in the distance. Mile after mile of orchards and fields zipped past us—the same orchards and fields Amá had worked for so many years, everything she had known.

"Isn't this fun?" she said, taking a deep breath.

We got off the train in Stockton and had to switch to a bus the rest of the way. So far we had walked, taken a taxi, driven a car, boarded a train, and now were on a bus, all to get farther and farther north.

The family couldn't wait until we arrived, so they drove an hour to meet us at our penultimate stop. We had arrived. Amá hugged her children, all of us, in the parking lot; she held them as if they were made of glass and would easily break, and they held her as if she was already broken, trying to put the pieces back together, though she would never look the same.

11.

Weeks later, still waiting to hear news from Apá, we sat outside in my garden, and I asked Amá what had happened while she was in detention.

They separated the men from the women. There were pregnant women and women with small children at their feet. There were women nursing babies and older women, and young women. Nobody slept. We couldn't sleep because they never turned off the lights, and there were no windows. I lost track of time. I didn't know if it was day or night. No beds, just the floor.

I was afraid I would miss them calling my name, so when I closed my eyes, I still tried to concentrate on the noises. Whenever the doors opened, everyone looked up and paid attention. Some women had been there for months. They gave us the same food every day—bean burritos or ham and cheese sandwiches on plain white bread with lots of mayonnaise. I saved extra food in my pockets for later. We lay down on the floor to sleep when we could. Someone had left a small blanket, so I took it and used it as a cushion. I used my shoes as pillows.

They took away our laces and everything in our hair, so I found a sock on the floor and used it as a hair tie. I met a nice woman from Guatemala with two small children.

They didn't let us use the bathroom when we wanted. They had their own schedules and took us in groups. We couldn't shower. I took some diaper wipes from the nursing mothers to give myself a sponge bath, just to wipe my hands and face with.

They called me into a room and sat me alone in front of a screen. They said a voice would ask me questions from the speakers. There was a camera pointed at me. They said I wouldn't be able to see them, but that they could see me. I answered their questions. I told them the truth and hoped they believed me. I went back to the large room and lay down on the floor. There was nothing to do but wait.

When they said I would be leaving, that they'd spoken to my son, I didn't believe them. It didn't really sink in until they took me and I saw the sunlight coming from a large door ahead of me. That's when they put on the monitor and told me I would be sent back into detention if I didn't follow the rules. The ink on my hand had washed away, but I remembered your number. After a while they let me go. I knew someone would find me.

[Fifth Movement as Bleach]

======

For years I kept dozens of copies of my "documents." I couldn't throw them away, I couldn't burn them. Among them was one with my name and a number whose individual digits added up to forty-four. The combinations that could add up to forty-four seemed infinite, and I was one among that endlessness. It was like choosing numbers for the lottery—my mother's birthday, my street address, the day my grandfather died.

*

I dissolved the copies. I dipped them into a bucket filled with bleach, glue, and water. I turned them into pulp; the image of my face broke apart, spilling its ink into the rest of the sludge. But here and there I could still see an eye, my hair, my chin. How stubborn I was.

I ran my fingers through the pulp and squeezed it between my webs. I wanted all of it to go away, to meld together like a ball of mating snakes, one unrecognizable from the other.

*

The water was a cloudy blue, like the sky in a midwestern spring— pockets of blue behind an overwhelming gloom, the blurriness of spoiled milk or of my paternal grandfather's eyes the last time I saw him before his death.

I wanted it to become something more than the sum of its parts—a rearrangement of the details of my life into a better outcome. Everything that went into the bucket was still there, nothing had gone away: the paper, the cotton in the paper, the dye in the ink, the glue, and the chemicals that gave the paper its clinical whiteness.

In the vat, the pulp would never return to what it was before. It was irreversible. There was a time I wanted to exist as a series of cyphers, to live in that impossibility of ever being put back together, by which I mean I wanted to not have a past.

*

It was a baptism of all my former selves, all trying to be redeemed. I had done wrong, I promised to do good. I dipped their heads in the water, rubbed their foreheads clean, and they all closed their eyes to receive something holy, the smell of bleach wiping everything away. They did what good Christian sinners do—disappear.

I slushed the mixture with my hands, making soft balls of pulp. In my hands, they could have been molded into anything I wanted them to be.

Fire would not do this. If I burned them, I probably would have kept the ashes and eaten them, or smeared them across my teeth and smiled at passing traffic. No one would know what I was smiling at, and they would all smile back.

*

I poured all of my names into bleach because I wanted them cleaned, sanitized, redeemed, rid of all their failures. And I thought long about the purpose of bleach—to whiten that which was not white—and my shame and disgust at how many times I thought of bleaching my own skin. All summer long, working construction to buy clothes for the school year, I wore long-sleeved shirts, large hats, bandanas around my face, and gloves. I wanted no part of my body to touch the sun, all to prevent myself from becoming any darker than I already was.

I was young; I didn't know how to love my skin, because everyone around me said that to be beautiful meant to be what I was not.

*

I began molding the mixture into a four-legged thing. It could have been a horse, or a dog, or a cow. I wanted to make a horse, but it wouldn't stick together.

The poet Richard Siken said that horses can run until they forget they are horses, running because that's the only thing they can do without having to tell their bodies how to do it. I wondered what I didn't need to tell my body how to do. When you are baptized, do you need to tell your body how to excise its sin, or does it just happen without you? Can you just toss your head back and let water, gravity, and the divine do the rest?

In that bucket I was creating a paper trail of my disappearances, of all the people that I was not. Maybe I could talk to them.

*

I made many more four-legged things and placed them in the sun to dry, to harden. I named each of them after famous lovers.

They were a record of myself that held my secrets. I could trust them never to tell what was written into them. The images and numbers were erased, but nonetheless they were there, coded. They were small vaults for which no one had the key but me—untranslatable, unbreakable.

They found Apá blindfolded and tied up by the side of a road. He lived. That is all I have to say about it.

At night, I press a flashlight against my stomach—the ring around it is like a small eclipse. It is no accident I am named after my father.

I love you, Daisy.

I am now six months sober, after filling in many boxes on forms with a blue pen. I want someone to take my picture, for it to feel like being touched.

I believe most in my body in the precise moment of pain, not in the reflection afterward. Memories lie to me, and this is why my body can never be a map.

I'm happiest locking myself in my room in the middle of the day and lying on the floor while playing Lana Del Rey as loud as my speaker will go, and pouring a little dirt from my houseplants into my belly button. There is always dog shit everywhere because we never bothered to house-train our two-year-old shih tzu–poodle mix. I can never keep up with anything in the house. "He hit me but it felt like a kiss," Lana sings, and I think of the first time my father hit me, as if I owed him money.

I thought things would be better by now; now that all the family is reunited.

I am starving myself. I consider the shame of letting myself go hungry, as if it's something I'm trying on, like a new sweater in the fluorescent light of a department store. "Chíngate pues," I hear people tell me. I go from 180 to 110 pounds in a year. This is called "learned helplessness," my therapist tells me.

I am slowly depriving myself of everything that gives me pleasure. Meat, alcohol, sugar, sex. I have isolated myself from the world and refuse to come out.

I consider how much I hate myself for my hunger. How I wish to disappear into nothing like my father.

Sometimes I don't realize what I am saying, say too much, and lose friends. Or I don't say anything for months and lose them as well. I want to know the perfect amount of myself to give to someone else.

In the morning, I make myself an espresso in a stovetop metal cup and watch the coffee pour from the little fountain on the top. I open the fridge and eat a pepper. I place the seeds under my tongue.

Standing alone in my kitchen, I think of the different ways I've ruined my life. Maybe I was meant to be taken in the field when Amá buried the seed, pregnant with me. Only when I lie underwater do I feel as I did before my mother left for Mexico. Even though she's back, it is different. It is only in that underwater solitude that I can learn to blame someone else for the person I've become since.

In that moment I hope that rising is like a baptism, and that I will be washed clean.

I imagine that being loved is like holding my breath underwater, temporary, something I can't hold for long. When I fell in love with Rubi, she said she loved me too, but then she left.

Though I know it will come, the feeling of rising to the surface still startles me—it's in that moment when I'm slowly starting to re-alize that although I still blame myself for many things that aren't my fault, I am still capable of being loved. She and I eventually got back together.

But I want to experience love the way I experience drowning—never coming back to the surface, never finding relief. Always just a click away from dying, which I admit is selfish, because it's easier to be desired than to go on with the work of desiring.

I know I can swim toward tenderness, but so many times I refuse.

I refuse because I imagine that stillness is part of tenderness, and if I reach that place of tenderness, I won't know what to do with the serenity.

I open the hot container of espresso, pour it into a small cup, and raise the cup to my mouth. I burn my tongue, yell, and wake up Rubi, who is sleeping in the next room, now pregnant with our child, who we will name Julián after my Amá Julia.

My child will know his grandparents by touch and not through a screen, or through my yelling as I push the phone to his ear.

I am always looking ten seconds into the future—looking for the nearest door to run through. Always needing to move.

Rubi is in the hospital maternity ward. Rubi is wheeled away. Rubi is lying unconscious on a surgery bed, with the doctor's hands inside her. No one expected a cesarean. They split her open and are taking things out and placing them in bags like shoes on a door rack. It doesn't look like they will be putting them back into her. The doctor reaches in and pulls out a small pink thing covered in blood, taking his first breath of this world.

He is screaming as if he has seen the future already and knows the past. They toss him around with towels to clean him, and though milky and gray, his eyes are already open. I am probably just a blurry shape and shadow to him, softening into the empty space around me, an interchangeable thing, just as my parents were to me in Tijuana. If I, too, am like the birds packed tightly together on a tree, and if a loud noise startles me, what would be left behind on the branches?

The nurse swaddles him tight and places him in my arms while the doctor staples Rubi's abdomen back together.

"Mijo, mijo, can you see me?" I say, and we are both shaking, as if we have either just finished, or are just getting ready to run.

ACKNOWLEDGMENTS

This book would not exist without people who believed in me long before I believed in myself and who continue to do so in days of uncertainty. First and foremost, I would like to thank Julia Kardon, my agent and friend, who read the essay that would become this book and who had the foresight to see and help craft its vision. Here's to many more shenanigans ahead. Equally important are my amazing editors, Sofia Groopman and Mary Gaule, who turned my chaotic ramblings into something worthwhile and to whom I am deeply grateful. Sofia, your kindness and generosity is unmatched—thank you. I feel incredibly fortunate to work with such a dedicated and talented team at Harper and further extend my thanks to the production and marketing teams, especially Emily VanDerwerken. To my family at Blue Flower Arts who have given me the support I need to focus on my work: Thank you, Alison, Barbara, and Anya.

I owe so much to Julia Kolchinsky Dasbach, who asked me to write when I felt I would never write again, and made me turn to prose for answers. Thanks to the editors of the following journals, magazines, and venues for publishing the first pieces from which many of the ideas in this book originated: *Buzzfeed*, *Construction Literary Magazine*, *Best American Poetry Blog*, *Washington Square Review*, and *PBS NewsHour*.

I am indebted to the love of friends who helped in more ways than I can name, who either fed me, housed me, or lent me an ear when I needed it most. Eternal love to Derrick Austin for being there through difficult times, Suzi F. Garcia, Britt Bennet, Rob Bruno, Lauren Clark, Vanessa Angélica Villarreal, Carolina Ebeid, Carina

Del Valle Schorske, and Gabrielle Calvocoressi among too many others to name here but who know who they are. Thanks also to my therapist, Kelly Schroeder, who kept me from falling to pieces throughout this process.

To my Canto Mundo, Kundiman, and Cave Canem families who came through for me in dire times and never wavered. My family owes everything to you. Gracias especially to Ross Gay, Kazim Ali, Sarah Gambito, Nicole Sealey, Carmen Jimenez Smith, Deborah Paredes, and Celeste Guzman. To my Ashland family for uniting around a love for our craft, dedication to our students, and allowing me to continue my passion for teaching.

I feel incredibly lucky to fall under the brilliant and caring guidance of Josh McKinney and Eduardo C. Corral, who for over a decade have advised me on matters personal and professional. Endless love and gratitude for you both.

I don't know what I did to deserve the gift of Sandra Cisnero's generosity. Thank you for all you have done for me and for looking through this book with a fine-toothed comb. I promise to pay the kindness you have shown me forward to younger Latinx writers.

To my father, mother, sister, and brothers: My love for you is endless. We are here, finally together. Los quiero mucho. To Rafael Zarate and Basilia Ayala, who have taken me in like their own son.

And last, to my wife, Rubi, and my son, Julian, who have my entire heart. May we always run out of breath dancing.

NOTES

FIRST MOVEMENT: DACA

1. For references to the strategies of the sovereign on the body politic to assert control, see Michel Foucault, *Discipline and Punish: The Birth of the Prison* *(New York: Pantheon, 1977).*

2. Details adapted from Jad Abumrad in "Border Trilogy Part 2: Hold the Line," April 5, 2018, *RadioLab*, produced by Matt Kielty, Latif Nasser, Bethel Habte, and Tracie Hunte, podcast, MP3 audio, 51:53, https://www.wnycstudios.org /story/border-trilogy-part-2-hold-line.

THIRD MOVEMENT: SENTENCE SERVED

1. *Merriam-Webster*, s.v. "decimate," https://www.merriam-webster.com/dictionary /decimate.

2. Line adapted from and in dedication to C. D. Wright's *ShallCross* (Port Townsend, WA: Copper Canyon Press, 2016).

3. From the opening line of Federico García Lorca's poem "Romance sonámbulo," in *The Selected Poems of Federico García Lorca* (1955; repr., New York: New Directions, 2005).

4. All historical details of the "El Paso solution" and others found here come from David Dorado Romo, *Ringside Seats to a Revolution: An Underground Cultural History of El Paso and Juárez, 1983–1923* (El Paso, TX: Cinco Puntos, 2005).

5. From Form I-485, Application to Register Permanent Residence or Adjust Status, Department of Homeland Security.

FOURTH MOVEMENT: GLASS

1. List form adapted from Danez Smith's poem "Alternate Names for Black Boys," in *[Insert] Boy* (Portland, OR: Yesyes Books, 2014).

2. "U and T Visa Law Enforcement Guide for Federal, State, Local, Tribal, and Territorial Law Enforcement, Prosecutors, Judges and Other Government Agencies," Department of Homeland Security, https://www.dhs.gov/sites /default/files/publications/U-and-T-Visa-Law-Enforcement-Resource%20 Guide_1.4.16.pdf, p. 4.

3. "A federal, state, local, tribal, and territorial law enforcement agency, prosecutor, judge, or other government official can complete [a certification] for a victim who is petitioning USCIS for a U visa." Ibid., p. 5.

4. "The decision whether to sign a certification is at the certifying agency's discretion. Each certifying agency should exercise its discretion on a case-by-case basis consistent with applicable U.S. laws and regulations, and the policies and procedures outlined in this guide as well as any internal policies of the certifying agency." Ibid., p. 6.

FIFTH MOVEMENT: ASYLUM

1. UN General Assembly, *Universal Declaration of Human Rights*, 10 December 1948.

MARCELO HERNANDEZ CASTILLO is the author of *Cenzontle*, winner of the A. Poulin, Jr. Poetry Prize (BOA editions) and *Dulce*, winner of the Drinking Gourd Prize (Northwestern University Press). As the first undocumented student to graduate from the Helen Zell Writers Program at the University of Michigan, he was a co-founding member of the Undocupoets Campaign, which successfully eliminated citizenship requirements from all major first-poetry book prizes in the nation. He lives in Northern California, where he teaches poetry to incarcerated youth and is on the faculty at the Ashland University Low-Res MFA program.